Getting Published

ABOUT THE AUTHOR

Alysoun Owen is the Editor of the *Writers' & Artists' Yearbook* and the
Children's Writers' & Artists' Yearbook and has commissioned several books on
writing and publishing for Bloomsbury. She has a degree in English Language
and Literature and has worked in publishing in the UK and overseas for
over 30 years and is a regular speaker at literary festivals and at publishing-
related events on how to get published. She runs a publishing consultancy,
www.alysounowen.com.

Writers' & Artists' Guide to

Getting Published

ESSENTIAL ADVICE FOR ASPIRING AUTHORS

Alysoun Owen

BLOOMSBURY YEARBOOKS
LONDON • OXFORD • NEW YORK • NEW DELHI • SYDNEY

BLOOMSBURY YEARBOOKS
Bloomsbury Publishing Plc
50 Bedford Square, London, WC1B 3DP, UK

BLOOMSBURY, BLOOMSBURY YEARBOOKS, WRITERS' & ARTISTS'
and the Diana logo are trademarks of Bloomsbury Publishing Plc

First published in Great Britain 2019

A catalogue record for this book is available from the British Library

ISBN: PB: 978-1-4729-5021-5; ebook: 978-1-4729-5020-8

Typeset by Deanta Global Publishing Services, Chennai, India
Printed and bound in Great Britain by CPI (Group) UK Ltd, Croydon CR0 4YY

To find out more about our authors and books visit www.bloomsbury.com
and sign up for our newsletters

CONTENTS

Introduction

How to get published? 1. Write a good book.
2. Read a good book – this one.

This quotation is from Charlie Higson's 2014 foreword to the tenth edition of the *Children's Writers' & Artists' Yearbook*. Higson, author of the *Young Bond* series which has sold well over a million copies in the UK, should know what he's talking about. This is an apt quote for this book too, even if it does stray gently into the realms of hyperbole. What it reminds us is that the book – the actual content, the writing, the illustrations, and the words and illustrations working together – is what matters most. The way in which a story, characters, tone, dialogue and setting come together as a work of alchemy is what puts the fledging writer at the front of the queue when it comes to getting noticed by a publisher's acquisitions or commissioning editor, or a literary agent on the lookout for new talent.

This is not a writing guide. It will touch on how to critically appraise your own work (or how you might ask others to do that for you). It gives advice on redrafting, editing and refining your work so that you might feel ready to start presenting it to the wider world. In short, it assumes you are contemplating the possibility of being published. It explores what you need to consider before you start submitting it to publishers or agents. It will provide a comprehensive description of what publishers do and how writers intersect with publishing companies and the individuals who work within them. It will describe all the constituent parts of the process from editorial, design and production, to marketing, rights and sales. It aims to demystify the various stages – and there are many – in bringing a book to physical fruition (digital or print or audio). As such it is an extension of the advice we already offer through the *Writers' & Artists' Yearbook* (WAYB) and the *Children's Writers' & Artists' Yearbook* (CWAYB). I will also mention the agenting process and how to get your work into good shape for submission, but this guide is not specifically about submission – that's just one part of the picture. The *Writers' & Artists' Guide to How to Hook an Agent* (James Rennoldson, Bloomsbury, 2020) gives in-depth hints, tips and advice on improving your chances of success in that arena.

Although the *Yearbooks* address these aspects, this book provides a broader canvas on which to be more expansive. The overview that *this* guide provides sets an overall scene: it provides practical, honest information borne out of years of experience, knowledge and working with authors, agents and publishers. The detail is as valid for those seeking publication via the traditional route – through an agent and publisher – and those intending to go it alone through self-publishing or hybrid models such as crowdfunding. It will provide you with the tools you need to decide what might work best for you and your writing and your longer-term writing ambitions. It invites you to think of yourself as a writer and to be professional about the way you approach your work. It encourages you to think about your book's route to market: how you understand what publishers are looking for, how they build their lists to develop an author's career as one ingredient in the wider publishing mix that forms part of their company's strategy. It considers how you might manage your own career as a writer, as an 'authorpreneur' with your own social media or sales strategy. This book will arm you with the inside knowledge and industry lingo you need to prepare yourself and your work for what lies ahead.

The economics of publishing will be touched on insofar as they help to shine a light on the unprofitable nature of so much of what this industry does and how an author's financial gain from publishing a book is calculated. Self-publishing may hold out the possibility of greater financial reward or at least a greater share of any profits that their book(s) may generate. The chapters in this book will invite readers to weigh up the pros and cons of different routes to publication: what might best suit their manuscript, how they might best reach their intended readership, and what skills, time and money they have at their disposal.

Each chapter concentrates on one main aspect of the publishing process and, with a range of case studies and examples, is intended to apply to all types of books: digital and print; fiction and non-fiction; books for adults, YA and children; and different genres, from fantasy and thrillers to romance and historical fiction. Most of the legal and financial examples provided relate to consumer, agented titles, rather than to non-trade i.e. academic or education books. It does not cover non-book content – writing for magazines and newspapers, for blogs and websites – other than tangentially.

This book doesn't claim to be a panacea for success, but if, having dipped into its pages, you feel better equipped to dust down your manuscript and, with a newfound confidence, understand what obstacles potentially lie in your path and how you might overcome them or better withstand them, then my intention will have been successful. What a book like this can do is help enhance your luck. Published authors – including multi-million-copy-selling authors – frequently cite luck as a major ingredient in getting published, and in the next breath recommend the *Yearbooks* as repositories of useful advice. Other writers suggest getting actively involved with writing communities, taking advice and solace from those who have gone before you. Learn from others' cautionary tales. There is a plethora of sites, individuals and experts ready to share their publishing stories: listen and learn.

It sounds glib to say that all successful writers were once unpublished. But it is true. Such writers are mere mortals too, however stratospheric their rise might seem to have been to superstar Gaiman, Rowling, Walliams or King-esque status. It's become a badge of honour for writers who have made it – once they have embarked on a successful career – to reference the number of rejection letters they received on their way up the greasy publishing pole. You'll be familiar with the concept of the stellar-author-with-most-rejections prize. Allegedly, Dr Seuss received 78 rejections; Robert M. Pirsig, author of *Zen and the Art of Motorcycle Maintenance*, 99 no thank-yous; and Stephen King's *Carrie* was overlooked 30 times before being published. Proof, if you needed it, that talent does get recognised, but that it might take some time. Perseverance on the part of the debut author is a laudable attribute, as is possessing the hide of a pachyderm. It is a difficult line to tread, but this book is intended to help you, encourage you and invite you to set realistic expectations. After more years editing, advising and managing book projects than I sometimes care to remember, and with seven years working on the *Writers' & Artists' Yearbooks* as Editor, I have amassed a working lifetime of case studies across different forms of publication. I am grateful for the breadth of publishing experience I have had the good fortune to have notched up across the last thirty years, as I was promoted through the ranks of desk-editor, development and managing editor to commissioning editor, working across print and digital, in the UK and overseas. I have always enjoyed marrying the strategic side of publishing (list-building, making money, improving workflows and systems) with the hands-on creative side. Nothing quite beats working closely with an author on their text or holding a finished copy of a book I have commissioned in my hand. I have learnt much from inspirational publishers I have met or worked for.

In my role as Editor of the *Yearbooks*, I have criss-crossed the country to give talks and lectures in local libraries, public halls, and at literary festivals. I have met hundreds of would-be writers (and successfully published ones too), who collectively, through questions asked at these events, have helped shape the context and the content for this book. Some of the advice will be applicable to all forms of writing intended for a 'public' audience; notably, how to be as professional as possible in approaching what can be a time-consuming, at times frustrating, but I hope ultimately rewarding experience.

CHAPTER I

Which publishing route to take?

The business of publishing

It helps to know how publishing works. It allows you to see where your own book fits into the overall mix and should provide you with some advance information on what to expect from your editor and the other professionals that you and your book will meet along its publishing journey.

There are two main routes to publication. The long-established way is to sign with a literary agent who negotiates with a publishing company to secure a deal on your behalf. Unless it is a work of specialist non-fiction or for the education or academic markets, you will probably need to go via an agent to reach a publisher, as most don't these days welcome unsolicited submissions (take a look at their websites to check for sure). The other route is to self-publish – now a reputable and realistic alternative. As in so many other areas, the web has been a galvanising force in book publishing. It has helped usher in ways of delivering new styles of content more quickly to a wider range of readers.

ONCE UPON A TIME

In Mainz in 1439, when Johannes Gutenberg – blacksmith, goldsmith, publisher and printer – built the first moveable-type printing press, could he possibly have imagined the explosive and far-reaching impact his invention would have? Hitherto books were mostly made and copied by hand. Crude, time-consuming block printing – where text and images were carved into wooden plates – was already in use, but books were expensive to produce. They were written in Latin, the language of scholars, and were very much the preserve of the educated rich. Gutenberg changed all that. He opened the way for the industry that we know now as publishing – which encompasses writing, printing and selling. That was almost six hundred years ago. In many ways, printing and publishing as businesses, although expanding dramatically and producing varied and new publications, followed a well-worn path, until the next great invention that revolutionised the way and speed in which we consume and have access to published materials. Tim Berners-Lee's World Wide Web was born in 1991. We can't imagine a time without it now: as consumers, and as writers and publishers, it has allowed us to create products, explore new relationships, and purchase in ways that were not conceived of when I first entered this business.

When I began work as an editor for Addison Wesley Longman nearly thirty years ago, we had a single computer in the department, solely for looking up sales and stock details, and which I probably consulted no more than twice a week at most. I dictated my letters and sent them to the company typing pool and could allow a leisurely two to three days for correspondence to leave the building. It would be a clear one-and-a-half to two weeks before a reply might come back from one of my American academic authors. The fax machine was the height of modern communication. I don't exactly hail from the era of hot metal type – though plenty of such presses and print works were still in existence, notably at the University presses in Oxford and Cambridge – but the fast, colour litho and digital presses that quietly speed their way through thousands of sheets of paper an hour were not yet a reality. Manuscripts arrived in large packages obediently typed in 12-point Times New Roman, single-sided and double-spaced. Editors wielded blue and red pens, marking typescripts, galley proofs and page proofs with the appropriate British Standard proofreading marks. Authors who delivered on floppy disks – though they were anything but – were considered ahead of their time. Publishers like Usborne and Dorling Kindersley (DK), ushering in a world of design-led, colourful and attractive books and novelty tie-ins, were decidedly cutting-edge. When I moved to Oxford University Press in the early 1990s, the trade and reference department I worked in prided itself on tagging all text – books such as Margaret Drabble's *Oxford Companion to English Literature*, Jancis Robinson's *Oxford Companion to Wine* and *The Oxford Dictionary of Quotations* – with rudimentary HTML. Our ambition was that one day such material might be used in environments other than print: we were proved right. How familiar digital publishing is now, but it was anything but then. I witnessed the dying days of the extravagant launch parties for new books and long, alcohol-fuelled publisher lunches. The latter still do exist but are more restrained – shorter and teetotal.

PUBLISHING TODAY

Some books are published because they are guaranteed cash cows for their publishers: a market has been identified and an opportunity has arisen to quickly take advantage of an immediate fashion or trend. Think celebrity memoir or self-help fitness manual, or a series of ghost-written children's books created to endorse the brand of an individual known for their successes in another profession – sport or music for example. But let's not be too sniffy (or jealous of billboards on Tube platforms and the brisk Christmas sales that such books might have). Many such brands were, after all, launched by different types of publishing platforms: Instagram, YouTube and a multitude of blogs and vlogs.

In what way does this matter to you or have any impact on your book? In some regards, these low-concept, high-selling books run in a parallel universe to the output of a debut novelist. But they do matter from a business point of view. The money your publisher makes on a sure-fire bestseller (once the not insignificant advance is paid off) can be invested in books that – ahem – might be less sure of immediate financial success. For more on the economics of publishing an individual title, see chapter 4.

Some books become overnight bestsellers, often against the likely odds. Who could have predicted that a book about divesting yourself of your possessions or one on cleaning your house would have such broad appeal, even if they were preceded by strong Instagram followings? The unpredictability of what will be a publishing success is part of the joy of being a publisher. It can provide both solace to a new author – write what you want to write and it may be a soar-away hit – and a worry, as there is no offer of certainty. A publisher may think your book is wanted / needed / will be enjoyed, but despite the book-buying statistics at their fingertips, they can't know for sure!

So where might your book fit in the publishing firmament? There is a wide range of publishing houses. The Big Five global conglomerates* dominate and together account for over 50 per cent of the total print market in volume terms (number of copies sold). Each of these is composed of dozens of **imprints**. At the opposite end of the spectrum are niche, one-person band operations, with a small output of just a few titles a year. There are all sorts of publishing companies in between: PLCs, limited companies, Arts Council-funded small presses, social enterprise operators and privately-owned businesses.

An imprint is a brand, composed of a collection or list of books with a similar approach or ethos, subject area or market. For an example of how a company might be structured around such imprints, let's take Bloomsbury Publishing Plc, a company with offices in New York, New Delhi, Sydney, London and Oxford. It has two Divisions: a Consumer Division and the Non-Consumer Division, differentiated by the two markets they serve. The Non-Consumer Division, as the name suggests, produces books and other content for groups of readers who have an academic, professional or specialist need. The imprints in this division are directed at serving a definable target market and include Green Tree (health and wellbeing), Osprey (military history), Hart (academic law) and Methuen Drama (plays and scripts). The Consumer Division is everything else: the trade fiction and non-fiction you find in bookshops and which individuals choose to buy rather than being required to for a course or career reading list. Bloomsbury's consumer division brings together its Adult

---

* Hachette Livre, HarperCollins, Penguin Random House, Simon & Schuster and Pan Macmillan.

Trade Publishing, Children's Books and Educational titles. In each of these are individual imprints including Absolute Press (cookery), Raven Books (literary crime, thrillers and suspense), and Bloomsbury YA (Young Adult).

Publishing has its own terms, often opaque to the outside world. 'Trade' means little to an author, but in publishing speak it's historical shorthand for the 'book trade' or booksellers and means books that tend to sell through retail outlets at what are known as trade terms, with discounts on the cover price of the books that are more generous than those on professional or academic works. Trade publishing is the arena in which a novel, children's picture book, YA dystopian trilogy, middle grade fantasy, or narrative non-fiction, such as memoir, popular science or World War II history intended for a general market (rather than a specifically scholarly one) will be published.

Publishers tend to be rather precious about their imprint name and associated logos or colophon — the image that represents their publishing house and appears on the title page and on the spine of its books. Readers are much less likely to be aware of them. Penguin's eponymous bird will be familiar to most, but who knows – or much less cares – what HarperCollins' flame logo looks like or that Chatto & Windus is represented by a pair of cherubs reading on a bench?

As an author, it's a good idea to be familiar with some of the lists and publishers who publish successfully in the genre, subject area or for the market you think your own book fits into. The publishers' pages of the most up-to-date editions of the *Writers' & Artists' Yearbook* and the *Children's Writers' & Artists' Yearbook* (new ones are published every July) are a good place to start. If you are writing children's stories, for example, then looking at well-established presses that publish specifically for this age range will help you see their current output (known as frontlist) and assess which titles stand the test of time to become backlist classics. Key names to familiarise yourself with in this sector are Scholastic, Nosy Crow, Chicken House, Egmont and Walker Books. If you are writing crime, see what Head of Zeus are up to; if you have a practical lifestyle manual up your sleeve, monitor

HACHETTE LIVRE
(France) owned by Lagardère Publishing, founded in 1826

HACHETTE UK
Also: Hachette Ireland, and companies in Australia, NZ, India and USA

OCTOPUS
Aster
Cassell
Conran Octopus
Endeavour
Gaia Books
Godsfield Books
Hamlyn
Ilex
Kyle
Miller's
Mitchell Beazley
Monoray
Philip's
Philip's Astronomy
Pyramid
Spruce
Summersdale

HACHETTE EDUCATION
Rising Stars

HODDER GIBSON
(Scotland)

HODDER & STOUGHTON
Mulholland Books
Coronet
Sceptre
Yellow Kite

HACHETTE CHILDREN'S GROUPS
Hodder Children's Books
Orchard Books
Orion Children's Books
Wayland Books
Quercus Children's Books
Pat-a-Cake
Wren & Rook
Franklin Watts
Little, Brown Books for Young Readers

QUERCUS
Joe Fletcher Books
MacLehose Books
riverrun

HEADLINE PUBLISHING
Wildfire
Headline Home
Headline Review
Eternal
Tinder Press
Wildfire

JOHN MURRAY PRESS
Two Roads
John Murray Learning
Nicholas Brealey
Hodder Faith
Jessica Kingsley

LITTLE, BROWN
Abacus
Atom
Blackfriars
The Bridge Street Press
Constable
Corsair
Dialogue
Fleet
Hachette Audio
Orbit
Robinson
Piatkus
Sphere
Virago

ORION
Gollancz
Orion Spring
Seven Dials
Trapeze
Weidenfeld & Nicholson
DASH

Example of a publishing company structure

Haynes Publishing's output; and if you have composed a historical or medical romance, then engage with Harlequin, which includes the Mills & Boon imprints. If you've dreamt of being published by distinguished literary houses such as Faber & Faber, Bloomsbury, the Penguin Press or John Murray, you can window-shop via their websites or sign up to their reader clubs to get news, updates and discounts on their titles.

What do publishers do?

Each **list** is run by a commissioning or acquisitions editor, or a body of smaller imprints might be grouped under a master imprint and this is likely to be overseen by an Editorial Director or Publisher who has a strategic role in managing the lists and their future development. The Hachette Livre example in the diagram opposite illustrates how many different lists or imprints some of the larger companies consist of. These will have been added over time as small, often independent publishers have been purchased. Each acquiring or commissioning editor is on the lookout for new books that will fit their publishing programme. In some publishing houses, these imprints act completely autonomously, and even in direct competition for authors. They each contract authors, for fiction and much narrative non-fiction via literary agents or may commission an author direct so their lists can develop and grow – and make money. List management includes planning for the future – as in any business – looking at three-year plans and schedules and plugging gaps, avoiding duplication, extending successful series or encouraging bestselling writers to turn in another title. There may be plans to tie a publication into a significant event to boost sales. In 2020 these might be the 200th anniversary of the launch of *HMS Beagle* that took Charles Darwin on his voyages, the birth of Florence Nightingale two hundred years ago or the thirtieth anniversary of the dismantling of Checkpoint Charlie that divided East from West Berlin. In 2022, there are likely to be books already planned to tie in with the Beijing Winter Olympics, the 50th anniversary of Bloody Sunday, the centenary of the founding of the BBC, or twenty-five years since the death of Diana, Princess of Wales.

The commissioning editor works as part of a wider team of publishing professionals, who together decide if a book is viable and should be published and when and how. Collectively, they then shepherd the book through its various stages from manuscript to final book and beyond. These people include:

- **Desk editors, copy-editors, proofreaders** and **indexers** (the latter three roles usually done by freelancers)
- **Designers** and production **controllers**
- **Publicity** and **marketing managers**
- **Rights, contract** and **financial experts**
- **Sales representatives** and **managers**

As you can see, a long line of individuals who – along with your agent, if you have one – will influence how your book reads and looks, and how it is promoted and sells.

As an author you don't need to have intimate knowledge of the ins and outs of the publishing industry, but it is useful to familiarise yourself with some of the processes and terminology and to know the latest trends and which books are doing well. You can do this by reading the book pages in the media, following Twitter, book blogs and news in The *Bookseller* or *Publishing News* (magazines to the book trade in the UK and US). The Resources section which starts on page 257 lists organisations, books and sites that you might find useful.

THE PUBLISHING PROCESS

What is the experience you might have once you are signed to a publisher? The standard process that you are likely to encounter is outlined below, but each publisher may have slight variants on this general workflow. Having a rough idea of what lies ahead means that you will be able to ask your editor what stages your book will travel through on its route to publication within their company. Questions such as: Will your manuscript be read in-house or by a freelance editor, or both? What's the lead time from receipt of manuscript to publication date? Who will you be working with on the marketing side of things and when might they be in touch with you?

Steps in creating a book (the traditional model)

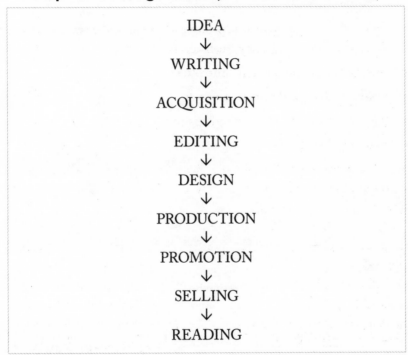

IDEA
↓
WRITING
↓
ACQUISITION
↓
EDITING
↓
DESIGN
↓
PRODUCTION
↓
PROMOTION
↓
SELLING
↓
READING

The publishing process consists of six main strands. Once your manuscript has been **acquired** and you have been contracted, a completed manuscript is delivered to the publisher and then **edited** for style, consistency, accuracy, structure and readability. Your raw manuscript is then **designed** – a cover is created, and the text and any illustrations are prepared to appeal to the intended readership, market or prevailing aesthetic trends. The designed text is then **produced**:

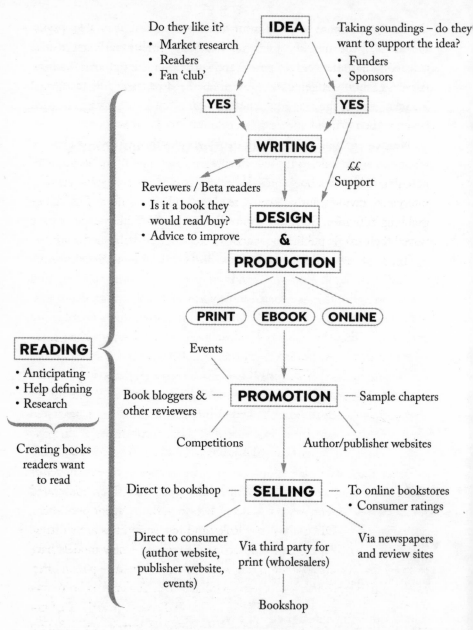

Do they like it?
- Market research
- Readers
- Fan 'club'

IDEA

Taking soundings – do they want to support the idea?
- Funders
- Sponsors

YES **YES**

WRITING

Reviewers / Beta readers
- Is it a book they would read/buy?
- Advice to improve

££ Support

DESIGN
&
PRODUCTION

PRINT   EBOOK   ONLINE

READING
- Anticipating
- Help defining
- Research

Creating books readers want to read

Events

Book bloggers & other reviewers —

PROMOTION

— Sample chapters

Competitions

Author/publisher websites

Direct to bookshop —

SELLING

— To online bookstores
- Consumer ratings

Direct to consumer (author website, publisher website, events)

Via third party for print (wholesalers)

Via newspapers and review sites

Bookshop

Subverting the standard model

the manuscript is typeset to form a complete set of 'printable' pages. Headings, page numbers, chapter headings, preliminary pages (the title, copyright and content pages) and endmatter (further reading lists, indexes, acknowledgements), will all be incorporated and translated into the right page size and binding style. The book, complete with cover, is then printed and/or converted into an ebook format.

Next comes **marketing** – your book becomes the preserve of a host of marketers and publicists if you are lucky and is brought to the attention of potential readers via book sites, blogs, newspaper and magazine articles, interviews, reviews, author events, readings and any number of headline-grabbing activities. So far, so controllable; the publishing experts have waved their magic publishing wands to create a well-published work.

The final part of the jigsaw and the most challenging is **distribution** – getting your book into the hands of your readers in the UK and internationally. This is where publishers can steal a march on self-published authors, particularly where print, rather than ebooks, are concerned. They have well-established agreements with bricks-and-mortar bookshops, library and other suppliers around the world and can sell in bulk – absorbing large discounts along the way – with online bookstores such as Amazon. Making any book stand out in a sea of publications is a challenge for publishers who are seasoned professionals – just think how inventive and entrepreneurial the lone writer or small independent press needs to be to get their work noticed.

Once there were clearly defined roles and names for the main actors in the publishing world: author, editor, agent, publisher. New compound nouns have now entered the lexicon: hybrid authors, agent-publishers, authorpreneurs, DIY-publishers. Roles and responsibilities are shifting. This is in part for pragmatic and economic reasons – new models have evolved, and agents and publishers want a share of the new pie on offer. They need to replenish the coffers that have been depleted as books get cheaper and Amazon and their ilk continue to discount heavily. That not only means snapping up successful self-published authors and offering them print contracts, but also offering self-publishing provider hubs and other author services, such as creative writing courses and paid-for events.

Where does the author fit in with all this? As obvious as it sounds, your role is to write. The publishing house wants to present your work in the best way possible to garner praise, sales and a clamouring from the market for your second book. You are the creator who sets the whole machine in motion. Don't underestimate the power that might come with that.

> *We publishers are middle-men; we don't except by accident, write the books we publish. We are entrepreneurs. We are not manufacturers. We don't actually print or bind the books we publish. Nor do we make the paper on which they are printed. We are publishers, that is we make public, we make known to the public, something that must otherwise remain private and inaccessible.*
>
> Geoffrey Faber, 1934[*]

A few years ago, writer and broadcaster (and distinguished former publisher) Robert McCrum fronted a series of short radio programmes – 'Publishing Lives' – on BBC Radio 4 (2013) on individual publishers who had shaped the profession. This quotation from Geoffrey Faber for me helps encapsulate what, in its pared-down, purest sense is what publishing is. 'It is the making public': the daring to share material. That's as true today as it was in the 1930s. In terms of the publishing industry, it is the reaping of financial reward that comes with such sharing. Publishing is a business: not a charitable enterprise per se, though books may of course be published by a charity or for a charitable cause. Books are not produced for the express purpose of satisfying the ego of an author, although that may be the overt or unintended consequence of publishing a work. The main driver, at least on the part of a publishing house, is to make money. Or *some* money, at least.

---

[*] From 'Are Publishers Any Use? A Paper read to The Oxford University English Club 15th February, 1934'; printed in *A Publisher Speaking* by Geoffrey Faber (Houghton Mifflin Company, 1935).

Different formats

The main publishing formats and the ones that most of you reading this book are probably interested in creating are:

1. Print
2. Digital
3. Audio

PRINT

Physical books remain the main format in number of copies produced each year and revenue derived from their sales, but ebooks have been giving them a run for their money until sales started to plateau and audiobooks are making significant inroads too. When I started out in publishing in the 1990s, there were two main formats for a book: print hardback and paperback editions. Specialist publishers offered ring-bound editions, usually for manuals and training materials. The hardback and paperback formats could be adapted to include flaps for paperbacks and flexi covers; and a softback (mainly Book Club) version appeared temporarily as a hybrid paperback in large format. There used to be distinct hardback publishing houses and separate publishers to whom the rights would be licensed to produce a paperback edition. There were different paperback options too: large format for more literary titles or mass-market for those that sold in higher volume, such as romances, sagas and thrillers, which were smaller in size and might be slipped into a large pocket or small handbag. These distinctions all seem rather quaint now. Publishers are more vertical in structure and can publish how they choose, in hardback and six months later in paperback or straight into paperback. There are fewer conventions to adhere to and a greater readiness to address each title's individual publishing needs.

Physical books show no sign of disappearing. In the wake of digital expansion, and because design is sometimes poor in ebooks, many publishers have continued to invest in producing beautiful books, objects that can be handled, treasured and displayed and not just for the well-established large-format photography and fine art titles that digital cannot yet better. The art of illustration is celebrated in a proliferation of graphic novels, quality picture books and in such oversized volumes as *Animalium* by Jenny Broom, illustrated by Katie Scott (Big Picture Press, 2017) and *Blue on Blue* by Dianne White, illustrated by Beth Krommes (Beach Lane Books, 2014) – they won't fit on the average bookshelf but are attractive and elegant.

Although self-published authors can make significant money if they publish ebooks, a majority still want to produce physical publications: perhaps to prove to themselves and others that they really have created a tangible book. In the *Writers & Artists* Self-publishing Survey in 2018, 86 per cent of our respondents said they wanted to publish in print.

Print on demand (POD) – whereby books are printed only when there is a minimum number of copies ordered via digital printing – means publishers tie up less of their cash in stock. This is particularly good for backlist titles, specialised titles with a limited sale and small companies or self-published authors who can't afford warehousing fees. Publishers have become better at inventory control in general, and now tend to print shorter runs more frequently. Books can stay officially in print forever rather than be made out of print, which was the case when it became no longer viable to print a small run of copies (fewer than five hundred, say) before POD became a central part of the publishing distribution chain.

DIGITAL

Digital or electronic publishing formats include single, standalone ebooks which can be downloaded from Amazon, Apple and other online bookstores and read on Kindle, Nook and other tablets and reading devices. The open standard ePub file format can be accessed on almost every e-reader or app, with the notable exception

WHO'S READING WHAT?

Of UK adults surveyed in 2019:

- 51% had read a book in the past year
- 40.6% had bought a book in the past year
- 34% of book-reading adults were categorised as 'heavy readers', which meant they had read 10 or more books in the past year
- The average spend per person on print books in the past year was £60.98; heavy book purchasers – those in the top 20% of buyers – spent on average £202.15

Reading habits based on age and gender

Compared to the average reader . . .

- Men are 40% more likely to read sci-fi
- Men are 50% more likely to read about sport
- Women are 58% more likely than men to read romance novels
- Women are 25% more likely to read contemporary literature
- 15-24 year-olds are almost 50% more likely to read fantasy or adventure books and 59% more likely to read sci-fi
- Those over 65 are 35% more likely to favour books about the home, gardening and DIY and 37% more likely to read historical fiction
- Of those categorised as 'heavy readers', 26% are more likely to be 65 and over

Interestingly, the surveying company refers to the annual spend of a keen book buyer as 'a whopping' £202.15 a year. Although the figure is up on previous years, whopping seems rather an overstatement. What a bargain books are.

Figures from Kantar's GB TGI consumer data Q1 2019 and Kantar's Worldpanel UK consumer panel 2019.

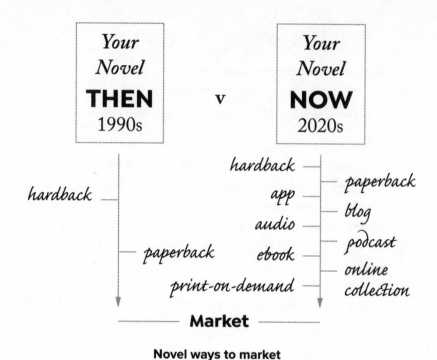

Novel ways to market

of Amazon Kindle which supports proprietary Mobi and AZW files only. Ebooks are often still an afterthought in the publishing production process. Increasingly, publishers are establishing more integrated workflows so that digital becomes another legitimate option rather than a secondary format.

Digital publishing is more than just individual ebooks – it encompasses blogs and apps and online collections of multiple books to produce collections of titles on a specific subject or for a target market. These include huge online databases of titles rendered in XML to provide full search capabilities, cross-title searching and linking to give users an enriched experience that goes far beyond the boundaries of individual titles. Collections of this sort include those invested in by the large academic and scholarly publishers including Oxford University Press, Cambridge University Press, SpringerNature and Taylor & Francis, who publish journals and monographs to a digital-savvy customer base in the form of libraries, academics, researchers and students. They want to be able to access, manipulate, share and save content wherever they are and whenever they like and can do so through these subscription platforms. Online services have enhanced the ways of delivering tailored content to users and provide new purchase models – temporary borrowing or ownership, institutional and individual subscription or perpetual access.

The advantages of digital are obvious: carriage, storage and warehousing are no longer an issue or a cost to the publisher; reprints become a thing of the past; and books can be updated swiftly. This is particularly useful for annual publications or for non-fiction titles with content that might need updating regularly. Digital books can technically be any length; their size is no longer constrained by print and paper costs or binding restrictions. Portability is enhanced. A whole collation of holiday reads can be downloaded at the click of a button. The speed with which a title gets to market is theoretically improved, though to be published successfully in ebook a title must first have travelled through the publishing 'sausage machine' and the standard editorial, design and production stages identified above. Quality should not be compromised – though often is – when producing an ebook. The stages in creating a well-conceived, well-edited book remain necessary: it's the manufacturing stage that has become more efficient, shortened and cheaper. Delivery is no longer to a bookshop via a warehouse but through virtual channels.

Digital-only or digital-first imprints, such as HarperCollins' One More Chapter, claim to 'close the gap between author, publisher and reader, reacting speedily to reading trends and publishing the best in commercial fiction'. In effect, they do what smaller and more agile operatives and self-publishers have been doing for a while: finding out what readers want to read, testing out ideas with readers and, through serialisation building up a loyal following in advance of full publication and then satisfying that demand quickly. In short, they establish a direct relationship with readers. For nearly a decade Sheffield-based And Other Stories have been asking readers what they want to read through reading groups that help assess new manuscripts. It's what underpins the crowdfunding concept too: finding out what a consumer wants and satisfying that demand.

AUDIO

Publishers are now setting up their own in-house audiobook service or production departments which can support the delivery of audio formats in the way that more traditional and established production departments (sometimes called content management departments) prepare print and ebook editions. For example, Penguin Random House (PRH) has expanded its audiobooks department in the last four years to twenty staff that work across editorial and strategy, identifying titles on the company's front and backlists that they think will have a substantial audiobook audience. They will consider the best way to publish in this format, make sure rights are cleared to use content for audio delivery, commission the best voice to present the material, determine how they might be paid, and decide whether it will be read by just one actor or be semi- or fully dramatised with a larger cast, with incidental music or other audio motifs inserted, and so on. They will also think about what the cover and associated branded materials look like, and if the file should be available at the same time as the print edition or ebook, in which outlets and in which formats – as a CD still or solely as a downloadable audio file via Amazon's Audible, Spotify or Apple Books. In short, the same thinking that goes into publishing a print edition is exercised by audiobook specialists.

Publishers actively developing their audio departments and output include Macmillan, Hachette, HarperCollins, and Bonnier in addition to PRH. The external companies that provide audiobook creation services and which smaller publishers will be dependent upon and which self-published authors can investigate if they are looking to self-publish their audiobook, include Audible, an Amazon-owned platform, Bolinda (Australian-based company), W. F. Howes (a long-established UK company that incorporates Whole Story), and ISIS Publishing. All are third-party publishers to whom audio rights can be licensed.

There are some all-inclusive packaging solutions too via Authors Republic which is particularly attractive to smaller publishers and to self-published authors.

The retailing of audiobooks is dominated, unsurprisingly, by Amazon's Audible service, US-based audiobooks.com and Sweden's StoryTel, via digital downloads and in the case of the latter via a monthly subscription streaming model. Other providers include Kobo, Google Play (for Android phones) and Overdrive, who specialise in the supply of audiobooks to the library supply market. Physical audiobooks are sold via the usual high-street bookshops and online vendors; WH Smith and Moto outlets stock titles that appeal to travellers, including children's stories and compilation collections.

Newspapers and online stores now include weekly bestseller charts for audio titles alongside their print book charts. The *Bookseller* and *The Times* introduced theirs in 2015. Podcasts and audiobooks are reviewed in the broadsheets and online.

PODCASTS

What's the difference between an audiobook and a podcast? Nothing, technically speaking. The file is the same, but the 'publishing' aspects are what differ: frequency, length, style, marketing, and naming convention. Podcasts tend to be less formal, journalistic, conversational and not heavily pre-scripted, but there are interesting ways in which a pre-set title might fuse with a more podcast-style delivery, which might involve audience and real-time listener participation via their smartphone. As for print books, building a loyal following and future market for the next product or output is what publishers are trying to do: creating a brand that is easily identified and that appeals to a broad customer base. The publisher's job is to continue to satisfy that consumer need and greed for new and enticing content in as many diversified ways as it can.

The Publishers Association's (PA) survey of reading habits of British adults (Kantar, 2019), found that lack of time was what stopped them reading. A fifth of book buyers consume audiobooks and this trend shows no sign of slowing. According to Nielsen BookScan figures, 40 per cent of people who listen to at least one audiobook a month discovered audio for the first time in the last two years (since 2018) and they are not necessarily readers of print books. You can see why publishers are keen to tap into this new revenue stream and appeal to a whole new host of consumers who are hungry to access stories in new ways. Audiobooks help solve a genuine problem and provide us with an alternative and effective way to engage with new writing on the go. National campaigns promoted by the PA such as #LoveAudio week, audiobook charts, reviews in the media and apps, such as titleShare which allows reviewers, bloggers and vloggers access to audiobooks in advance of publication, all help put audio at the heart of the publishing ecosystem.

NEW FORMS

Digital and self-publishing have encouraged experimentation and creativity, which have enlivened the wider publishing industry:

There has been a new wave of **short fiction**. Short stories, agents and publishers have long told us, don't sell. Self-publishers have proved them wrong. Writers can develop the art of concision through very short flash fiction or other micro-fiction, such as Twitter fiction, and are being encouraged to do so through writing competitions.

With **episodic** or **serialisation** or **subscription publishing**, we see a return to the days of part-works and Dickensian periodical publishing. Mills & Boon and Reader's Digest have done it for years – sending a loyal readership regular instalments of their literary pick-me-up. Writers (and publishers too) are using such digital part- or episodic publishing to test the waters, get feedback from readers, build a readership, and offer free taster content. Hugh Howey released *Wool* – the first in his highly successful self-published trilogy – chapter by chapter.

Work-in-progress books, with the reader as muse, influencer and in some cases co-writer, are possible through writing share sites and start-ups such as Leanpub (www.leanpub.com), whose digital-only publishing encourages 'books-in-progress' – with reader rewriting and editing encouraged. It works particularly well for text that may be regularly superseded or which dates quickly, such as computer manuals or political reportage.

The **interactive novel** allows readers to select (from a set of pre-defined options) the way the e-story they are 'reading' develops; a sort of html-linked *Dungeons and Dragons* or *BeastQuest* for grown-ups. Coliloquy (www.coliloquy.com), a US company which specialised in this form, published well-known writers such as Amy Tan and Stephen King, but is no longer active. Interactive stories are also published in print; Puffin publish the *You Choose* series by Pippa Goodhart, illustrated by Nick Sharratt.

These creative options set new demands on writers and readers. Writers may want to pursue such options because they like the creative freedom (or discipline in the case of constrained forms such as flash fiction), and because they provide more direct ways to engage with readers. This is something traditional publishers seem to have been reticent about to date, but they are catching up.

Routes to publication

AGENT-PUBLISHER ROUTE

Most writers still aim to be published by an established publishing house and (with a few exceptions referred to in chapter 3) are likely to need an agent before having their manuscript considered by a publisher. The main focus of this book is on writers who are seeking such representation and want to know what publishers will do with their manuscript once it has been delivered.

There used to be three main ingredients in the recipe for publishing success: write a great book; find a dynamic literary agent; and cross your fingers. Luck does pay a huge part, as anyone who has submitted to publishers and agents and received rejection letter after rejection letter will confirm. Knowing something about the process that will turn your prose from a Word manuscript into a finished book might help improve your chances of finding an agent or publisher.

There are other ways to get your book into the hands of readers. The rise of self-publishing has been phenomenal and shows no immediate signs of slowing. Delivering content more cheaply without the need for expensive kit or training is a reality. Worlds that were once the preserve of a creative elite are now more accessible, and markets that authors either didn't know existed, or didn't know how to reach, have been identified and satisfied. It is a very exciting time to be a writer, a reader and, despite the doom-laden prognostications of nay-sayers within and outside the industry, a great time to be a publisher. Publishers who are nimble, creative, innovative, market-driven, energetic, and niche will survive and new ventures will be set up (just as we see old ones close, amalgamate and restructure), and amongst these will be author-led businesses.

SELF-PUBLISHING

Self-publishing offers a genuine, good-quality alternative which keeps the writer at the heart of the publishing process. The writer herself can make informed decisions about layout, cover design, pricing and delivery options. Writers frustrated with the publishing establishment – the closed world of agent and publisher – have other avenues in which to test-drive their writing on potential readers or engage with them directly via social media and through share sites such as Wattpad (www. wattpad.com). They can capitalise on their own contacts or benefit from a hardworking approach to publicity and sales opportunities.

The DIY approach to getting published can be highly rewarding. Some authors have done extremely well financially from this route, but tend to be the exceptions to the rule. And while self-published authors do get to keep the majority of any revenue from the sale of their books, typically 60 per cent from sales via Amazon's Kindle Store versus 15 per cent or so from a book published traditionally, remember that a self-published title may be very cheap (less than £2) and publishers do know how to promote and sell books: it's a tough call for the individual new writer to establish a foothold in a more established market. Spending time, effort and money are what successful indie authors do to improve their chances through intelligent metadata tagging of their book title and deftly crafted blurbs, which are packed with key search terms to help send the book up the Amazon and Google listings. Don't despair if that sounds too daunting. There are plenty of individuals and businesses who are eager to sell you their services and support you in your self-publishing venture. As you would when scouting for a plumber or builder, invest time in understanding what it is you need help with and ask for written quotations for any work tendered for. True self-publishing when you perform all aspects of the publishing process as well as the writing yourself – editing, designing, producing, marketing and distributing – is hard. It can be free, straightforward and easy via platforms such as Kindle Direct Publishing (KDP), but to produce a professional book that is free from spelling errors, has a great page design and quality photography, requires real skill, investment and doggedness. Writers are rarely hotshots at cover illustration and text design. You might be, but it may be more productive to employ experts to help you with things such as blurb writing, cover design, page layout etc.

There are two main avenues for these paid-for services – outsource a discreet part of the process to a vetted individual or series of individuals (such as a copy-editor, a proofreader or designer) or sign up to a self-publishing provider company who will do all aspects and in effect become your packager in exchange for a fee. There are many such providers: be careful what you sign up to, read contracts carefully and ask to see examples of other books they have created. I recommend that you don't part with any cash until work has commenced. Phased payment plans are fine, but don't hand over hundreds or thousands of pounds in advance: any reputable provider should be running a legitimate business with good cash flow; you wouldn't pay your plumber in advance of your dripping tap being fixed.

The biggest difference between self-publishing and the more established agent–publisher route, apart from access to distribution channels, is money: who pays for what. Publishers carry the costs for all aspects of creating, distributing and selling your book. As a self-published author, you will bear these not inconsiderable costs yourself. Paper and print and storing printed copies of a title can be pricey and intimidating: how do you sell copies of your autobiography piled high in your garage or spare room? Print on demand (POD) has made this less of an issue and ebooks have revolutionised the world of all publishing; POD has become *the* viable route for the self-published. There is plenty of support from those who have gone before. Self-published or indie authors are generally a generous breed, happy to share advice, knowledge, pitfalls and successes, everything from finding a suitable editor to using social media to help drive sales. The Alliance of Independent Authors (ALLi) is a good place to start; find them online at www.allianceindependentauthors.org.

Some authors are plumping for the self-publishing route lock, stock and barrel. Take Brenna Aubrey, whose debut romance novel *At Any Price* was self-published on the Kindle Store in December 2013, and which thirty days later had earned her over $16k. She turned down the $120k three-book deal she was offered by a mainstream publisher not only because on her past record she could make more money the DIY way, but because it allowed her greater control as a writer over her work. Author Adam Croft claims to have sold 150,000 copies of his thriller *Her Last Tomorrow* earning £2,000 a day in royalties at its peak. Within three months of self-publishing his first novel *Killing Hope*, Keith Houghton had six-figure sales. His books have now sold over 500,000 copies.

CROWDFUNDING

Crowdfunding is a way to pay for your writing and fund its publishing: you pitch your idea, wait for bids of support and when you reach the reserve price, write the book which you will subsequently distribute to your backers. Crowdfunded publishing models straddle self-publishing and traditional publishing and are becoming a viable option for writers. You can go it alone and pitch your book idea on one of the well-established creative platforms to raise small investments from a wide pool of individuals, such as Indiegogo (www.indiegogo.com) and Kickstarter (www.kickstarter.com). As an author you then arrange for the production and distribution of your book using the monies raised, relying on providers of professional services such as those used for the self-publishing model.

Other platforms, specialising in book projects only, promote writers by hosting their concepts and the bidding process, but include an editorial vetting phase similar to that undertaken by mainstream publishers. You submit a proposal to the crowdfunding publisher to their required specification (check online to see what this is in each case). As the author you are likely to be very involved by sharing sample content, details of your life story or research that supports the rationale for writing the book you are pitching. You might offer incentives to would-be investors to entice them to fund your idea, such as naming a character in your book after them, listing their name as a sponsor in the book, inviting them to a launch party or providing them with a deluxe bound edition of the title, all with different pre-set levels of pledge related to the exclusivity of each enticement. Successful players in this area include Pubslush (www.pubslush.com) which describes itself as a community that connects writers with publishers; Publishizer (www.publishizer.com) which acts as a broker bringing together authors and potential publishers – traditional or crowdfunded operators; Inkshares (www.inkshares.com) and Unbound (www.unbound.com), which like other curated crowdfunded platforms, publish books that hit a pre-order threshold. They then assign an editor to work with the author and arrange the production, print and delivery of copies. The attraction of the crowdfunding model for publishers is knowing *before* investing in an author or title that there is a market for the book.

In the case of Unbound, which accepts submissions via agents as well as from authors direct, the costs are calculated according to the needs of the project. The target amount will pay for the professional-quality editing, production, publicity and distribution costs that the publisher incurs plus a contribution to the publisher's general overheads or running costs. Authors receive a profit-share after costs of 50 per cent. That's significantly more than a typical royalty arrangement with a traditional publisher, but shy of the 60 per cent income share on copies of self-published titles sold through Amazon's CreateSpace and Kindle Direct Publishing (KDP). Unbound, unlike most publishers, encourages authors to get in touch with each other to share experiences via an online forum. This can provide emotional support and lead to practical benefits as authors help promote one another's books.

Crowdfunding can be a fruitful option: it allows authors to 'test' their book idea – is there *really* a market for it? – to have significant input in how their book is pitched or 'sold' to potential micro-patrons; to share more of the profits when a book becomes successful and exceeds its initial reserve fund; to be in direct contact with their readers and build a loyal fanbase. Unbound published Nikesh Shukla's *The Good Immigrant*, which went on to win the 2016 Books Are My Bag Readers' Choice Award; this was followed by *The Good Immigrant USA*, published by Hachette. *Good Night Stories for Rebel Girls* by Elena Favilli and Francesca Cavallo (Penguin Random House, 2017) started as a Kickstarter campaign aiming to raise $40,000. It raised over $650,000 and has since sold over 1 million copies and has been translated into forty languages.

OTHER OPTIONS

New initiatives, creative hubs and collectives abound and often appear with fanfare before gently fizzling out when the harsh realities of the economics of publishing bite and previously offered sponsorship disappears. Exciting ways to access and provide books are good for the industry and introduce new ways of doing things, but the long tried and tested methods die hard and remain at the forefront of getting a new book from manuscript into the hands of readers, bankrolled by large publishing conglomerates and their international holding groups.

Some of the options below provide writers with greater choice, opportunities and freedom to experiment. Be wary, as some of the 'innovative' approaches offered might not be as attractive as they first seem. Exercise due diligence around companies offering to help you publish your book, don't ignore instinct, common sense or any research you do just because you are desperate to get your book in print.

Agent-assisted publishing There was a flurry of excitement a few years ago when a number of literary agents decided to diversify and extend their remit into producing books as well as acquiring new talent. In the main they looked to their authors' out-of-print backlists and to experimenting with e-publishing. Examples include the late Ed Victor's Bedford Square Books. Agents soon realised that although creating a book is not that difficult, finding buyers is a whole other ball-game. Some 'agents' will offer to publish new writers and will ask them to contribute financially to agent-assisted self-publishing (AASP); but why would an author be tempted by this? The agent is acting like a self-publishing provider service but also takes 15 per cent of any author earnings. You are advised to give such deals a wide berth.

Author cooperatives These range from practical support networks of writers who share their specific skills with others, like the US-based Book View Café, to online communities of authors offering a form of quality assurance to readers.

Fanfiction publishing Fanfiction is written by devotees of a published author's work, is shared online and is based around the characters, themes or storylines from the original books, but is not usually authorised or professionally published. Publishers and agents may follow trends in fanfiction, and conventions such as the Young Adult Literature Convention (YALC) or Comic-Con can be fertile ground for finding out what devoted readers are writing and sharing. Famously, E. L. James' *Fifty Shades of Grey* started out as self-published *Twilight* fanfiction in ebook form before being taken up by an agent and the print publisher Vintage.

Hybrid publishing is an attractive option for authors who want to explore both self-publishing and traditional publishing routes. A hybrid author might retain digital rights for a title and self-publish digitally but be published traditionally in print. She might write across different genres, some more suited to self-publishing, or may wish to juggle the demands and creative freedoms of self-publishing with the collaborative benefits of working with an agent and publisher because it is fun and might be one way to forge a more lucrative writing career.

Partnership publishing is akin to self-publishing or vanity publishing, though often presents itself as a more 'respectable' model where publisher and author share the costs of producing a book to professional standards and thus share in the risk of the book being a commercial success or otherwise. As with self-publishing, there are reputable operators and others to steer clear of. With no standard code to which companies need to adhere, you are advised to read any small print in contractual letters carefully so you know exactly what you might be signing up to. An author might be seduced into 'buying', i.e. paying up-front for the printing of a minimum number of copies. How might you store or sell 1,000 copies of your book? Check to see what marketing support and access to sales channels the publisher provides.

Social enterprise publishing There are organisations with social enterprise at their heart which offer publishing support – expertise and funding – to those who might not otherwise be published. These initiatives, many not-for-profit charitable operations, are motivated by social, community and environmental objectives rather than by profit. They include the likes of Comma Press, Dead Ink Books and Lantana Publishing.

Sponsored publishing is, as the name suggests, book creation where the costs have been underwritten wholly or in part by a third party such as a professional institution or society, charity or business that has a vested interest in supporting the project. This might be a company that wants to provide a book about their organisation to give away free to clients or a charity that funds a book that will give advice for individuals and supporters of a rare medical condition that it represents and wants to see more widely discussed. Some foundations might also offer sponsorship to authors from disadvantaged backgrounds, such as the Arkbound Foundation, which works with Luna Press Publishing.

Vanity publishing is when an author pays to have their book published, but has little say over how this is done, unlike in true self-publishing where an author pays for the services she specifically chooses. The term is used pejoratively for providers who take overall control, may retain copyright and offer little in return. A vanity press may do a scant amount of editing and serve up print copies to an author for a hefty fee and provide no help in promoting or selling the books. Authors are advised to avoid such publishers. You can find some useful advice and details of some companies to avoid at http://vanitypublishing.info/.

NOT QUITE SO NEW?

Before we get carried away and imply that the old models are passé and no longer relevant, that the trio of author-agent-publisher that has lasted for decades (the first literary agencies were established around the 1880s), is on its last legs, let's not be too hasty to usher out the old just yet.

Self-publishing might not be quite as revolutionary as we are sometimes led to believe, though its reach is profound. Self-publishing and sponsored publishing have always been around, with authors paying in part or full for the production costs of their works. In her book *The Naked Author: A Guide to Self-Publishing* (A&C Black, 2011), Alison Baverstock provides this anecdote:

> In 1797, a manuscript was submitted to a London publisher by the proud father of an unknown author. *First Impressions*, a three-volume novel, was offered for private publication; the writer's family would pay . . . to mitigate the publisher's financial risk. The publishing house turned it down.
>
> Revised and renamed, it was finally published fourteen years later to good reviews . . . [and is] today . . . a cornerstone of English literature.

She is describing Jane Austen's *Pride and Prejudice*.

Beatrix Potter, James Joyce, Virginia Woolf and William Blake self-published to get their work in print, as more recently did already established authors Timothy Mo, David Mamet and Roddy Doyle. What's good enough for Dickens, Proust and Mark Twain should be good enough for anyone reading this book.

Some writers are trying all avenues. After publishing the twelve books in her *Mira James Mystery* series traditionally and being disappointed with the income she earned, Jess Lourey negotiated to have the rights reverted and redesigned and republished the books herself on Amazon. Susan Hill, author of *The Woman in Black* and a prolific back catalogue of works across several different genres, is a traditionally published author who has experimented with self-publishing and has set up her own publishing company Long Barn Books. She is perhaps the ultimate hybrid author.

Deciding which route to take

How you decide which publishing route to pursue will depend on you and on your book. Ask yourself how much control, beyond writing, do you want? How much time, energy and skill do you have to publish your own book? How willing are you to work with self-publishing provider services that can help you take this path? It may depend on how patient you are: do you want to spend time looking for a literary agent when you know that the odds are stacked against you as a debut novelist? Have you already tried to get a publishing deal or exhausted all possible agent avenues and are ready to try the self-publishing route instead? Do you have a quirky book idea that doesn't appear to fit the mainstream or do you have a sponsor lined up to finance part or all of your editorial, production or distribution costs? Do you have professional skills and expertise as an editor or PR or sales manager and think you could translate these into the publishing arena? Are you impatient to get your book to market? Have you researched all there is to know about search engine optimisation (SEO), BIC and Thema codes, Amazon and Google rankings, and have heard that publishers may not be as knowledgeable in these areas as you might be yourself?

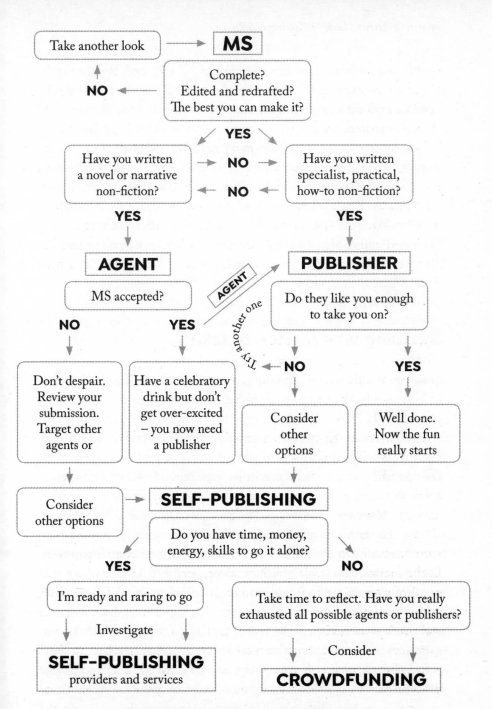

Which publishing route shall I take?

Do you want to keep a higher percentage of the revenue from each copy of your book sold? Do you think you might make more money publishing yourself or via a crowdfunded publisher in ebook than with a traditional publisher?

Whatever your circumstances and motivations, it is good to remind yourself *why* you are embarking on a particular route and to consider what might be the best way to publish your particular title: do you know you can reach your target audience without the need of Geoffrey Faber's middle-man publisher (see box on page 16)? Take advice from authors who have already been published – what do they recommend? What worked well for them and what worked less well? Which areas might you be able to successfully outsource? What resources are there to give unbiased and clear, reliable advice? Are there events or conferences where you can engage with publishing experts and other authors to help inform your views? Go with your gut feeling too. In the end it may fall down to personal preference and situation: do you have time and money to devote to self-publishing in a professional way?

WHY CHOOSE THE SELF-PUBLISHING ROUTE?

You might opt to self-publish your book because you think you can do it better and quicker than a publisher, or you have professional contacts who might be able to help you in an exchange of skills (you write a cover blurb and edit their text in return for them designing a front cover or explaining the finer points of keywords and SEO). You may be happy to research and sign up to paid-for services that you trust on recommendation and so have some creative and business control over how your book develops and gets produced and distributed.

Certain types of book are readily suited to being self-published: titles that may be too niche or innovative for a publisher and do not fit neatly into a pre-existing publishing list; titles that publishers might eschew such as erotica or that few agents represent such as fantasy and its panoply of sub-genres. Your book may not be commercial: you might be creating a title for a specific, local audience: a family memoir, a charity cookbook, local history or walking guide perhaps. It might be a work of art or of love.

If you have been frustrated by an inability to hook an agent or engage a publisher with your manuscript and you are impatient to get your writing into print or ebook (to tie in with an anniversary, for example) or because you have decided to bypass the traditional agent-publisher route on principle, then self-publishing could help you realise your literary ambitions. Established authors may find that their earlier works are no longer in fashion and their publisher is no longer promoting them strongly in backlist and looking to move the titles into print-on-demand or put them out-of-print altogether. If that happens – and the publisher is amenable *and* the author's original publishing contract allows – an author might decide to have a go at self-publishing (possibly in ebook only) to see if they can revive their backlist. Contracts usually include a reversion clause which indicates that when a title sells fewer than a certain number of copies the author or their agent on the author's behalf can ask to take back the publishing rights.

Whatever your reasons, the self-publishing route is not an easy one, but many authors attest to it being a very rewarding one. Having learnt new skills while navigating the vagaries of the publishing process, some then choose to share these skills with other aspiring self-published authors or set up small publishing companies themselves; in effect joining the traditional model but reinventing it in ways that allow for greater nimbleness, efficiencies and a personal approach. If you can't beat 'em, join 'em.

Self-publishing is not so innovative: it uses the same terminology, the same expertise and the same processes as mainstream publishing. What is new is the ability of all publishers (self- or otherwise) to be in touch direct with their readers and their purchasers by harnessing new technology. The fact that self-published authors have embraced this so readily is what has helped to disrupt the existing publishing structures.

PUBLISHERS – WHAT DO THEY OFFER?

- Track record: they know what they are doing
- Kudos: brand can matter
- Quality control: design, editorial and production skills
- Market knowledge: sales and marketing expertise
- Contacts: across the media and selling outlets
- The whole package: the complete process
- Support from an expert in-house editor and design, production and marketing colleagues

Why self-publish?

- Speed to market: you want to get your book out into the market quickly
- Control and ownership over your own work
- Because you can: relatively easy and cheap to do so
- Flexible: an opportunity to explore new formats
- You have direct access to your market and readers
- You think you can make money and want to keep the lion's share of revenues
- You have been rejected by agents and publishers too many times
- You have the requisite skills or know people who do
- You want to: and have the time, energy, passion and money to do so

The pros and cons of each route

	Traditional publisher	Self-publishing	Crowdfunding
Agent	Most authors of fiction need one; an agent is likely to get you a better deal than you get yourself	You don't need one; you don't have to share your earnings (they typically take 15% commission)	You don't need one (see self-publishing column)
Funding	All stages from manuscript delivery to final copies are paid for by the publisher	You will need to fund all stages in producing and selling your book	Individuals pledge money to fund the production of your book
Copyright	Is retained by you – make sure you don't assign it to a publisher	You retain copyright in your work	You retain copyright in your work; make sure you don't assign it to a crowdfunding publisher
Control	A publisher will have a clear sense of how they want to present and publicise your book based on their experience and expertise	You can publish your book how you see fit: choose your own design, cover and have full control; but do you know what you don't know?	You can have full control or work with a publisher
Market	They can take a while to get to readers – up to 12 months from MS delivery	You can get to readers quickly, but how will you identify and reach them?	You have a market – readers who have signed up to buy your book in advance

	Traditional publisher	Self-publishing	Crowdfunding
Publicity	Have contacts with reviewers and media outlets	Do you have access to lists or contacts or will you have to create these?	You have already promoted your idea in advance of publication
Sales	They can exploit existing rights contacts and have established sales channels	You manage distribution; with limited access for print distribution	Confirmed sales: books are pre-ordered by readers
Author income	May offer an advance; royalties will be around 15% of cover price or even lower if based on net receipts	Author keeps around 60% of revenue but cover price is usually low	Author may share 50/50 in earnings after costs

Advice for whichever publishing route you take:

1. Do your homework.

2. Decide what's right for you and your book.

3. Don't rush.

4. Think about what your intentions are.

5. Be professional.

6. Do your best.

Your aim should be to produce the most attractive and readable book possible. There is a mountain of badly produced self-published books, and a sizeable pile of others that are poorly written or edited. It is all too easy to write a good book and publish it badly: to attach it to a cover that doesn't properly reflect the content or saddle it with a boring blurb that fails to catch the attention of potential readers.

We haven't really departed from the basic premise that a book is something we read for pleasure or information and is composed of written words and images. We may be able to do that in more convenient ways than Gutenberg and his contemporaries, but the human need for stories and the way in which we mentally digest narrative hasn't changed that much.

Whichever route you plump for, the quality of your writing is what matters: having something to say and saying it well. Which takes us nicely onto the next chapter, which considers how to make your manuscript submission-ready to send to a publisher or literary agent or to be uploaded to a self-publishing platform.

CHAPTER 2

Writing, editing and perfecting your manuscript

Being a writer

A writer is a person who writes.

John Braine[*]

TAKE YOURSELF SERIOUSLY AS A WRITER

If you take your writing and your ambition to be a published author seriously, then others might too. That means calling yourself a writer at functions when you are asked what you do, rather than telling people that's what you *want* to be. As Sarah Crossan, Carnegie Award-winning author, muses in her Foreword to the *Children's Writers' & Artists' Yearbook* (2019 edition; Bloomsbury, 2018):

> Rather than going to the cinema when friends asked, I started to say, 'Sorry, I can't. I'm writing.' When they seemed irritated by my resolve, I didn't care. If I wanted to achieve my dream of writing for a living, I had to believe in myself, otherwise no one else would. I found a way out of my shame and into a pattern of work that I loved.

Sarah became committed and professional in her approach to developing her craft. How much time and money you can commit to doing this will depend on your individual circumstances. You might think you have a book in you (who doesn't!), but if you don't know how to release it into physical form, then it is no more than a fantasy.

---

[*] From *How to Write A Novel* (Methuen, 2000, original published in 1974 as *Writing a Novel*, Eyre Methuen Ltd).

For thriller writer Claire McGowan completing her first full-length novel (proving to herself that she actually could) and paying for some writing advice were the first stages in turning her dream of being a writer into a reality: 'Spend money. Invest in your writing. Whether that's purchasing a Moleskine notebook or attending a writing course.'

Why is it so difficult to call yourself a writer? Is it because there isn't a clear route to the profession, no standard qualifications? There are creative writing courses that result in certification – MAs, PhDs – and increasingly combined BA and undergraduate programmes, but most writers don't follow structured academic apprenticeships. Such courses are expensive, take time and are not always very compatible with a full-time job or raising a family. Few can jettison a career whilst they write in the hope that their first novel will be an overnight success. Most need to do the literary equivalent of a Hollywood wannabe waiting tables whilst honing their skills in the hope of being talent-spotted by an agent.

Most likely as a fledging author, you will be dipping your toe in and out of the literary waters in a cautious and possibly apologetic way. How dare you have the temerity to suggest that you can sustain a 300-page romantic fiction, police procedural or fantasy doorstopper that readers might actually want to read. If you do want to be a writer, then WRITE.

DEVOTE YOURSELF TO YOUR CRAFT

Commit to your writing. Be confident that wanting to be a published author is a realistic ambition, if you put in graft, think positively and accept that there are likely to be knockbacks along the way to achieving this goal.

If you are spending time attending conferences and festivals, researching compulsively online and in libraries, working creatively with children in a school, you are raising your profile and immersing yourself in the world of books and words, being advocates for your craft. But you are NOT writing. Don't kid yourself that you are. You may be involved in a very positive way, interacting with your potential audience and readership and you may be doing something that you enjoy. John Braine cites the possibly apocryphal tale of Sinclair Lewis arriving drunk to a Harvard lecture on writing and yelling at the assembled audience 'Hands up, all those who want to be writers?' Of course, all hands went up. 'Then why the hell aren't you at home writing?' he asked, before staggering off the platform. He had a point.

Being strict with yourself and establishing a routine and self-discipline is an important part of proving that you truly are a writer who takes your chosen profession and your craft seriously – seriously enough to carve out minutes and hours each day to dedicate yourself to it to the exclusion of all other distractions.

You might be networking in writing environments and amongst writing communities out of financial necessity to supplement your paltry and unsteady income from the sales of your books. It's not true that 'thinking is writing' – as I heard at a recent 'How to Get Published' day in Bristol. At best it is research, and useful preparation, but is more likely to be an example of procrastination. I should know. I'm an arch putter-offer. It's easy to faff, delay and find displacement activities to fill the hours when you *could* be writing. There's nothing quite like a publishing contract with a submission deadline you have signed up to and a firm publication date in sight to make you get your scribbling skates on. But you are not going to be forced to write (the publisher can always take back the advance they entrusted to you). Writing has to be an activity you want to do or want to make yourself do. You can improve your chances of completing a manuscript by getting down to it and getting at least some words on the page, by being organised, focused and doggedly rigorous with yourself.

When I commission pieces for the *Writers' & Artists' Yearbooks* each year, agents and authors will not infrequently politely decline a request to compose a short piece, the reason being that the author is very busy writing to a deadline and is not to be diverted by other projects. These writers are committed, disciplined and know that they lose focus every time they are tempted away from the task in hand.

MAKE A PLAN AND STICK TO IT

Many authors recommend setting achievable goals. Creating a realistic timetable to which you will work is helpful. You can then reward yourself if you hit word count or the date you set for writing a complete first draft of your first chapter, or your synopsis, or the pen portrait of your main protagonist. Breaking down your goals into manageable chunks is a good idea. Setting a mountain of a goal is not. Aiming to write 1,000 words a day before lunch is a more realistic ambition than a wide sweep of a target such as 'I'm going to write my memoir'. When you achieve your pre-set goal, reward yourself. The promise of a run round the block or bar of chocolate might be just the incentive you need to keep your target in sight and not be diverted from your writing.

Victorian novelist Anthony Trollope would get up at 5.00 am, review the previous day's output and set himself the task of writing around 2,500 words for two and half hours, by the end of which it was time for breakfast. He sat literally 'watching the clock' with his watch beside him and maintained this strict regime most days. He would make a note of when he diverged from this habit so that he might rebuke himself for any dilatory behaviour. 'In this [his diary] I have entered, day by day, the number of pages I have written, so that if any time I have slipped into idleness for a day or two, the record of that idleness has been there, staring me in the face, and demanding of me increased labour, so that the deficiency might be supplied.' Most of us may not share Trollope's work ethic, but we can't deny it bore fruits as far as he (and, let's face it, his publisher and ultimately his devoted readers too) was concerned. His output was prodigious; he wrote forty-seven novels in addition to his short stories, plays and non-fiction in fewer than thirty years, all the while working full-time during the early years of his writing for the Post Office and later campaigning to become a Liberal MP for Beverley in Yorkshire's East Riding. He devoted his final years completely to his writing career. Trollope claimed that he never submitted his work late and always hit his deadlines.

Producing a set number of words each day is something many writers advocate. In their book *Willpower: Why Self-Control is the Secret to Success*, psychologists Roy F. Baumeister and John Tierney (Penguin Books, 2012) suggest keeping track of how much you write is useful:

Monitoring is crucial for any kind of plan you make – and it can even work if you don't make a plan at all. . . . Even a writer who doesn't share Trollope's ability to meet a daily quota can still benefit just by noting the word count at the beginning and end of the day: the mere knowledge that you'll have to put down a number will discourage procrastination (or the kind of busywork that might feel virtuous but doesn't contribute to that word count).

WHO SAID WRITING WAS EASY?

Most authors will tell you a fair amount of hard slog and graft is involved in writing. Prolifically successful writer Roald Dahl – who famously had a shed at the end of his garden in which to write – said 'Two hours of writing fiction leaves this writer completely drained. For those two hours he has been in a different place with totally different people.' Writing can be physically and emotionally taxing. Philip Pullman, author of the *His Dark Materials* trilogy, knows a thing or two about getting on with it: 'If you only write when you want to, or when you feel like it, or when it's easy, you'll always be an amateur.'

Being rigorous with your time and keeping to your targets is a step in the right direction. There are no stringent rules about where and how to manage *your* writing time. But carving out a space and time when you can devote yourself to it and dismiss all other distractions will help. Start by switching off email and social media, finding a conducive place to write, being consistent and establishing a regular pattern of working. Every writer works out a pattern for herself. Grabbing thirty minutes first thing in the morning or last thing at night when children, paperwork, household chores or the day job have not yet invaded or have been 'put to bed' might be all you can manage. John Braine (whose advice seems just as pertinent now as when he first shared it in 1974) suggests that 'the will to work' itself is 'all the seclusion that one needs' and that 'the lack' of quiet or solitude should be 'no barrier to writing'. If you wait too long to locate the equivalent of Virginia Woolf's 'room of one's own' you might be waiting rather a long time. A study, garden room or spare bedroom might be a luxury most writers don't have; a kitchen table, local café or booth in your town library (those that are left) can provide the 'seclusion' you might need.

Writing, we have determined, is hard and it is work. It can be pleasurable, too, in spite of – or because of – the challenges it poses. The pleasure can be found in the execution: the process of getting thoughts out onto the page, unpacking an idea so that it is rendered in a linguistically articulate and felicitous way. And it can be found in the completion: having a sense of achievement of minutes or hours or days well spent with a text to show for the endeavour: some text, any text, raw material that can be manipulated further through rewrites and edits. To return to Braine (you can tell I'm a fan), if you write you are a writer. If you want to be a writer but fail to write, then you are a procrastinator.

So, you have found the will, the rigour and the wherewithal to sit down to write. As Stephen King puts it in his wonderfully readable *On Writing: A Memoir of the Craft*, '. . . there you are in your room with the shade down and door shut and the plug pulled out of the base of the telephone. You've blown up your TV and committed yourself to a thousand words a day, come hell or high water.'

WHY DO YOU WRITE?

There are two reasons why people write: for pleasure or to pay the bills. Ideally, you'll do the former in order to successfully fulfil the latter. That's basically what publishers are looking for: bankable, saleable authors who will help fill their coffers. It also helps if you have something worthwhile, interesting or entertaining to say.

It's a much-referenced adage that writers write because they 'have to'; they are driven by the creative urge (and not motivated by money) that has to be satisfied or they will have a life devoid of meaning. That's possibly true. If so, why not toil away in your own little garret and forgo the need to be discovered and have others read your work? Writing may be a solitary art, but I'm not convinced that it is as self-effacing or unselfconscious as the must-be-creative-at-all-odds would have us believe. There is surely an element of vanity in the desire to be published, particularly in wanting to have a novel published – and while novels are most definitely necessities, it is still seen as rather a luxury to spend one's days hunched over a MacBook Pro or Underwood typewriter rather than toiling at more practical tasks in a 9–5 job.

WHAT KIND OF WRITER DO YOU WANT TO BE?

The writer comes in all shapes and sizes: part-time, full-time, or with very little time (an hour or two snatched across the week). They might only write what they want to, write to commission or work as a jobbing hack. They might desire to see their name in lights or are happy to ghost someone else's life or story idea. They might earn income through an agent–publisher royalty deal or on a work-for-hire fixed-fee basis. They might want to write just one book – to prove to themselves and others that they can – or they might map out a writing life in a more professional, business-focused way.

You might choose to raise your author profile and your bank balance bit-by-bit, by writing comment pieces for blogs and magazines or drafting copy in a more commercial direction, such as speechwriting, marketing copy, instructions for manuals, products and services.

You might write a book or a series of books from which you can spin off a whole range of narratives and creative propositions, shaping stories for beyond the page or Kindle for comic books, audio or video games.

You might have a grand plan – a real sense of what kind of author you want to be, where you want your career to be in five years' time and how you will measure your success: will it be by selling over 20,000 copies of your first psychological thriller or winning a national prize for your literary debut? Your imagined goals might be more realistic and contained: getting your title onto the shelves of Waterstones or your local independent bookstore and garnering a fistful of five-star reviews in the Amazon bookstore. Will you feel you've 'arrived' when you can balance your work and writing lives in a way that suits you and brings pleasure rather than stress? Or when you have jacked in your day job altogether?

Jo Nadin, a successful full-time writer of books for children and adults with over seventy titles to her name, has built a life around books. She teaches creative writing at Bath Spa University, supports celebrity writers with fashioning their story ideas into a publishable format, writes books for schools, co-authors titles, appears at festivals and makes school visits to inspire the next generation of novelists; and amidst all this, she still finds time to create her own original narratives. She is proud to call herself a jobbing writer and is a perfect example of the writer who has established, over time and through hard work, a strong reputation. Being effective as a writer can be as much to do with being an efficient, organised and directed human being.

Now comes the big question: What are you going to write about?

WRITING ABOUT WHAT YOU KNOW . . . OR NOT

According to King, you should write 'Anything you damn well want.' The writer is mistress of her own universe. A writer is usually commanded to write what they know or to write from experience. Your novel might be more successful if you do. But what does successful mean? It's two things: a book that will appeal to readers and therefore will sell. Happy readers will recommend your work to other potential readers, by word-of-mouth, via blogs or online starred recommendations. More readers equates to increased book sales. That results in a happy author and a happy publisher.

A WRITER'S INTENTIONS: ASK YOURSELF

- What are you writing?
- Why are you writing?
- Who are you writing for?
- What are the intended consequences of putting these ideas on paper or screen?
- What experience do you want your reader to have?
- How will you reach your readers?
- What can you do to up your chances of getting published?
- What kind of writer do you want to be?

TOP TIPS FOR WRITERS #1: KEEP FOCUSED AND KEEP WRITING

How do you keep yourself energised and focused and ensure that you just keep writing?

Read, read, read everything – trash, classics, good and bad,
and see how they do it. Just like a carpenter who works as an
apprentice and studies the master. Read! You'll absorb it. Then write.
If it is good, you'll find out. If it's not, throw it out the window.

William Faulkner

1. **Read:** This is the single most repeated piece of advice that authors hand down. It's unlikely that you will know what stories others might want to read without cultivating a reading habit of your own. Most successful writers own up to being voracious bookworms in their childhood and creators of stories too; even fashioning mini books complete with illustrations, cover designs and blurbs in some cases. They talk about books being part of who they are.

   Don't despair if you've been an unenthusiastic reader to date. It's never too late to start immersing yourself in the works of those writers that are successfully being published in the genre you think you want to write in.

2. **Don't be discouraged** if you don't think you fit the 'typical' writer mould. There is a shared view – and about time too – that the world of books will be enhanced by encouraging a much greater diversity of voices in the publishing business itself by employing a wider range of individuals beyond white, middle-class university graduates with an English degree. When commissioning new books, publishing editors *are* now looking for wider ranges of experience, seeking out new writers from groups traditionally underrepresented in the book-o-sphere (notably BAME and LGBTQ+ writers), who have interesting and (hopefully)

commercial stories to tell. Employing a wider spectrum of people in the industry (yes please to more graduates with scientific, technology and business backgrounds too) can only be a good thing: the theory is that they will be able to spot and nurture the unsung voices from the world's they hail from. There have always been publishers and agents who have been searching for startling new writers with something to say: a good editor or agent should always be on the lookout for talent and not purely for the competent or talented from their own tribe; but now – thank goodness – there seems a genuine attempt to be proactive in this area.

New voices include those from economically deprived sectors of society. There have been notable successes for writers such as bestselling exponents of the thriller Kimberley Chambers (market stall trader and taxi driver before turning to writing), Mel Sherratt, who self-published before getting picked up by her agent Madeleine Milburn, and more recently Kerry Hudson, who grew up poor in 1980s Aberdeen, and is the author of award-winning and brilliantly titled novel *Tony Hogan Bought Me an Ice-cream Float Before He Stole My Ma*. The award-winning author of *My Name is Leon*, Kit de Waal, also editor of *Common People: An Anthology of Working-Class Writers* (Unbound, 2019) and Natasha Carthew, who writes both adult and YA books, have been spearheading new initiatives, including the Working Class Writers' Festival planned for 2020.

3. **Carry a notebook** or (dicta)phone with you wherever you go. Jot down ideas and plotlines – however slim or outlandish – on your phone. Get into the habit of writing things down. It will help in forming a regular pattern of writing time and will remind you that writing something – anything – can encourage your creativity. Allow your imagination to run riot. Think of the 'what if' and the 'what next', the dot, dot, dot of a situation.

Scribble away when moments allow – on train, bus or tube journeys or whenever you can snatch a few minutes to yourself.

Note down a well-crafted line or combination of words when they come to you. Be inquisitive and nosey; listen in to conversations, observe the tone, phrasing and vocabulary that are used by individuals who might provide ingredients for characters in the current book you are working on or ones you have yet to write. Develop the art of overhearing – being as subtle as you can – so that your writing can be as authentic as possible. Be magpie-like and pick up shards of shiny details about the way that places look and people act and talk and interact with one another and to a situation. Take time to look and observe and digest. Keep your eyes and ears attuned to the world around you. This is the best and most original research you can do as an author.

4. **Stop procrastinating**, set yourself goals, targets and timetables that you can stick to.

5. **Find a place to write** that suits you and work out your own routine that means you actually get on with what you are supposed to be doing. Turn off email and social media alerts so you don't get distracted by them. Consider scheduling a set time of day when you will look at your emails.

6. **Write what you want to write** and not what you think the market wants. You will only know if what you want to say in print is of credible, readable or marketable value if you have a go and then present a finished version to an agent or publisher and to other critics during earlier drafts. Agents and publishers can help you turn your words and ideas into a presentable document that is appropriate in style, tone and length for the readership for which it is intended.

7. **Keep going**. Just get things down and get to the end of a piece of prose (a scene, a chapter or a complete manuscript): avoid pausing to refine and tweak on the way. You can't call yourself a real writer if you don't finish things off. You might be in the middle of your narrative and you get bogged down: a scene just won't work, a character starts behaving erratically, you lose your ability to render realistic dialogue. You are dispirited. The end of your novel seems

a long way off and you are bored. Ride the potholes in the road. Don't go around them but confront them head on. It might be a bumpy ride, but you'll get to your intended destination in the end. You can revisit the problem areas once you have completed the full manuscript and are ready for your rewrites and edits. Conversely, coming to a halt and deciding you have reached the end of your novel is hard. Really hard. You may enjoy living with your characters so much that you don't want to stop spending time with them. Perhaps that means it is time to plan a sequel or another book in a series. If motivating yourself to start your novel is difficult, then letting go and tying up the ends to come to a convincing denouement can be even more taxing.

8. **Get a cat** (advised Muriel Spark, it helped her concentrate) or invest in quality gin (recommended by literary agent Ed Wilson) or drink cocktails when you get stuck (Sophie Kinsella) or *never* drink and write (F. Scott Fitzgerald).

9. **Get a change of scene**. Make a curry. Jog, run or take your dog (or someone else's dog) for a walk. Take regular breaks and time off to allow your brain to breathe and ideas to reach you spontaneously. Have quiet, contemplative moments – go on a writers' retreat if you have time, money and inclination to do so – look out for discounted rates and prizes given in competitions such as those offered by Arvon (fifty years old in 2019) and the annual *Writers' & Artists'* Short Story competition. Find something that is different from sitting in front of a computer screen for hours on end or bashing the keys on your typewriter or gripping your 'good luck' writing pen. In short (and so as not to contradict the advice given in point 4 above), create a daily schedule that allows for routine in an environment conducive to writing AND give yourself time to go off-piste, to take inspiration from the world outside your writing shed: whether that's a beach, woodland or countryside, a park or Italian coffee shop down the road where you can indulge in a pick-me-up double expresso.

10. **Try not to get down** or lonely or anxious. Learn how to cope with being ignored or rejected. As mentioned already, you'll need to develop the hide of a rhinoceros. Engage with other writers – see ways in which you can do this in Top Tips For Writers #2 on page 71. As a writer starting out, you might not feel confident sharing your new-found passion with your friends and family. You may not know other writers or how to meet them. Most writers will have felt something similar and might feel that those in their immediate circle of friends and colleagues do not understand that aspect of their life. It has never been easier to find the writing support and camaraderie that you seek.

11. **Enjoy yourself** as you do all the above. Spending time with your characters and finding out what happens to them, how they will react to the challenges and events that your story throws at them, should be an absorbing and exhilarating experience. Occasionally making yourself sit and write might seem like a chore. That's fine too. Most jobs have tedious aspects which can seem less than enlightening or purposeful. Plough on. Put an off day down to the usual ups and downs of life. Don't indulge the instinct to imagine you are having writer's block. Now there's a luxury your average worker doesn't ever get to experience. Writing *is* hard and time-consuming and frustrating. But every time you feel sorry for your writerly self, just remember you are not being sent down a mine, having to scrape veruccas off wrinkled feet or cold-call people who have no desire to speak to you, much less purchase the insurance policy or phone package that you are trying to fob off on them.

Who are you writing for?

It is a good idea for you to have a sense of what your market is. Who are your writing for? What is the age, experience or possibly gender of your likely reader? What do you want to get across to your reader? Are you writing a novel for adults or YA or a cross-over readership or are you not quite sure yet? If you are writing non-fiction is it for a reader with some, a lot or no prior knowledge of the subject? Your reader might be an imagined individual or group or a specifically identifiable peer group with whom you are sharing some up-to-date information, via an academic paper for example. In all cases, as the writer, you should have a clear sense of what you are writing and what your aims are.

In any business there are likely to be standards, norms, template documents that text will adhere to. Writing is no exception. To be convincing for the intended readership, your manuscript will most likely conform to certain conventions that have been developed for a particular style or type or genre of writing. Think how different in tone, length or use of vocabulary a news story might be from an experimental, literary novel, or indeed how one journalistic piece in the *Telegraph* might differ from a write-up of the same news item in the *Daily Mirror*. Or how the *Daily Mail's* print edition compares to its online version. The audiences are different, so the text is presented to appeal to these different constituencies of reader; they conform to each publication's 'house style'. This might cover the nuts and bolts of punctuation and spelling conventions (e.g. -ise rather than -ize spellings) as well as the preferred format for a strap- or by-line to accompany a piece, and the general tone or political leanings that the article writer might adopt to appeal to their readers. The newspaper or magazine editor aims to know who buys their publication so they can deliver what their readers want and more importantly so that they can keep them buying the next edition and not lose them to a rival publication.

What has this got to do with book publishing? Lots. It's an example of how we expect – even if that is subliminally so – what we read to conform to what we have read before. We expect the novels that we read, if we are English speakers, to start on page 1 and for each sentence to be read comprehensively from left to right. Each time we turn the page, we expect the story to continue in a logical way so we can follow the narrative. Notable exceptions, when an author plays around extensively with form and style, can understandably be a more challenging read – Joyce's *Ulysses* or *Finnegan's Wake* or Ernest Vincent Wright's *Gadsby* (when no word containing the letter 'e' was included). In a similar vein, freeform writing eschews some of the usual rules of punctuation and structure, such as in the more recent award-winning titles *A Girl is a Half-formed Thing* by Eimear McBride (Bailey's Prize for Fiction 2014) or *Milkman* by Anna Burns (Man Booker Prize 2018).

There are conventions for most genre fiction. Crime novels tend to have a flawed but intelligent detective accompanied by a professional sidekick, a trail of clues that pepper the story which the reader will use to try and solve a mystery, and a resolution during which the 'bad' character of the story faces a comeuppance. A psychological thriller will focus on the state of mind of the protagonist and is often told through their eyes in the first person. In the case of an academic title, there are critical peer review stages that are undertaken to establish the credentials and quality of the ideas and research contained therein and standard structures and ways of presenting that conform to norms that have become established over time: such as where, how and why footnotes and bibliographical references are cued to a text. Such conventions confer a level of authority on a text, which fulfil the expectations of the readership.

How to improve your manuscript

Writing non-fiction is the art of persuasion. Writing fiction is the art of making up stories. In the latter case, it can be an escape route from real life too. George Orwell implies that it was his awkwardness that led him to write, to escape the loneliness he encountered as an only (and what he deemed an unpopular) child. Taking solace in the world of make-believe, he created stories from an early age and 'created a sort of private world in which I could get my own back for my failure in everyday life!' The reasons Orwell was compelled to write are surely amongst the reasons why we read books: to escape the humdrum or the disappointing or the horrors of life in the real world.

This book is not about how to improve your writing. There are some excellent books and other resources to guide you in that (see the reading lists that start on page 259). But it is useful to be reminded of the core elements of any text that you need to get right as you produce a persuasive piece of non-fiction or an absorbing work of fiction.

STRUCTURE

As a writer, there will be all sorts of stylistic, structural and creative concerns that will pre-occupy you and which you will consider as you write. You will need to learn how to structure your story, creating a narrative arc that is convincing and which engages your reader, so that she reads from page one through each chapter and sticks with you and your characters and your story to the very end of the book.

WORDS, WORDS, WORDS

Do you enjoy words – the pleasure of the sound of them rolling off your tongue? Do you delight in the rich eccentricities of the English language and of the thousands of words it has imported into its lexicon from other languages across cultures and time? Do you get excited by the meanings that words convey and how these evolved? As a writer you should care deeply about words: what they can evoke, how they can be employed, why one word is better than another in a particular context. Words are the writer's essential tools: their bricks and mortar. Your task is to select, combine and craft them into strings (sentences or dialogue or verse lines) that can create atmosphere and a sense of place, and evoke emotions and help you develop a complete world in which your characters live, act, interact, talk, develop, rise and fall, win and lose.

FIND YOUR VOICE

There are aspects of the craft of writing that can be taught. And you can learn how to improve your work. By far the best way to become a better writer is – yes, you guessed it – to read the work of published writers (which I have reiterated several times). Try to work out what it is that works for you in their writing, that persuades you they have written a good book: maybe a fine sentence, an engrossing opening paragraph, or a knock-you-between-the-eyes twist of an ending. There is no need to become a literary critic overnight or spend all your time analysing the structure, tone, style and pace of other writers' work: but having a readiness to learn from examples of successful writing will undoubtedly have a positive impact on your own work. Don't fret about inadvertently copying another writer's style or story: the chances are you won't. You do need to be clear about attribution even in your notes, though. Lots of plagiarism cases involve authors saying they have accidentally not credited another author during the writing process. You are bound to be influenced by what you have read: just in the way you unconsciously imbibe everything else that is going on in the world around you. You will colour any story with your own approach: that *je ne sais quoi* that is the essence of you as a writer and which is in effect the unique 'voice' that you possess.

It might take time to find your voice and to be confident with letting it be heard or read. The next best thing you can do, after reading, is practise. Write lots and often. Emulate great writers by aping their style: the pared-down prose of Hemingway, the lengthy sentences of Henry James, the raw Scots dialect of Irvine Welsh or the Jamaican *patois* of Marlon James, a five-line limerick in the style of Edward Lear. Write a pastiche. Write practical, functional prose, for example copy for a new brand of washing powder or instructional prose to inform a reader how to make a coffee or wire a plug. Practise being nimble with words. Learn how to write with confidence for a specific market. Write something. Anything. Foster the urge to write. Make it part of who you are and what you do. Flex your writing muscles.

What makes a good book?

How is 'good' writing defined? This is of course subjective, there is not a checklist against which a writer can assess their work, but there

quest title cover brand
authenticity conflict relatable
surprise pace strong plot illustrations
anticipation
dilemma
world building rhythm convincing climax / anti-climax
struggle cadence character humour
empathy

This word cloud includes the features that debut authors at a recent
Writers & Artists Writing for Children workshop considered most important.

Essential ingredients for a novel

are standards (i.e. well-received published books) against which it can
be judged. We all have preferences about what we like to read, which
genres, styles and approaches we enjoy. I may prefer a literary, ruminative
style full of parenthetical phrases, sub-clauses, lengthy description and
convoluted sentences, akin to the florid – and what some frankly would
deem long-winded – style of Henry James. Hemingway's clipped prose
might be more affecting to you.

I read 'bad' writing every week – text that is flabby, dull, dripping
with adjectives, adverbs, clichés and pedestrian dialogue, that tells
rather than shows the action of a story. To avoid writing poor prose,
consider the building blocks for any story:

Theme: What's your story about? What's the impetus that compelled
you to write it? Can you encapsulate the story in a couple of choice
words or sentences? You don't need to have chosen an 'issue' to explore
in your novel, though you can. Is it a story exploring themes of loss,
growing up, love and death (most books have these somewhere at their

heart)? What other topics are woven in: poverty, loneliness, slavery, immigration, obsession? Have a go at summing up some of your favourite novels or one you have read recently. Can you distil them down to a theme or two and can you do the same for your own book? This can seem a little reductive, but all books are about *something* and it's good to be reminded of the point of your story while you write and subsequently pitch it.

Plot

Plot is no more than footprints left in the snow after your characters have run by on their way to incredible destinations.

Ray Bradbury

As you edit and refine your manuscript, ask yourself what purpose every element in your text has: are all the scenes, characters, twists and dialogue all necessary for advancing the plot? Do they enhance the reader's understanding of a character, their emotions and motivations? Can your reader follow what is going on and are you keeping the reader's attention?

Is the **setting** – the time, place and context of your novel, also called 'world-building' – convincingly imagined? Is the stage for your action and on which your characters act out their emotional and physical highs and lows, well-conceived, consistent and clearly developed?

Is your **main protagonist** and the other characters with whom he or she interacts well-rounded and someone your reader can like, dislike, care about, be fascinated by? Do they sometimes behave out of character?

Is **conflict** explored and then resolved by the end of the novel? There might be obstacles that your protagonist is forced to confront and overcome, actual or emotional. Your story does not have to have a conventional or happy ending, but some sort of resolution is usually expected.

Why does this all matter and what's it got to do with getting published as opposed to the writing process? If you know what your novel is *about* then it makes things much easier for you to convey that to others. That becomes very important and useful when you are making your pitch to an agent.

To keep a reader engaged, absorbed and loyal to your story, so that they read to the end, you need to imbue your story with these key ingredients:

- **Drama and action:** the detailed plot twists and turns which can be psychological, emotional or physical – the showing of what's happening to your characters.

- **Pace:** moving the story forward and providing moments of tension, a range of **tone** to heighten or lighten a mood and provide variety of style.

- **Gaps:** by this I mean allowing your reader to do some thinking, to let their own imagination fill in spaces between your words.

- **Dialogue** can be a good way to keep your narrative flowing. Do your characters sound realistic when they speak? Are their characters depicted through what they say and how they say it?

- **POV** (point of view): this might be first person, third person, internal voice, omnipotent narrator, or a mix of some of these. Chapters told from the perspective of different characters to paint a broader picture of how events can be interpreted in multiple ways can work well if adroitly handled; master storyteller Peter Carey shows how it can be done in *A Long Way From Home* (Faber & Faber, 2017). It's not an easy option and can mean yo-yoing between voices which might mean your story can become repetitious, disjointed and lacking in pace.

If you are writing non-fiction, you'll need to consider similar aspects. Is your theme or idea clearly defined, structured and delivered? Is the book organised in a logical, clear way? Are headings and non-textual materials used appropriately for the topic? Is the pace and tone suitable for the intended readership? Do you need to cut or explain jargon, expand on areas or trim when too much detail is included? Are you assuming too much or too little prior knowledge from your reader?

If you consider the elements referred to above, you will go far in **finding your voice**. Write with passion and fervour. Don't get stalled by being over-concerned about the genre you are writing in. Write the book you want to write and leave the worrying about where to slot it on the Amazon store or bookshop shelf up to the publisher's marketing or sales departments. Voice is what makes a writer's 'style' unique. If you practise writing, it will emerge: you will recognise it when it does. There are practical aspects to help you find this inner narrator. Adopt the active voice – which *shows* the reader what's going on in the story: 'Don't tell me the moon is shining; show me the glint of light on broken glass.' (Anton Chekhov). In the same way, direct speech, i.e. dialogue, rather than reported speech, makes for a more active and dynamic story.

BEGINNINGS AND ENDINGS

How you open and close your story is important. The start of your book will determine if you have captured your reader's attention and encouraged them to read on. Your ambition for your ending should be that it does not disappoint your reader and will leave them reaching for your next book.

Opening sentences, paragraphs, pages and chapters should hook the reader. The best openers encapsulate the essence of a story and are as a result memorable and often quoted:

- *It is a truth universally acknowledged, that a single man in possession of a good fortune, must be in want of a wife.*
- *It was the best of times, it was the worst of times . . .*
- *Aujourd'hui, maman est morte. / Today, mother died.*

> – *Mr and Mrs Dursley, of number four, Privet Drive, were proud to say that they were perfectly normal, thank you very much.*

Opening lines that plunge you straight into the action of a story immediately pique curiosity. As a writer you want to draw your reader in, giving them just enough detail to arouse their interest – who is this character, what incident is being hinted at, what's going to happen next, what has led to the incident described, how is the drama of the plot going to play out, why should I care?

By the end of your first chapter you should aim to have established:

- Who the story is about
- Where the events are happening (and when if it is historical fiction)
- The moment of narration – is it the story's present or part of a backstory?
- Who is telling the story (is it told in the first or third person?)

And to have:

- Hinted at the tone, atmosphere and action that are to follow
- Displayed your voice
- Captured the reader's attention and held on to it: why should they care about your characters or the dilemma they find themselves in?
- Dropped into the story at a significant event (or perhaps even an insignificant one)

Backstory can be filled in over the course of the novel if it needs to be. Avoid over-explanatory text and lengthy description if it's not in keeping with the overall tone, pace and intentions of your novel.

Knowing where to stop is a necessary part of writing and concluding your story in a way that does not disappoint the reader that has stuck with you up to that point is a challenge. Consider if your ending:

- Suits the narrative you have chosen
- Ties the threads of your plot lines too cleanly
- Provides some hope and a form of resolution
- Avoids any clichéd cop-outs in the vein of 'it was all a dream', which is likely to infuriate your reader
- Leaves enough frayed edges to allow for a sequel

Finishing your book should not be because you have run out of creative steam. It might have been exhausting to get there and you might not want to say goodbye to characters you have been living with in your head and on the page for months or years, but a novel is an artifice with a set of conventions with which it needs to be bookended, so try your best to conclude it well. If you find it hard, then you are not alone.

E. M. Forster in *Aspects of the Novel* (Penguin Classics, 2005, first published by Edward Arnold, 1927) wrote that the ending of nearly all novels is a let-down: 'This is because the plot requires to be wound up. Why is this necessary? Why is there not a convention which allows a novelist to stop as soon as he [*sic*] feels muddled or bored?'

Finding advice you can trust

Authors need readers. It's a good idea to have your manuscript read as you develop it. You don't need to ask for these beta readers or critical readers to comment on every stage or too early in the process. It's best to get them to read a complete chapter, better still a full manuscript so they can provide meaningful feedback. Make clear what you are asking their advice on, and what sort of feedback you are expecting – detailed checking of facts by a content expert or notes from a reader who fits the demographic of your target audience? Is the story gripping, readable, convincing for them? And importantly, if you are inviting their candid commentary, are you sure they will provide it and are you ready for any negative views? Ideally your critical readers will be people you already know and trust. Avoid asking those too close to you. Friends and family might be tempted to give too whitewashed a view so as not to hurt your feelings. Apart from liking you, what credentials will your mum or best friend or partner have to allow them to appraise your writing in a dispassionate or meaningful way? If they are professionally engaged with writing or publishing or a profession that relates to content or characters or a plotline in your book, then they may be best placed to guide you.

However, you may need to cast your net more widely to find readers who will be a better judge of your manuscript and its state: is it nearly ready for submission? Does the ending work? Is it riddled with plot holes? Is some of the dialogue wooden? Is the story confusing: are there too many sub-plots, minor characters or time shifts crowding the narrative? You will know which sections of the book are working better than others and where you think you need specific input. Be self-deprecating enough to both seek and then accept criticism gracefully, but don't assume that one reader has the monopoly on knowing if your manuscript hits the mark or not. Some people will not like your book. That's life. Don't fall into the Slough of Despond because the first person who reads your manuscript doesn't respond to it the way that you had hoped. Ask someone else, take wider soundings. Is there a pattern to the responses? Do they suggest that there are weaknesses that it would be foolish or arrogant not to address?

If you don't know anyone who might be a reader in your immediate circle, then there are other ways to seek useful input.

Join a creative writing group to share your work, make writing friendships and receive advice from a tutor. Regular meetings help provide a structure to your writing life and deadlines to which you need to produce some content ready to be read and critiqued by the group. The experience is likely to be more rewarding if the group is no more than eight or so individuals who are at a similar stage in their writing, so ask around for any in your area.

Develop relationships online There are numerous writing communities online that coalesce around a genre or style of writing and share sites like Wattpad, Inkit, Litopia, Worthy of Publishing.

Be inspired by initiatives such as National Writing Day and NaNoWriMo (National Novel Writing Month) when you are encouraged to commit to writing and recording 50,000 words across the thirty days of November.

Seek out a mentor in an informal or more formal (paid) capacity. A writing group or course might not provide you with the one-to-one support you think you need and which a mentor can give. As well as providing feedback on your work, a mentor can advise and support you about publishing more generally and help to demystify the process of submitting to agents. There are some well-established projects, including Gold Dust Mentoring or those offered by The Literary Consultancy, the National Centre for Writing, and Jericho Writers and newer ventures such as the Megaphone scheme for BAME writers and the Killer Women Mentoring Scheme directed towards BAME and working-class female crime writers.

Pay for an editorial service if you think this will boost your confidence, help iron out a structural, plot or style issue that is vexing you. Thoroughly research the options and associated costs and editorial credentials of those offering these services. Word-of-mouth recommendations are preferable to a Google search in determining what support you might need and who might be able to provide this.

Sign up for a creative writing course There are numerous short, part- and full-time writing courses, everything from three-year degree programmes to one-year MAs and higher-level PhDs. A publisher-led course might span a weekend or several evenings across three or six months, such as those run by Faber & Faber or Writers & Artists or the literary agency Curtis Brown. Creative writing charities such as Arvon, Writing North or Literature Works put on workshops, residential courses and other events. However, you do not need to pay to attend a course to be a successful writer. If you are tempted to attend one, you need to decide if you have both enough time and money to do so and be very clear why you're signing up.

Ask yourself if it is the right course for you and your writing. What are your expectations, and what do you want from the course? For example, do you want to be inspired by guest lecturers (established writers) that teach on a specific programme? Do you want to have your draft manuscript critiqued in detail by an expert tutor and work towards completing a final, publishable manuscript as part of a PhD thesis? Do you want to spend a weekend with other debut writers to inspire you to devote more time to your writing? Do you need the routine and rigour of a residential week away from domestic chores or your regular job to make yourself concentrate on completing the last chapter of your novel? Whatever the impetus or motivations, consider if it is the right time for you to attend. Is your manuscript advanced enough for it to be a beneficial experience? Will it be value for money? What will you hope to have achieved by the end of the course, and will that take you further forward in being able to finish your book, find a publisher or be signed to a literary agent?

Attend events, conferences and literary festivals to hear from other writers and to network. These may provide you with the opportunity to meet other individuals who, like you, are starting out as a writer and who don't know people in publishing, don't have friends who write and who are seeking camaraderie and emotional support. Creative writing workshops can be particularly productive. You might find yourself working with others with whom you can explore some of the highs and lows of the creative process and can thus help one another to write better, gain confidence and feel less isolated. Writers like to be amongst other writers: people who 'get them' and understand why they have the urge to write. There are a huge number of literary festivals around the country, from the well-established Hay, Edinburgh and Cheltenham festivals showcasing hundreds of authors to more boutique weekend events where it is possible to hear, meet and learn from authors with a local connection. Festivals increasingly have practical how-to writing workshops alongside their speaker and panel discussions.

Look out for **open-pitch sessions** where you can rehearse your submission technique and meet agents, such as those run at the London Book Fair or at the Winchester Writers' Festival or offered by publishers. Penguin Random House's WriteNow programme aims to find, mentor and publish writers and illustrators 'from communities under-represented on the UK's bookshelves'.

WAYS TO IMPROVE YOUR CHANCES OF GETTING PUBLISHED

Be positive
'The worst enemy to creativity is self-doubt.' Sylvia Plath (works include *The Bell Jar* and *Ariel*).

Work hard
'A professional writer is an amateur who didn't quit.' Richard Bach (works include *Jonathan Livingston Seagull* and *Stranger to the Ground*).

'Nothing will work unless you do.' Maya Angelou (works include *I Know Why the Caged Bird Sings* and *Letter to My Daughter*).

Keep practising
'Even if it isn't the piece of work that finds an audience, it will teach you things you could have learned no other way.' J.K. Rowling (works include the *Harry Potter* series, *The Casual Vacancy*, and the *Cormoran Strike* series under the pseudonym Robert Galbraith).

Experiment
'Experimental fiction is something you write for the love of it. It is rarefied. But it is important because it often forms the foundation of our creative ecosystem.' Eimear McBride (works include *A Girl is a Half-Formed Thing* and *The Lesser Bohemians*).

Get to the end

'I may write garbage, but you can always edit garbage. You can't edit a blank page.' Jodi Picoult (works include *My Sister's Keeper*, *Small Great Things* and *A Spark of Light*).

'Abandon the idea that you are ever going to finish. Lose track of the 400 pages and write just one page for each day. It helps.' John Steinbeck (works include *Of Mice and Men*, *The Grapes of Wrath* and *East of Eden*).

Editing

'The first draft plunges on, and about a quarter of the way through it I realise I'm doing things wrong, so I start rewriting it. What you call the first draft becomes rather like a caterpillar; it is progressing fairly slowly, but there is movement up and down its whole length, the whole story is being changed. I call this draft zero, telling myself how the story is supposed to go.' Terry Pratchett (works include the *Discworld* series and *Good Omens* written with Neil Gaiman).

Be part of a writing community

'I have never found anywhere, in the domain of art, that you don't have to walk to. [...] There are, of course, roads. Great artists make the roads; good teachers and good companions can point them out. But there ain't no free rides, baby. No hitchhiking.' Ursula K. Le Guin (works include the *Earthsea* series, *The Left Hand of Darkness* and *No Time to Spare*).

Find a conducive place to write

'At night, when the objective world has slunk back into its cavern and left dreamers to their own, there come inspirations and capabilities impossible at any less magical and quiet hour. No one knows whether or not he is a writer unless he has tried writing at night.' H.P. Lovecraft (works include *The Rats in the Walls*, *The Call of Cthulhu* and *At the Mountains of Madness*).

TOP TIPS FOR WRITERS #2: HOW TO FOCUS ON BECOMING A *PUBLISHED* AUTHOR

No one can drag you into the ranks of published authors. Here are some of the ways you might do that if you set your mind to it.

1. **Read** See what I did there? This is number 1 under Top Tips for Writers #1 too. A writer should always be a reader first. Romance writers such as Katie Fforde and Sophie Kinsella, as well as numerous others, advocate writing the books you'd like to read yourself.

2. **Research,** or at least have a passing knowledge of, the publishing industry and the potential market for your book; understand what routes there are to this market and consider how other writers have had their books packaged successfully to reach it.

3. **Go to festivals** and other events to network and be inspired.

4. **Use social media effectively** to gain followers by sharing reading and publishing-related tweets. Avoid any hard selling of your book – that is likely to alienate rather than appeal to prospective readers. Think about what you post: would you want an agent or publisher to see it?

5. **Promote yourself** effectively through your website if you have one, especially if the content of your site relates to what you are writing about, and post blogs that might be of interest to other writers struggling to get a foot on the publishing ladder.

6. **Enter competitions** and ply your craft through practise and gaining confidence. If you make it onto long- or shortlists for reputable competitions that will count when you start to approach agents.

7. **Don't do anything you don't want to**: If you are not a social media junkie or WordPress savvy don't despair. You should concentrate your creative efforts where you choose and decide what input you want or need from external forces. Are you content to read extensively, visit bookshops and surf online, but eschew groups and events if they intimidate you or detract from the little amount of precious time you have available?

8. **Learn from others**; take advice from experts (you are doing that already by reading this book).

9. **Join a creative writing class,** go on a writing retreat, share thoughts, fears and your writing via online writing communities.

10. **Take yourself seriously.** If you don't, why should anyone else? Invest in yourself and your writing by paying for a writing class or buying a subscription to a writing magazine such as *Writing* or those published by Writer's Forum or Mslexia. By investing in advice and resources, you'll be able to think about your writing as a potential business and not just a hobby. What return might you get eventually on this modest investment?

And one for luck . . . (because all authors need a healthy dollop of that):

11. Consider the **self-publishing** or crowdfunded route if you think these might suit you and your writing or if the traditional agent-publisher route seems too insurmountable a challenge.

Redrafting, rewriting and editing

> *edit* v. (edited, editing) prepare written material for
> publication SYNS correct, emend, revise, rewrite,
> reword; shorten, condense, cut, abridge.
>
> *Oxford Dictionary & Thesaurus*

The very first editor of your manuscript will be you. Editing means refining and improving. It can include trimming extraneous, repetitive text or cutting scenes that are not essential for the plot of your novel. It might mean moving sections of your story or non-fiction guide to a different part of the narrative from where it was first positioned to provide greater drama or clarity. Editing includes adding detail as well as taking it away. It has the express purpose of improving a piece of writing. And if you're thinking that you don't need to edit your text if professional editors will come in later and tidy up your linguistic or plot-related mess, think again. There are several reasons why editing at all stages in the development of a manuscript from initial idea through writing and final polishing for publication is a good idea. These are:

1. To add clarity and sense to a text
2. To make the text more readable
3. To render the text appropriate for its intended readership
4. To ensure a text looks professional

There is a tsunami of professionals who can be described as 'editors'. It is used to describe the individual who oversees the editorial direction, tone and type of content of a magazine or newspaper or news website. In book publishing there are editorial directors, editors-in-chief and editors-at-large who sit at the top of the editorial hierarchy, with development editors, desk editors, sub-editors, copy-editors and proofreaders further down the scale in seniority, each in turn performing a more hands-on interaction with your manuscript than the last. Some publishers employ fact-checkers or sensitivity readers.

Redrafting and rewriting are really different ways of editing: they may be on a grander scale, but editing does encompass restructuring and overhauling of manuscripts as well as the close refinements that we usually associate with the process, such as checking spelling errors and grammatical infelicities. Editing is all about helping you communicate better. Redrafting can help heighten elements of a narrative to enhance the funny or sad or dark bits. Roald Dahl, who wrote twice a day for thirty-five years, said that writing 'disgusting characters is more fun. The only way to make them truly disgusting was to re-write again and again. Making the character more disgusting each time.' His novel *Matilda* sat as an idea in his files for twenty years. He claimed that in the first draft Matilda was a very naughty child. The first chapter was titled 'Wickedness' and Matilda was so naughty that the headmistress Miss Trunchbull seemed relatively pleasant. As Dahl proceeded with further drafts and Matilda became nicer, Miss Trunchbull became nastier.

IMPROVING AND REWORKING MY MANUSCRIPT

Many writers (me included) display a curious combination of confidence and insecurity. You need to be a bit pleased with yourself to believe you have something that's worth sharing with the world, but also have a healthy dose of insecurity (realism?) to be able to look critically at your work and give yourself honest advice.

The 2007 version of *Flirty Dancing* wasn't something I knocked out in a few weeks. It took over a year to write and I had spent hours tweaking and fiddling with words, sentence structure and punctuation. I was pretty sure it was close to perfection so when I sent it to three publishers I was feeling quietly confident. Then I got three rejections, the insecurity kicked in and I decided I was stupid to think I could ever be a writer. I wasn't just being a quitter. I'd sent the MS off when I was pregnant and I now I had another, noisier, project on my hands. Fast forward four years and prompted by my mum repeatedly saying, 'I really loved that dancing book', I read it again.

What a difference four years can make. Although I could see that *Flirty Dancing* was well written, the distance allowed me to see its limitations: it was safe and pedestrian, dull, like that grey cardigan that goes with everything. I was certain it wasn't good enough to be published, but I wasn't sure what to do to it …

And that's when confident Jenny took over. Rightly or wrongly, I generally believe that given enough time (and by using my brain and working hard) I can achieve anything. So I strapped one child to my chest, put the other in a pushchair and went to the library where I took out every teen romcom I could find. I read them and made a list of all the reasons (big and small) why these books were better than mine. It went something like this: make it funnier, try the present tense, make Bea's voice stronger, use punctuation for humour, stop describing colours, take out uncertainty (*quite*

& *a bit*), make Pearl meaner. By now I was itching to get started again and as soon as I began editing the most magical thing happened: as I improved one aspect of the book it revealed other areas that needed attention. It was like cleaning a house: it's only when you vac one carpet or declutter one surface that you realise what a flipping mess the rest of the place is.

I edited my book in this way for around two years. As I worked I realised I was slowly, but surely hiding my voice and letting Bea's shine through. I took out descriptions that were clearly written by a 35-year-old English teacher and details that were only interesting to the person who had been living with this story for several years. I snuck in more hooks to intrigue the reader (Why is their dad in Mexico? What is the present? What is the warm squidgy thing?). As my confidence grew I became less controlling and left spaces for the reader to fill in the gaps. For example, I took out the line '... in what I hoped was a calming voice' on the opening page because I trusted the reader to work that out from the dialogue.

Flirty Dancing 2013 involved much more work than *FD* 2007 and yet it feels lighter and more spontaneous. But there was a problem. I knew that I couldn't just make my book *as good* as the ones that were already being published, I needed to try and make it better in some way or different. An added benefit of having scrutinised the competition so thoroughly was I began to see my strengths more clearly. I realised I was good at writing comedy so I made my book funnier. And then, one wonderful day, I knew *Flirty Dancing* really was ready to share. All I needed was a killer opening sentence. How did I write that? I didn't. My sister did. Did I mention how helpful family can be?

Jenny McLachlan writes funny books for children. Her teen books, including the *Ladybird* series, are published by Bloomsbury; *The Land of Roar* is published by Egmont.

Flirty Dancing 2007

'Bea!' hissed a Marmite-scented voice in my ear 'HAPPY BIRTHDAY'

'It was my birthday three weeks ago. Go away, Emma.' I rolled over and tried to go back to sleep.

'Got you a present.'

'Present later, please,' I mumbled.

'No, NOW!' Emma screamed. My sister was three and could go from cute and quiet to violent and loud in less than a second. Sensing a tantrum on the way, I turned on the light.

Emma was standing there, wearing nothing but a T-shirt and a pair of wellies. Her face was red and angry and she was holding something behind her back.

'Present later?' I asked again in what I hoped was a calming voice.

'Ok,' she said and backed out of the room keeping her hands behind her back. She had a funny little expression on her face that could only be described as 'sneaky'.

I turned off the light and snuggled down into my lovely warm bed. Little did I realise that I had just made a big mistake... a very big mistake.

Flirty Dancing 2013

A small naked person is licking me. I don't panic - this happens a lot. The naked person starts kissing my face. I smell Marmite and banana…hang on…the person is not entirely naked. It's wearing wellies. *Wellies?* This is new. And *totally* unacceptable.

I grope for my phone…5.34 a.m.

5.34 A.M.!

'Bea!' Emma cries. 'Happy Birthday!'

'Go away. It is not my birthday.' I try to push her out of my bed, but she resists and we start to scuffle. Mistake. For a three-year-old, my sister's a mean wrestler. I briefly consider being grown-up, but before I know it, we're having a proper fight.

'I got you a present!' comes her muffled voice from somewhere around my feet.

'Present later?' I could probably sleep with her down there. It's not so bad. Quite cosy and -

'PRESENT NOW!' she screams. She's clearly in one of her extra-special moods so I say what I always say when I want to get rid of her. 'Did you hear that?'

'What?'

'I heard Dad's voice…He's home! Dad's home!' (He isn't. He's in Mexico.)

'Daddy!' She shoots out of my bed and down the stairs, leaving me to roll over and snuggle my face into something warm and squidgy. A forgotten piece of banana, perhaps?

I sniff it. It's not banana.

THE DIFFERENT TYPES OF EDITING

Editing encompasses a wide range of tasks, each with the intention to improve the quality of what is being conveyed by a piece of writing. Below are some of them. In chapter 5, we will consider in detail the various editing phases performed by an agent, publisher or editing services company.

Manuscript assessment: Does your book idea have legs? Is the story you want to tell best told in fiction or as memoir? Why not test it out on author share sites and at a writers group? It's useful even at this early stage to consider what are the salient aspects of your book (what in chapter 3 we will discover is the 'pitch'): who is it for, what's it about, what will entice readers, what is the storyline or incentive for sharing your experiences, ideas or information if you are writing non-fiction? If you think your manuscript would benefit from some early assessment, you could consider a manuscript critique service, such as those offered by The Literary Consultancy (TLC) who provide bursaries under their Free Reads Scheme, Cornerstones, Jericho Writers and Golden Egg, who specialise in books for children, as well as those offered by Writers & Artists. Whenever you decide to part with money for a service of this kind, always think about the input you are looking for and if it is the right time for you to seek such advice. Assess carefully what each service is providing and ask the provider who will be reviewing your text about their credentials for doing so.

Structural editing or development editing provides in-depth feedback on the aspects of a manuscript that make it convincing as a complete narrative. It considers the success of its component parts as highlighted above under 'What makes a good book?' on page 59, as well as the use of appropriate language for your readership, and technical features such as characterisation (fiction) or reference styles (non-fiction).

Redrafting might include editing as you write to make the text enticing and readable, keeping your audience engrossed, or a revision of your manuscript once you have a full first draft. It's a good idea as a way of keeping track of each draft of your manuscript to include the version number and date in the file name and to keep them together in an online folder. You might like to keep a spreadsheet on the go too with the status of each draft.

Content editing includes fact-checking, source checking and legal reads to ensure that there is nothing incorrect, libellous or potentially harmful in the book (in the case of a non-fiction title on medical prescribing for example). For fiction it might include consistency checks: does a character's eyes or hair colour or age change inadvertently midway through the narrative? If not checked at the redrafting stage, it might incorporate double-checking of chronology, that events and dates match up; or if a sub-plot is not worked through and there are holes in the story.

Most types of writing require some **research**. It's obvious in the case of academic writing or how-to books that these will be products of extensive and often lifelong research or experience in a formalised professional capacity. Facts will usually need to be checked and double-checked (sometimes by the publisher but the onus will usually fall upon the author) to make sure your reader has confidence in what you say. A fantasy novel may require some library or Google research if real scientific knowledge underpins your narrative. Some authors employ or forge strong contacts with professionals who work in the environments they depict in their books, the most obvious being crime or police procedural novels. A book will be let down by some basic errors in the ways that a crime might be investigated and the formal processes that detectives or forensic or firearms teams might carry out. The way your cast of characters respond *emotionally* is up to you, though: that's where you bring in your creative flair.

Historical novels demand that you get your facts right, too. Establishing a convincing setting in time and place to set the scene for your characters and how they might behave will be important. Anachronisms are acceptable where they have been deliberately employed.

Anything *is* possible in a novel – that's why it's called fiction – but try not to let yourself down by being sloppy with detail and inaccurate with your fact-checking. If you hate having to check facts get someone else to do it for you. Your publisher will ask your copy-editor to keep an eye out for elements in your text that might require factual review.

Copy-editing is a thorough tidying-up of copy or words for sense, accuracy and to a house style and includes checking for accuracy of spelling, grammar and punctuation.

Layout editing includes cutting or amending text to fit a space, format, page design or template. This is particularly relevant for illustrated books or books designed spread-by-spread when it is important that specific text appears on a particular page.

Proofreading is what happens when your book is in page layout (or proof), when the text is set in the font that it will appear in the final book. It's a chance to do a final set of checks and balances to ensure no errors slip through to the published version.

You do not need to employ a professional editor to review your manuscript *before* you submit to an agent or publisher, but you should always check your own work carefully for errors. If you want to self-publish your book, seek some professional editorial support, even if it is just a final copy-edit or proofread.

EDITING YOUR OWN WORK

As you edit and refine your manuscript prior to submission, ask yourself what purpose every element in your text has: is the plot device, character, event, or piece of dialogue necessary for advancing the plot? Do you think it will enhance a reader's understanding of a character, their emotions and motivations? As you edit, there are choices you have to make as a writer: it is part of the decision-making that goes into perfecting your manuscript.

Never junk text you have deleted from your manuscript; it may be the germ of a new novel or a sentence that might sit well within a chapter you've not yet written. Save it somewhere so that you can revisit it for another project.

There are some standard editing rules and plenty of books to guide you in spelling, grammar and punctuation which insist you should avoid splitting infinitives or starting a sentence with 'and' or 'but'. But rules are there to be broken as long as it makes sense for your narrative to do so and readers are able to follow what is going on.

That means you can:

- **Make up words.** Shakespeare, Lewis Carroll, Dr Seuss, J.R.R. Tolkien and Roald Dahl all did (respectively) with 'bedazzled', 'chortle', 'flunnel', 'tween' and (my favourite) 'scrumdiddlyumptious'.

- **Defy the usual rules of punctuation,** such as removing speech marks, as Frank McCourt does in his memoirs and Julie Myerson does in *Something Might Happen* (Cape, 2003). Cormac McCarthy doesn't favour them either. This may be a decision you make for a good reason, but is it always clear to the reader who is speaking? McCourt, Myerson and McCarthy know how to handle their narratives to avoid any incomprehension that missing speech marks might engender; are you able to manage your text as deftly? If in doubt: leave them in.

- **Use the passive voice.** Although the active voice is usually preferred, it might be useful to use the passive when the identity of who is performing an action needs to be concealed (e.g. that of a killer in a murder mystery) or an author wants a variant sentence structure for effect.

Formatting and layout

The way you present your work matters. After spending time refining your writing, as a final task you should format your text in a consistent and professional way. A poorly formatted manuscript should not detract from the *content* of the book and how a story is told. There are some simple steps to follow before submission.

- Take **time** to check the preferred layout and format for your whole manuscript.

- Make sure that you include who you are and your **contact details**. I recommend including these in a header or footer on each page as well as on the front page of your manuscript.

- Always **number** your manuscript in a single consecutive system and make sure that the pages referenced in a contents page or in cross-references if you have them match up.

- Always include a **title** and subtitle if you have one.

- For non-fiction, you'll need a clearly laid out **contents list**, which should include all your chapters as well as any preliminary or endmatter such as further reading or glossary. The contents list can also include the main sections within each chapter if you think that would be helpful to your reader to indicate the topics covered in each. It allows a publisher or agent to see at a glance what you are including.

- Include **breaks** in your text, paragraphs, sections and chapters. Most books, other than picture books or perhaps a novella, will have chapters. These might not have titles but should be indicated in some way even if only by a number (1, 2, 3 or I, II, III). If chapters have been dispensed with for other reasons, then you will need other ways to break up the text. Perhaps you have decided to tell your story from different characters' perspectives or in a series of diary entries in which case you should clearly indicate where one section ends and the next begins. Don't deliver a long screed of dense text which will be daunting to any reader. You want to encourage them to turn the page.

- Include **images, tables, maps** or references to these as well as any pictures, illustrations or photographs that you envisage appearing within or alongside your text and indicate where they might come. For fiction, you don't need to provide any illustrations; in fact, you are actively discouraged from doing so. For non-fiction, though, they may be an essential part of your book so should be referenced if they are not all provided at this stage.

- Use a recognisable **font** that is easy to read. Serif fonts tend to be better on the eye for continuous text, such as 11- or 12-point Times New Roman, and make sure you have formatted the whole manuscript. If you want headings to be in a larger font size, make sure you retain those.

- Allow your text to 'breathe' by formatting as double or one-and-a-half line **spacing** and with each new paragraph either indented or preceded by an extra line space.

- Supply your manuscript as a **single file**, not broken up into separate files for each part or chapter. A reader will want to scroll through the text and not waste time opening a series of files.

- **Name** your digital file appropriately: the title of the book, your name and the completion or submission date would suffice.

- Use a **standard format** that is recognised by most text processing programs such as Microsoft Word or Google Docs. Make sure it can be downloaded to an eReader. Some agents like manuscripts submitted as a PDF, so check their submission guidelines.

- Use editing or writing **software** if you think it will help you (there is a list on page 285). Use spelling and grammar checks judiciously as you might not want to standardise your writing to their rules.

- Make sure your manuscript is **complete** and all the chapters are the final versions and that you haven't inadvertently left in paragraphs that should have been deleted or moved to another chapter as part of cut-and-paste during your redrafting.

- Don't be too clever with **formatting** unless a range of fonts and layout are an essential part of the book's design as might be the case for a picture book or teen guide or a novel composed of newspaper articles, diary entries or emails.

- Be **functional**, cooperative (i.e. follow submission guidelines) and don't reinvent structural, grammatical and other conventions unless there is a very good, creative reason to do so.

- Think about who will be **reading** your manuscript and make it as pleasurable an experience for them as you can by producing it to a neat, easily navigable, **professional** standard.

- Always keep a **copy** of the latest version of your manuscript: make sure you have backed up any work you have done.

Are you ready to submit?

How do you know that you have written a good, saleable story? How do you judge when your work is ready to submit – to an agent, publisher or an online self-publishing platform? Well, *you* don't. The point of publishing is that professionals help take that decision away from you. Editors and agents make informed, critical judgements about your work and the likelihood of its success in the crowded books marketplace. Ultimately the market decides. Is the market ready for your book?

You may never feel totally content with your manuscript and might be tempted to keep tweaking and amending, never totally satisfied or confident that you have written the masterpiece that you set out to create. If you are genuine in your desire to be a published author, at some stage you'll need to hand your manuscript over to professionals who will make a judgement on its merits. There is no such thing as the perfect manuscript, but there is 'the best you can make it' manuscript and that is what you should be aiming to produce.

If you follow the advice in this chapter then you will have improved your chances of developing a manuscript that is well crafted, well presented and of which you can be proud. Don't ever send off a manuscript that you know is lacking. You may be aware of aspects that would benefit from external input from an agent or an editor and will subsequently find their input invaluable. Be practical and honest enough to ask yourself if you have produced a credible manuscript that fulfils the key points in the following checklist.

Can you answer 'yes' to all these questions? If so, you might just be ready to press the send button on your laptop.

1. **Have you finished your manuscript?** It is essential to have a complete manuscript, even though you may not need to send it initially to an agent or publisher. Three or four beautifully crafted chapters don't prove you can sustain a convincing, readable narrative. You may be able to start a story, but do you know how to conclude it? An incomplete manuscript is not a book – it's still work-in-progress.

2. **Has someone else read your manuscript?** As suggested above, it's a good idea to get constructive criticism of your work at stages in its evolution. This is as much to instil you with the confidence you might need to let go and send your manuscript out into the world. Another set of eyes that you trust can help you see details that you can no longer acknowledge yourself because you are so close to your text. You shouldn't be timid about sharing your writing. Authors need readers.

3. **Have you read your manuscript one more time?** Take one more look at your manuscript – ideally after you have finished what you consider to be your final, well-polished version and which you have put away in a metaphorical drawer for a few days or weeks. Look at it again with fresh eyes. Are there any inconsistencies or factual errors, spelling or grammatical mistakes that you missed before and can be tidied up? Read the full manuscript as a reader would from start to finish. Are there any weak spots, superfluous content, or sections that sag? Read your manuscript out loud to get a sense of how the language, cadences and rhythms of your prose (or verse) sound.

4. **Are you proud of your manuscript? Do you *feel* that it is ready?** Listen to your inner voice and instinct. If your hunch is that a twist in the plot is not quite working or your protagonist is

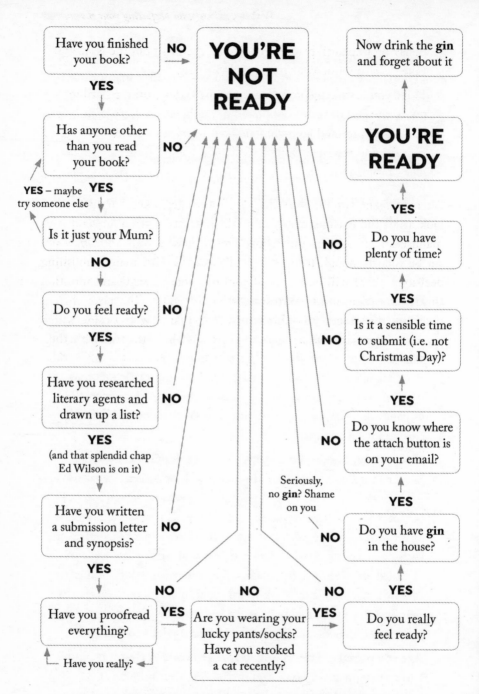

Are you ready to submit your manuscript?

behaving implausibly out of character, then sort out the issue and take time to refine your manuscript further.

5. **Have you formatted your manuscript?** After working hard to get to the end of your book, having sought advice from your beta readers and refined your copy in what seems an endless round of redrafts and rewrites, don't forget to set your manuscript out in a clear, professional way.

Literary agent Ed Wilson's diagram (opposite) takes a light-hearted look at all the reasons why you might not yet be ready to send your manuscript off to him and fellow agents or why your book may not yet be robust enough to be self-published. As with many publishing decisions, there will be a mix of common sense (head) and intuition (heart) that determine your submission schedule. The next chapter describes the process of submission to agents: how to decide which agents to approach, what to send them and how to deal with their responses.

CHAPTER 3

Submitting your work to a literary agent

Congratulations: you should now have completed a well-crafted manuscript that is ready to be considered for publication. If you have followed the advice offered in chapter 2 of this guide and have considered the publishing routes available to you discussed in chapter 1, then read on. If you are hesitant and want to test one more time whether your manuscript really *is* ready for submission to a publisher or to a literary agent, take another peek at agent Ed Wilson's diagram 'Are you ready to submit your manuscript?' on page 86. Take a large swig of the drink of your choice as you do so!

This chapter is long. It needs to be as there is a large amount of practical detail to cover and its inclusion is likely to be one of the main reasons you bought this book. It brings together all you need to know about literary agents – who they are, what they do, and how you go about finding one that might be appropriate to represent you and your work. It covers the submission process: what materials you need to assemble and why when approaching an agent (or publisher) for the first time. It also touches on the psychological toll the process might take on you. Each part of the process is described in general terms – what it is you are most likely to encounter and what you typically need to do to get the attention of an agent.

Although this chapter is about approaching agents, it is possible to pitch your book idea or submit your manuscript direct to a publisher in some cases, as outlined below. The advice on what to submit and how to present it is as valid for pitching to publishers as it is for agents.

What is a literary agent?

> *It's the best feeling in the world discovering new talent
> and nurturing debut writers.*
>
> Hellie Ogden, agent at Janklow & Nesbit

Literary agents form one third of the publishing triumvirate of author–agent–publisher, who together usher a manuscript into print, digital and audio editions. Agents have three main roles: they are **creatives**, **negotiators** and **sales people**, combining good communication skills with a creative flair and a nose for what sells – to publishers and ultimately to the book-buying public. A 'good' agent – i.e. one you might want to represent you – will combine these attributes in equal parts and, crucially, an agent exists to serve you, their author. A sizeable part of their working day, over 90 per cent, is devoted to managing the careers of their established list of authors: their existing clients. That means making sure the author is well-served at each stage in their writing and publishing life: juggling everything from contract negotiations to publicity support, putting them forward for new commissions or events, liaising with a colleague or sister agency in the selling of subsidiary rights or hosing down a stressed author who is suffering from 'writer's block'. It could mean spending a morning working with a well-established author, who already has seven titles under their belt, on their latest pitch to their publishing house, and an afternoon hands-on editing a manuscript for the agent's newest debut signing.

So how does an unknown writer who has sent in their unsolicited manuscript get a look in? Agents get a lot of these – 100 or so a week – and that's on top of any manuscripts or treatments for new books they have actively asked to see. Together, these unsolicited submissions form the 'slush pile' and it will take agents a not inconsiderable amount of time (that last 10 per cent of each day plus their evenings and holidays) to look at these. Why do they bother? Because authors are an agent's bread and butter and they *really are* on the lookout for the next bestselling talent.

Who would want to miss a potential new literary sensation? Agents tend to love what they do. That's why most of their reading of scripts takes place out-of-hours and the nitty gritty of negotiation, pitching and communication with existing clients and homegrown and overseas publishers eats up the hours of any standard working day.

DEBUNKING SOME MYTHS

The responses here aim to dispel some of the incorrect assumptions that authors sometimes make about agents and the whole submission process. Agents really do want to find brilliant new books, and so breaking down any obstacles or prejudices to allow them to do this effectively is in their interests as well as yours.

Here are my top ten agent myth busters.

1. **Agents don't read all the submissions they receive.** They do – or at least someone in their agency (a reader or a junior agent) will usually do an initial sifting for them. From the slush pile, the assistant extracts submissions that look promising. The agent will look them over to decide if they want to read the full submission.

2. **Take representation as soon as you are offered it.** Don't be panicked into accepting the first deal you are offered. If one agent wants to represent you, might others too. Go back to all those you submitted to and let them know that you have an offer and see what that might trigger in your favour.

3. **Agents don't talk to their competitor agents.** Publishing is a small world. Agents within an agency will know what has been submitted to their colleagues (so don't submit to more than one agent at any one agency, it will waste their time and yours) and they also talk to agents at other agencies via their professional networks and at rights fairs. They may well discuss maverick submissions doing the rounds and will certainly follow the publishing news on who is signing up which new authors.

4. **'I don't understand why agents don't give more detailed feedback.'** The agent's job is not to critique submissions in any

detail. They receive up to 100 unsolicited scripts a week; it's inevitable that a good proportion of these will receive a standard rejection letter.

5. **'I've been told I shouldn't submit to more than one agent at a time.'** That's not true. You'd take forever trying to get a deal if you waited for each agent to reply to you before submitting to the next. Agents assume you are applying to several (relevant) agents at different agencies simultaneously.

6. **You need to have connections to get an agent to notice you.** It does probably help and gives you a potential head start, but only if you have produced a manuscript they can't ignore. The quality of your writing is what matters, not who you went to school with.

7. **Once you have an agent you will get a publishing deal.** Not necessarily. An agent takes you on believing that you should be published, but it's the first step on your publishing journey and they then pitch to publishers who may not see a market for your work.

8. **Agents only want to represent blockbuster bestselling titles.** Different agents represent different genres and a range of authors. Agents and publishers are hoping to make money from publishing your book: editors' lists are composed of bestsellers, slow-burn and mid-list titles.

9. **You need to submit the whole package for a picture book – illustration and text.** No, you don't. In fact, if you are an amazingly talented storyteller it's unlikely that you are an equally brilliant illustrator too. Check out the agent guidelines and don't waste money on getting pictures created. Publishers will match an illustrator of their choice with an author.

10. **You must have an agent to get a decent publishing deal.** Agents might want you to believe so and it's true they will probably get you a better deal, but there are some smaller publishers who encourage direct submissions.

Looking for an agent

Most debut writers tend to see the agent–author relationship as one where the agent holds all the cards. It can seem like that, but it should be a joint venture, a business relationship based on mutual respect (and often more than that).

An agent is just as keen to find you as you are to hook them. They are on the lookout for the best new writing from writers they can work with effectively. See it as a two-way beauty contest. They are on the lookout for the best new writing from writers they can work effectively with and you are on the lookout for the agent who can bring out the best in you and give you the support that you need. Ask yourself: is this an agent I can work with? That said, the odds are not in an unpublished author's favour when it comes to submission. Few debut novelists get taken on; agents might sign up two or three new writers in a year from the thousands who approach them. By buying this book and taking on board its advice, you might just up the odds a little. Armed with your new-found knowledge about how agents operate, you are forewarned about the potential obstacles in your way, are aware of the time it might take to get noticed, and are prepared for how that might tax your patience along the way.

So how should you go about looking for the right agent for *you* and *your* work? The three main maxims that underpin all the advice that follows are:

- Research thoroughly
- Take your time
- Be professional

These are equally relevant when approaching a publisher direct.

Research
Use resources such as the *Writers' & Artists' Yearbook* or *Writer's Market* to narrow down the agents who might represent your genre and the age range you are writing for. Look them up online, follow them on

Twitter, attend events where they are speaking. Do they seem like a good fit for your work? Draw up a shortlist and have a clear sense of why you will approach each one: this will become very useful when you are drafting your cover email (usually still referred to as the cover letter).

Do you write across several genres and age ranges? If so, can you find an agent who represents them all? A larger agency is likely to have agents who collectively represent authors writing for adults, children and YA, which might be advantageous if you do too. A boutique agency might be more specialised.

Take your time
You've sweated blood and tears over your manuscript: put the same effort into perfecting your submission. It's your chance to promote your work, so take a deep breath and follow guidelines. Draft and redraft your submission email. It all sounds like common sense, doesn't it? But you'd be amazed how poor so many submissions are. Take time to get it right.

Be professional
Let's assume that your manuscript *is* ready to submit – that it has gone through various drafts and rewrites and really is the best it can possibly be. This is your one shot at impressing an agent with your pitch, so don't blow it with an ill-researched and rushed 'application'. Treat it like a resumé for a job and make a good impression.

Types of literary agencies

Getting published is a long process; success doesn't come overnight, so who you share your journey with is important. Big agency or small agency, it's all about best fit and only you can decide which is right for you.

Gill McLay, children's agent and owner
of the Bath Literary Agency

No two agencies are the same. Agencies are composed of individual agents, each a personality with their own favourite genres, skills and passions. You'll have worked out by now, in your quest to be published, how personality-driven the whole publishing world is: it's a very subjective business, in all senses. The broad structures and functions of an agency or publisher might not differ wildly – but there will certainly be agents who are professionally better at representing thrillers and other commercial fiction than literary novels. There will also be agents who – as individuals – you could work with better than others.

To find the right agent for *you*, ask yourself some key questions:

- Do you want to be a big fish in a small pond? Do you want to be taken on by an agent in a larger, well-established agency or by a newer, boutique sole-agent agency?

- Do you want an agent with editorial skills to help shape your writing, or are you keener on someone who comes from a brand management and marketing background?

- Do you need an agent to be based in the country, state or city where you live?

Small vs large agencies

To some extent the size of an agency should be immaterial, as it's an individual agent who you work with. Larger agencies do have the advantage of employing staff who specialise in rights, contracts, legal, accounts and admin support and they might have a team that deals with TV and film in addition to book rights. A smaller agency will only have a couple of these specialists and sometimes might not have any; your agent may coordinate all these aspects themselves. Do you want to work with a team or have one contact who deals with all your concerns and queries?

Well established vs more recent agencies

Older agencies obviously have a track record: evidence that the agents are doing a good job, if you like. Though remember that a busy agent may not have lots of extra time to devote to a new author. Younger agents, those just starting out or those who have been recently promoted from an assistant agent role might be good ones to target. They may be actively looking to build a reputation and client list for themselves. Likewise, experienced agents who break free from one of the more established agencies to set up their own business might be hoping to attract new talent. Look for agencies established in the last few years (the *Writers' & Artists' Yearbooks* include wherever possible the year they were founded).

An agent's previous experience

Knowing something about an agent's professional background and approach will be helpful. Many agents were once publishers, working in the rights, editorial or sales areas of the business. Do you want an agent who will edit your manuscript closely and suggest rewrites? Or an agent who looks at the bigger picture, scouting for new opportunities for you beyond pitching and selling your individual titles? The best agents do offer both aspects but may have a natural bias in one area.

An agent's specialisms

Agents tend not to be complete all-rounders, but rather provide expertise for particular genres and markets: specialising in non-fiction, or children's picture books (possibly representing both illustrators and authors). This expertise is likely to reflect their reading passions; a good sign as it suggests they will know how to sell your work and where it fits into the market. Their website profiles and those on LinkedIn will indicate what areas they cover as well as those they don't. Their Twitter feeds are good for this too. Agents as a breed are inveterate tweeters and like to share news, views and stories about the publishing world and books more generally. They will tell you what they are reading, who is their favourite writer or hint at what they are currently on the lookout for (a dystopian novel for adults, psychological thriller, police procedural, high-concept fantasy, cosy romance, etc.).

Increasingly agents are seeking out new voices representing sectors in society that have been long under-represented, such as writers from lower socioeconomic communities and those from LGBTQ+ or BAME groups. They are rightly identifying new markets which might be served by publishing a more diverse range of authors who reflect a wealth of experiences which they can pour into their writing. Some interesting initiatives have been established in the wake of this recent call to make publishing more pluralistic and reflective of the society we live in. Agencies who are or have actively targeted traditionally marginalised voices with open submissions for BAME un-agented writers include (in the UK) The Good Literary Agency, Greene & Heaton, Darley Anderson Children's Book Agency and Andlyn. Some of these initiatives are time-sensitive, but new ones are announced frequently – sign up to writing newsletters and The *Bookseller* for updates.

Location

Where an agent is based matters less in terms of the speed and frequency of communication, but meeting your agent in person rather than via Skype or Google Hangouts might be more meaningful. Some agents will represent you in all markets, i.e. globally, but more often, your agent will live and work in the same territory as you. They are typically operating out of the main publishing centres of New York or London, though regionally based agents do exist of course. This might be a consideration: how easily will you be able to travel to see your agent? What might be the practicalities and cost?

Do you have to have an agent to succeed?

In this chapter there is a whole heap of information and advice on what it is agents do and how they can support, manage and help authors. You might assume that means they are essential to publishing success.

Most fiction authors have an agent and many non-fiction writers do too. An agent is not essential but is usually the debut novelist's route into being conventionally published. It should be remembered, of course, that hooking an agent is just the next step on the publishing ladder: it doesn't guarantee you a publishing deal.

Self-published titles – as the name suggests – circumvent the need for both agent and publisher, although increasingly agents pick up authors who are initially self-published and sign them up for print editions of their books, with the author retaining digital rights (see page 31 in chapter 1, where the rise of the so-called hybrid author is discussed). Academic, reference, professional and educational works tend to go direct to a publisher and may often be commissioned from the author (as an expert in their field) by the publisher. If your book is for a niche sector on a subject that might only be published by a handful of specialist publishers and is aimed at a clearly definable readership (members of a specific learned society or special interest group for example), the publisher may very well accept submissions direct from writers with the right credentials. Let's say you're writing a book on a medical condition or a history of railways in twentieth-century India or a repair manual for a specific make of bicycle . . . You might not find an agent who represents something quite so targeted. Check the publisher websites and follow any submission criteria slavishly.

Small publishers might not work with agents; newly established publishers likewise: they may be actively looking to work with new authors to establish a list. For all the above reasons you might have to or be advised to go to a publisher direct. But if you are writing a novel and want to be published by an established trade publisher, why might you want to go it alone and not have representation? Reasons could be that you have the skills and contacts to negotiate contracts on your own behalf (for example, if you once worked in publishing or know people who can and do give informed advice). You might not want to share your financial winnings with a third party (agent) and you may once have had an agent who didn't perform as well as you'd hoped. Whatever the reason(s), as long as you have time, clear intentions and the confidence to stride out alone, there is no reason not to if the publishers you approach are happy to receive unsolicited manuscripts.

Bestselling children's writer Philip Ardagh doesn't think you need an agent to succeed: 'I enjoy the getting-to-know aspect of developing a relationship with publishers and, when it comes to contracts, I have a very useful not-so-secret weapon. I may not have an agent but I can call on the contracts experts at the Society of Authors' (www.societyofauthors. org; the US equivalent is The Authors Guild www.authorsguild.org). Philip struck lucky with his first book by going direct to a publisher but does advise newbie authors these days to stick to getting an agent first. So – yes, you can succeed without an agent, but it's best to try and hook one if you can.

Putting a submission together

> *When I read a manuscript, I'm looking to connect with a voice, a concept, a character and a story, a book with something to say. I'm looking for clarity and intent in storytelling, and to be taken somewhere new.*
>
> Julia Churchill, Children's agent at A.M. Heath

There are three parts to the submission package that you need to send to an agent. Do check to see what specific requirements each agent you plan to contact requests, as they may differ slightly from each other. Details will be on their website along with instructions on how to contact them. Some agencies have submission forms with fields you need to complete when prompted and you should upload your documents in the format that they request. Such forms will go to a central agency submission inbox. Other agencies provide an email to a general account which you should use, or to a specific agent or to their assistant if they have one. Double-check which method is preferred by each agent and stick to their instructions *to the letter*. If you don't conform to the simple steps that the agents ask you to follow, it will look as though you couldn't be bothered to do your research properly or present your submission in a professional way.

If there is a single submissions email for an agency, do still address your cover email or letter (more on that below), to the specific, named agent that you have identified on your list of 'targets'. Assume that most agents expect to receive digital submissions (there are a few exceptions, so do check). If you post a submission, keep a copy of your manuscript and include a stamped addressed envelope with the correct postage if you want to have it returned to you.

The usual three ingredients in a submission are:

1. A cover email or letter (in the US this is also called a query letter)

2. The first few chapters from your manuscript

3. A synopsis

Some agents also ask for a writing CV, but this is not by any means standard. This would include details of any previous publications and unpublished work including blogs you might have contributed to, writing courses and events you have attended or creative writing groups you belong to. If you have won any prizes for your writing or been shortlisted, then the writing CV is where that should be mentioned, along with any other professional credentials you think will strengthen your submission. In most cases, if you have this kind of relevant experience then you would include a line or two about it in your cover letter or email.

The submission package is your professional calling card, a way to ply your literary wares, and so should be as focused and clear as you can make it. Many, many submissions are poorly put together, riddled with spelling, grammatical and factual errors (one agent I spoke to suggested that 75 per cent of unsolicited scripts she received were in this state). Your aim must therefore be to sit somewhere amongst the well-executed 25 per cent of submissions, which will immediately bump you up the slush pile.

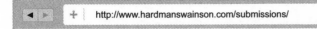

http://www.hardmanswainson.com/submissions/

Submissions

Please direct your submission to ONE agent (more info <u>here</u>) and send by email to: <u>submissions@hardmanswainson.com</u> and not to our personal email addresses.

We welcome submissions and are actively seeking to represent both established and new talent.

We accept submissions of literary fiction, women's fiction, historical fiction, crime and thriller, horror, YA, middle grade, memoir, narrative non-fiction including popular science and history, other quality non-fiction.

We are very selective in taking on new authors so don't be disappointed if your work isn't for us. Please don't send us poetry, plays / screenplays / scripts, or very young children's / picture books.

We are interested in international fiction, but US authors may be better served by an agent in the US in the first instance unless there is a compelling reason to have a UK agent.

FOR FICTION

Send a covering email, and attach a one-page synopsis as well as the full manuscript.

Please direct your submission to ONE agent (more info **<u>here</u>**) and send by email to: <u>submissions@hardmanswainson.com</u> and not to our personal email addresses.

FOR NON-FICTION

Send a covering email outlining your book, why it has a place on the bookshelf and why you are qualified to write it, along with a proposal and a sample chapter of the whole work, if it is completed.

We want to see everything in one hit, so please include the sample material along with the query – either as an attachment or in the body of the email.

Please direct your submission to ONE agent (more info **<u>here</u>**) and send by email to: **<u>submissions@hardmanswainson.com</u>** and not to our personal email addresses.

A note about rejections:

We read everything we receive, but for the majority of those we cannot represent we simply don't have the time to give feedback. We receive a huge number of submissions every week. This is a very subjective business, so it is worth persevering with other agents, but if you find you are being rejected repeatedly by agents and publishers then it may be worth your while seeking advice from a literary consultancy who read and critique for a fee. Please see our resources page for more information.

Sample agent submissions webpage

COVER EMAIL

This is more usually referred to as the cover letter, though in reality it will usually be an email to which your manuscript sample and synopsis are attached. Some agents ask to receive the manuscript chapters within the body of your email. If that's the case, then insert them below your introductory email text. The email's purpose is to provide an agent with clear, concise and coherent information about your book so that they will want to find out more about you and your writing. Its task is to draw the agent's positive attention and encourage them to read your sample chapters straightaway. Don't fall at the first hurdle by fluffing your cover email. Don't agonise over it, though, either. It doesn't need to be a piece of perfect prose, but it does need to be competent and should demonstrate that you are able to marshal your ideas and language coherently. If you follow a few simple rules as outlined below you should be able to create an email that properly reflects the content, approach and value of your book.

The basics

Only send your submission to agents who represent the type of book you have written. It's astonishing how many people contact children's agents with adult novels and vice versa, or send a fantasy or detective manuscript to an agent who only handles non-fiction. Always check that an agent is open to receiving unsolicited submissions; some will close their books temporarily. Some well-established agents may only take on authors that they have actively approached themselves and who have a 'track record' in a related sphere, such as being a journalist or screenwriter. Address your email to the right agent and spell their name correctly. Agents get particularly peeved if addressed with the collective: 'Dear Sirs . . .', especially as so many agents are female. It suggests you haven't made any attempt to research agents in any detail and that your cover email is a generic version that has not been personalised to suit each agent you are writing to. You might not actually write a different email to each one but do give the impression that you have. Check before you fire off your emails that you have changed the name of the agent to reflect the agency you are sending it to and that the 'subject' line of your email is amended too if necessary. I suggest you also remove 'FW:' as it looks a bit sloppy, even though agents will be expecting you to submit to several of them at the same time. Don't ever send a group email or copy in all the agents you want to approach.

Getting the agent's name right is a simple first step. It will immediately endear you, as will a line or two making clear why you approached the particular agent. Do you follow them on Twitter and noticed that they were looking for a middle grade romance? Did you hear them speak at a recent event or meet them at a one-to-one pitching or agent speed-dating session (which agencies, writing festivals and bookshops sometimes run)? Are you inspired by the writing of other authors they represent? You can find out who these are by looking on the agent's website or in the acknowledgements page of published novels; agents are invariably mentioned. It's best not to mention that you've already been rejected by thirty other agents and they are your last hope or to pretend that you love reading the works of other writers they represent when you don't or if your own work is very obviously different.

Check your cover email for spelling and grammatical errors – there are no excuses for letting them slip through. Avoid gimmicks, jazzy fonts, overtly formatted design and coloured type: the agent wants to be able to read your email clearly at a glance. Use a font that you would employ when sending any official or business correspondence to someone you don't know. It's fine to use first names if that's your style. Remember to include your full contact details – don't just rely on the 'From:' line in your cover email. Always provide a phone number and I recommend including contact details within the manuscript itself in case it becomes detached from its cover email at any time. Include a title for your book. It might not be the one under which it ultimately gets published, but it helps make it seem more like a real proposition and shows that you have thought about this crucial marketing aspect.

Try to show that you know something about the market and age range you are writing for and refer to the genre you are writing in. Include word count and mention if the book will be one in a trilogy or longer series, though concentrate on pitching one idea well at this stage. Adopt a polite, personable and professional tone. You can see what this is in the sample 'good' email on page 109. The 'poor' cover email (on page 107) needs rather more work to persuade an agent to turn to the author's manuscript. In short, try not to alienate the agent by being clumsy, rude, arrogant, ill-informed or confusing.

The pitch

> *You want to make the agent want to read your work. And you might only get one go at making your big sales pitch to an agent.*
>
> Philippa Milnes-Smith, agent at The Soho Agency

The core of your email is the pitch, also referred to as the elevator pitch. This is a brief, persuasive summary – rather like the blurb on the back of a published book – that you can use to spark an interest in your manuscript. A good pitch should last no longer than a short elevator or lift ride of 20-30 seconds, hence the name. It should be relevant, interesting, memorable and succinct and around 100-150 words only. Why is your book unique? Why should the agent want to read and know more? These simple questions might help you craft a concise, convincing and captivating pitch.

What's your objective?

Know why you are creating a pitch. Think about who will be reading or hearing it. A bit like writing a whole book – consider your reader, which in this case is an agent or a publisher.

Succinctly cover key plot points or themes

- Introduce the main protagonist and point of the story (theme)
- Indicate, if relevant, where and when is it set
- Highlight the main actions and emotional highs and lows

A good pitch will indicate the WHO, WHAT, WHEN, WHERE, HOW of your story.

Make your pitch:

- Enticing
- Concise
- A good example of your ability to write

Styles to consider and to avoid:

- Questions can provide a sense of the arc of the story – 'Will she find her way home?'
- Avoid telling the agent what she must think – 'Readers will love the character of Jilly, a sassy, red-headed 14-year-old girl who has dark secrets, magical powers and an unhealthy interest in the occult.'
- Cull any extraneous description and redundant words (think like a poet!) – 'Fourteen-year-old Jilly Markham carries a dark secret . . .'
- Overt marketing copy should be avoided – 'This book is a sure-fire bestseller in the style of . . .'
- Rewrite dull descriptions – if *you* can't get excited about your story or characters, why should an agent or a reader?

Try and get across the essence of your book. Be positive and confident with what you and your pitch have to offer. Practise, test it out on others: does it tell them enough or too little about the story? Read it out loud: does it sound convincing?

Examples

Breakfast with Tiffany is a cookbook of breakfast and brunch recipes from around the world, with a healthy dose of spiritual nourishment whisked in too. Award-winning blogger Tiffany Fey weaves together stories and traditions from her travels in Asia, Europe and beyond. Alongside her recipes she offers inspirational advice for the start of each new day in this thought-for-the-day meets Jamie Oliver guide.

* * * * * * * *

'The Beachcomber': Disgraced national newspaper hack, Tommy 'Chopper' Burns, returns, a shadow of his former bombastic self, to the northern seaside town of his birth. With his career in shreds and his personal life in tatters, he looks to his past glories and to those he left behind thirty years before to help rekindle his fortunes. When the body of a young woman is discovered on the beach within days of Tommy's arrival, some murkier details from his past start to resurface. But could this be the biggest investigative scoop of his life, helping him prove he's not quite washed up yet?

STRUCTURE OF A COVER EMAIL

Have you included:

- A title
- Introductory sentence making clear why you are approaching this particular agent
- Word count and genre
- Age or market you are writing for
- Elevator pitch
- Relevant biographical information
- Your contact details

From:	jrush@timewaster.com	01/04/2019
To:	jenny@writeoffliteraryagency.com	
Subject:		

Dear sirs

I'm half-way through my YA thriller-western cum fantasy noval and want to give you first refusal on it. I attach my favourite chapters, numbers 3, 9 and 15 to give you a flavour of my writing style. I've not read anything like it before and all my friends say it is exciting, original and worthy of being published. i hope you agree.

A spaceship has landed in rural Ohio on the night of the Black Hawk ceremony, an annual ritual of the Shawnee tribe when they ward off wild animals from the plains where they live and farm. Who are the strange visitors from outer space and what are they doing in the American Midwest? Do they come in peace or war? Themes of identity and colonialisation are explored through a thrilling fast-paced story.

I think the book will be about 150,000 words when finished and it will be one of a series of five books. I'm also planning on illustrating the stories myself and enclose some rough copies of some of my drawings.

I think this could be as BIG for you as other series such as Harry Potter or Paul Pullmans.

Cheers. 😊

J. Rush

What's wrong with this letter? The pitch itself might be somewhat intriguing, but notice the following, which should be avoided:

- The letter is not addressed to a named agent
- The text includes factual (e.g. Paul Pullmans instead of Philip Pullman) and spelling errors (e.g. noval)

- The tone is overly familiar
- There are some grand claims which might be hard to substantiate!
- The manuscript is very long and is not yet completed
- The author claims to be an illustrator *and* a writer and has provided 'rough' drawings for a chapter YA novel, which are usually not illustrated
- A random set of chapters and not the first three are being submitted
- Friends' recommendations are not a good indicator that a book should be published
- The author has not given any information about herself or provided a phone number

What's good about the letter opposite?
The author has spent time researching a suitable agent for her novel.

- She is familiar with the agent's client list
- There is a clear sense of who the book is aimed at and where it sits in the market
- The pitch is concise and provides enough detail to suggest an interesting plot and some broad themes
- She has included relevant professional and writing experience
- Follow-up contact details are provided

SAMPLE OPENING CHAPTERS

If you are writing fiction, in whatever genre, you will usually be expected to submit the first three chapters of your novel. Some agents stipulate a minimum number of words or pages. For picture books you should submit the full text for several picture books or as a minimum the full text of one and fleshed-out details of other titles you have planned or written (see Submitting picture books, page 115 for more detail). Your sample chapters are the most substantial part of the submission

From:	linda.luck@gmail.com	03/05/2019
To:	susie@oneworldliteraryagency.com	
Subject:	MS Submission: Carrie Brady and the Midnight Gang	

Dear Susie,

I'm a huge fan of James Stride who you represent and his Light Fantastic novels. I am sending you the first three chapters of my own YA novel, along with the synopsis and author CV as requested on your website for all new submissions.

'Carrie Brady and the Midnight Gang' is a 65,000-word novel that weaves magic realism through a contemporary narrative. Carrie Brady is a normal adolescent schoolgirl leading a life without adventure, until tragedy strikes and her mother becomes seriously ill and dies within a few months of her cancer diagnosis. Left to support her bereft father and her younger brother as best she can, her mental health starts to unravel. She spends nights wide awake and days hardly functioning and drifts without purpose. That is until the midnight gang enter her world during the night and whisk her away to places and experiences she could only once imagine. This is a story about triumph over adversity, a coming-of-age narrative of learning to cope with anxiety and trauma and the power of stories to heal a broken heart.

This story has evolved over several years and is inspired by my work as a counsellor with vulnerable young adults and their families.

I was shortlisted for the 2018 Writers' & Artists' Short Story Prize and have recently completed an Arvon novel writing course.

Thank you for taking time to read the sample. I can be contacted by email or on 78000 00000.

With best regards,

Linda Luck

linda.luck@gmail.com

Good submissions cover email

package: they show that you can write and sustain an absorbing narrative. You want to draw them in with your narrative – with the first words, lines and pages – so that the agent turns avidly from page one to two and from chapter to chapter, and then wants to read more, so will – you hope – call or email to ask for the full manuscript. Make sure you have one.

As noted already, your manuscript should be ready for submission (remind yourself what that means if you need to by returning to chapter 2). The start of each chapter should be clearly identified, so include chapter titles if you have them, and remember to paginate the documents. It's a good idea to include a header or footer too with the name of the book and your key contact details: your name, email and phone number. PDFs or Word files are usually requested (again check what specific requirements each agent gives on their website or call their reception if you are unsure what the brief is). Even though most agents will read online and many like to download onto their reading devices to digest the unsolicited submissions on the hoof when shuttling from one meeting to the next or during the daily commute (thus favouring PDF format), some might print out your text. If you've forgotten to include page numbers in your manuscript and it gets dropped, an agent is unlikely to spend her time marshalling it back into some semblance of order. Prologues are not chapters, so can be snuck in. As you refine your manuscript, consider if it is really necessary to flesh out the back-story or whether this information might be more effectively and deftly woven into your narrative. Some agents love prologues, others hate them (one children's agent has a real aversion to maps at the opening to middle grade or YA novels)! Unfortunately for you, you are unlikely to know each agent's particular creative foibles. Don't fret about what you can't pre-empt or control. Concentrate your efforts on presenting your manuscript in its best possible light. Chapters that are not too long, peopled by strong characters, with moments of suspense and intrigue that display your skill with dialogue and pace will appeal to an agent on the lookout for a gripping plot.

THE SYNOPSIS

> *A synopsis is a straightforward chronological account of the most important things that happen in a story.*
>
> Madeleine Milburn, director and agent at
> Madeleine Milburn Ltd.

What is a synopsis? Why is it necessary, what's the point of it, who reads it and why is it so damn difficult to write?

A synopsis is a factual description of what happens in your story and who it happens to. It's an opportunity to expand on your one-paragraph elevator pitch which you have used to grab an agent's attention in your cover email. It includes just enough detail – in the order in which it happens across the book – about the key characters, the actions, highs and lows and final acts of the story. It's a vehicle for showing an agent that your book has a structure, however loose, that contains all its moving parts, and that you have some sense and control over how the narrative is delivered.

A typical synopsis for a standard-length novel should be no more than a page or two of A4 text or equivalent, 1,000 words maximum, and clearly structured to reflect the main parts or 'acts' of the book.

It might include an introductory, one-line statement outlining the concept of your novel: setting the scene and time in which it is set if you've not already included these in your cover email. It should introduce the main characters and hint at why the reader might become invested in him or her and should focus on the main events and dramas of the novel. These can be real or imagined difficulties that your protagonist might need to overcome or psychological traumas he or she must address. Agents will want to know what happens at the end of your novel: spoilers in a synopsis are acceptable, indeed necessary. In contrast, it's good to keep a sense of intrigue in the elevator pitch. If the cover email is the vivacious, slightly enigmatic and intriguing character who you want to get to know better, then the synopsis is her reliable, steady and fleshed-out best friend. The two have their respective strengths, different purposes and support each other.

A synopsis should not be a long exposition of what the novel is about or a detailed action-by-action, blow-by-blow description of who did or said what to whom. It's a good discipline for a writer to take stock of where their story is headed. If writing the synopsis is proving so difficult, perhaps you should take a look at your story arc. Is there too much going on in each part or chapter? Or not enough? Is there a clear sense of progression as the story unravels and heads to its conclusion? Why might a reader want to keep reading – are there enough dramatic moments or emotional highs (and lows) to keep them gripped? Or so many that that the story appears muddled and undisciplined?

The synopsis is not expected to be an elegant piece of creative writing: it doesn't have to be written in the style of your novel, but it *does* need to be engaging enough to ensure an agent or publisher reads to the end and is convinced by the storyline you present. They will be asking themselves whether this sounds a promising, interesting, and sustained narrative. Does this author seem to know what they are doing? Are they in charge of their material? Can they sort the wheat (overarching storyline) from the chaff (the colourful detail)?

WHAT TO AVOID WHEN SUBMITTING

This is a selection of things to avoid that agents repeatedly mention.

DON'T

- Submit if you are not ready
- Over-inflate your successes or your work
- Compare your writing to that of literary greats (let the agent decide!)

- Apologise for your writing
- Be too wacky or wordy in your cover email
- Try too hard to be funny – it might backfire
- Worry about being rejected – most manuscripts are
- Phone to discuss a manuscript (always email)
- Forget to follow submission guidelines
- Send to every agent within an agency
- Be rude, hectoring or sloppy
- Chase too soon after initial submission
- Say that your work is recommended by your mum, friend, partner or any other person close to you
- Submit several ideas in one approach or claim to write across multiple genres, ages and formats: stick to getting a positive response to one fully fledged idea first

NON-FICTION SYNOPSIS OR PROPOSAL

The synopsis for a **narrative non-fiction** title should also make clear what or who the book is about and how it will be executed, what the approach will be and what each chapter or set of chapters will cover. In that sense it is not dissimilar to a synopsis for a novel. But it will differ in a few crucial ways. It should indicate any ancillary materials which will complement or enhance the main text, such as maps, a chronology, glossary, etc. A book that is based on research or a topic that is being presented in a new light or for a non-specialist readership, would usually have foot or end notes, a further reading list or bibliography to confirm the credentials of the work and of its author. An agent needs to be convinced that a book about an historical period or individual or one on a political, social or contentious topic has been rigorously researched and the thesis which underwrites it is convincing and delivered in such a way as to be engrossing for its intended readership.

Probably the most straightforward synopsis to write is for **practical, how-to non-fiction**. This is a chapter-by-chapter outline of what will be included in the book. There should be a clear sense of order and of what each chapter will cover. The non-fiction writer should ask themselves: what's the point of my book and what is the benefit to the reader? And then work out how to convey that to an agent or publisher.

For certain types of book, such as an **academic monograph, textbook, reference title,** or title for an **educational** market, you are less likely to need an agent and might be approached by a publisher rather than having to approach them. There may be templates that a publisher provides for prospective authors to complete with their idea (a New Book Proposal Form). Such forms are used by a publishing editor to make an informed judgement on the book's uniqueness, sales potential and suitability for their list. The detail the author provides will be used by the editor to persuade their colleagues from other parts of the business (rights, sales, marketing) that the title is a viable publishing proposition. There is more about the purpose and content of Proposal Forms within publishing houses on pages 134–5 in chapter 4.

Whether you are pitching your non-fiction idea to an agent or to a publisher, the synopsis or proposal should cover the following:

- **Practical details**: title, subtitle, number of words, structure (number of chapters, illustrations, endmatter).

- **Authorship**: your credentials, professional role or qualifications that make your equipped to write the book. It should also mention any other books you have written or other experiences you have that are linked to the book you are writing (e.g. speaker events, training you offer, social media following).

- **Description**: what the book is about, its theme, and your approach to the topic and material. As such it's an expansion of what you will have hinted at in your cover email.

- **Content breakdown**: what each chapter covers – 3-4 sentences for each one should be plenty; use of bullet points is acceptable to indicate the full range of topics or themes.

- **USP**: what is your book's unique selling point? What is the potential sales hook? It could be you, or a topical theme presented or interrogated in a new, original way. It could be a new exploration of the work or life of a writer, sports personality or other historical figure.

- **Market**: linked to the USP: who do you imagine to be the readership for your book? Are there any specialist interest groups that you have a link to? If you are a member of a society, organisation or institution or you can define a group of experts, professionals or passionate hobbyists that your book is likely to appeal to, then include that too, particularly if you have statistics to back any claims that it is 'essential' reading for such individuals. Avoid the woolly and meaningless term 'the general reader'.

- **Competition**: how unique is your book? What other titles are there already on the market that cover a similar theme or subject? In what way does your book differ? Does it treat the subject in greater depth, is it more up-to-date or more accessible? If there are no other titles might that mean there is no market for it? Is it written by a team of writers or an individual with greater expertise (a university professor, say) or someone with a more personal connection to a story? For example, are you the great-granddaughter of the subject of the biography you are writing, or are you a journalist who has exposed the hot political scandal on which your book is based?

SUBMITTING PICTURE BOOKS

Picture books are short, so make sure that your submission conforms to the word length that the agent or publisher stipulates. Agents will usually represent individuals (an author or an illustrator) rather than an illustrator-writer team. You do not have to go to the expense of commissioning artwork for your picture book text. An agent will be interested to know if you have ideas of how your words might be visually complemented, but they are more interested to see that you have a clear sense of how picture books work, spread-by-spread. An agent would like to be reassured that you have more than one picture book idea and if you are an illustrator will need to see a full, online portfolio of your work.

SUBMITTING POETRY

An agent is unlikely to be particularly helpful in your quest to be a published poet and most do not represent writers who only write poetry. More established writers who make a name for themselves with other forms (children's or adult novels) may already have an agent who then looks after their poetic output, though they may not know as much about poetry commissions and readings as you do through your own networks. You may choose to hold on to that precious 15 per cent commission that an agent would cream off your earnings: which in the case of poetry are likely to be slim pickings. Poets tend to submit direct to publishers (few agents represent poetry) only once they have a sizeable body of work to form a collection and after having work featured in magazines and pamphlets. To have a hope of getting your poems in print, you'll need a body of work to form a potential collection with which to tout around the few specialist poetry publishers.

SUBMITTING SHORT STORIES

Short stories, rather like poetry, are difficult for agents to place, unless they come from the pen of a well-known and bankable writer. Nevertheless, there has been a resurgence in the form in the last few years, in part because of digital channels that offer short-form publishing and self-publishing. But you don't need an agent to get your individual short stories or story collection online. If you are a debut short story writer and want to try the agent route, then check if they do represent the form (most won't actively encourage short story submissions). If your stories have been longlisted or shortlisted for or have won short story competitions and you have had work published in journals, magazines or elsewhere then this would strengthen any pitch. You will need to provide at least three stories (equivalent to the first three chapters of a novel) and have a clear sense of what you are offering an agent: does your writing show real flair and potential? Beware, an agent might try and persuade you that you could tackle longer forms and your short stories might start to morph into novel-length narratives. For an unknown, it is useful when pitching to consider how your stories 'fit' together, what other than you links them. Is there an overarching theme? How can you string them together like beads on a necklace to make them seem a more realistic proposition for agent or publisher? For example, is each story told by a different person who lives in a housing block or street or does the character in one story then appear in the next one and so on through a chain of stories? These may seem a bit gimmicky but indicate what a publisher might consider when thinking how to wrap your stories together into a coherent, saleable product.

SUBMISSION CHECKLIST

Before you click send on your submission email, check that you have:

- Addressed it to the correct agent
- Spelt the agent's name correctly
- Corrected any spelling errors in your cover email
- Provided a clear, upbeat and full description of your manuscript
- Provided all your contact details, including phone number
- Attached the correct version of your manuscript
- Numbered your manuscript and provided the first three chapters only (or equivalent)
- Attached a synopsis (and any other documents) if asked for
- Followed all the agent's submission guidelines

SUBMITTING GRAPHIC NOVELS

You don't need an agent to get your graphic novel published. The world of graphic novels is still bijou enough to rely on personal contacts. You can get to know the editors and publishers in the business at conventions and by sharing your work with them online. Not having an agent will not count against you; most agents are not familiar with the vagaries of the comics industry.

SUBMITTING SPECULATIVE FICTION

Surprisingly, for such a popular genre there are few agents who represent science fiction and fantasy specifically. Agents tend to favour books and genres that they like to read for pleasure themselves and so steer clear of territory they think they are less able to wholeheartedly champion. They are missing a trick: there is a huge appetite amongst the reading public for speculative fiction and its sub-genres, dystopian, steampunk and fantasy, to which fan sites, self-publishing and mainstream imprints such as Gollancz, HarperVoyager and Angry Robot can attest. Increasingly agents *are* looking for novels in this genre and there are some who do specialise in this area (such as London-based Zeno Agency Ltd), but you can approach publishers, particularly smaller presses devoted to the art of sci-fi writing, direct. More established presses will insist you reach them via an agent: a bit of a vicious circle? It may be why so many sci-fi authors opt for self-publishing straight into ebook as they know their readers and know how to reach them.

Waiting to hear back

Just as it's a good idea to be professional and organised in the way you set out to locate and then approach agents, an efficient system for monitoring the agent responses when they come in is helpful too. A simple spreadsheet where you can input the contacts (name, agency, email) and dates when you sent out your submissions, or notebook set aside for recording this information by hand, can be useful for several reasons. It might make the whole process more businesslike (which it should be) and it will help you keep track of which agents you have heard back from and so know which to chase gently for a response in due course. If you are lucky to get interest from an agent, then politely letting the other agents on your 'list' know might encourage them to move your submission right to the top of their slush pile. If you have the agent details clearly in one place, it will be easier for you to follow up with them quickly. The spreadsheet or notebook might be a useful location in which to record the nature of the responses you get and thus see if over time there is any pattern that might mean your submission needs a review and overhaul. For example, if different agents independently refer to a fault in your story arc or have reservations about the age range you think you are aiming your story at, then listen to what they are saying. If you do get some specific commentary on your text or idea such as this, then you are already well ahead of the average submitting author.

Dealing with rejection

Rejection is a fact of life. As a writer you have to accept that. Learn to cope with it. But try to avoid it when you can by putting your best efforts into putting a well-thought-through pitch together and contacting agents only when you have a complete manuscript that has been reworked until it is as good as you think it can be. Don't mess up the opportunity to submit at the best time, in the best way and to the agents best suited to your work. Most authors get rejected by agents. Multiple times. And most authors receive standard rejection letters.

If you do see a glimmer of positive support for your work from an agent, then pat yourself on the back. Reflect on the advice and see where your manuscript might be improved. In some cases, the agent you have contacted might not be taking on any new clients or they may be looking for specific types of work and your book might not quite fit their wish list, however well-written it is.

Continue to refine your writing and your submissions. Don't set out to fulfil lower expectations than you set yourself. Avoid being unduly apologetic: 'I'm trying to be a writer but I'm not very good . . .'. In which case you shouldn't be wasting your time or that of an agent in trying to be one. Stand tall metaphorically, though try not to be arrogant or bumptious. A sprinkle of positive energy and self-confidence won't go amiss. If you are not confident about your writing why should anyone else be?

And if at first you don't succeed, try, try again. If you get rebuffed by all the agents on your first hitlist, consider who else you might target and prepare a new round of email submissions. It's a good idea not to contact too many in one go; perhaps test your submission on up to ten agents to start with and in some cases (such as fantasy) you probably won't have even that many to send your work to in total. Don't assume the agents you first approached are the bad guys in this relationship and are misguided, stupid or unable to see the true merits of your oeuvre; reflect on what you have sent them. If all your replies have been short generic rejection letters, then see that as an opportunity to revise your submission. Does your manuscript need more work? Could your cover email be made more enticing? If you made the mistake of divebombing over thirty agents from the off and they all rejected you, you might have blown your chances with that manuscript. Put it to one side and try writing something else. It might not be your first work that stimulates an agent's interest. Most agents do respond to submissions, though I'm sorry to say that some don't. Do check if it is stated on the agent's website that you will only receive a response if the agent wishes to see the full manuscript and if you have not heard from her within a stated set of weeks, resist chasing for a response. Never, ever hound an agent or imply that they are discourteous or rude if they don't reply to you. Give agents time to read your submission and don't chase too early. Leave at least four to six weeks before sending a gentle and professionally polite nudge by email. They are entitled to stipulate their own terms of engagement. If you don't like their approach, strike them from your target list.

Being taken on by an agent

If an agent (or publisher) is bowled over – or even mildly intrigued – by your cover email and has read your sample chapters and wants to read more, they will phone or email and the speed with which they do this after submission might suggest how keen on your writing they are. Try to remain calm and don't act too keen. It might not lead to anything substantial or to you being taken on, but it does suggest that you might have something to offer the publishing world and reading public. Sending your full manuscript for the agent to review is a major milestone and you've come further than most if you reach it. An agent may engage in some creative discussion with you at this stage if your full manuscript fulfils the promise of your sample and, if they feel the work has strong potential, they may invite you to a meeting. Never agree to representation as soon as it is offered or over the phone. Think about what kind of agent you would like to represent you and refer back to the questions you asked yourself on page 94 under 'Types of literary agencies'.

Some agents may ask for exclusive reading rights; it's up to you if you wish to offer them that, but I wouldn't recommend it. If one agent is interested, then let all the others you sent your sample to know. Like bees round a honeypot, they are likely to be drawn to your submission straightaway, moving it to the top of their pile so they can check what they might be missing out on. This puts you in a strong position, especially if they too request the full manuscript and then go on to have active discussion with you about representation. Well done if so, you've hit the jackpot if you have several agents interested in your work. Avoid the temptation to sign up too swiftly, take time to consider what each agent has to offer, speak to them and visit them in person if possible.

CHOOSING WHICH AGENT TO REPRESENT YOU

When my YA manuscript was ready, I bought the invaluable *Children's Writers' & Artists' Yearbook* and borrowed back copies of the adult edition from my local library. In the directory section I circled agents who were accepting my genre and transferred their details and submission requirements onto a spreadsheet. I used this to track and date responses and ensure I didn't accidentally query agents from the same agency. My cover letter was brief and focused on my novel's hook, my motivations for writing and comparable titles. While reading the UKLA longlist (a fun part of my job as an English teacher) I made a note of the agents mentioned in the acknowledgements of contemporary YA novels I had enjoyed that were comparable to mine in voice, setting or intention. I mentioned my admiration for these books in my cover letter. This demonstrated to the agents my research and respect for their work, and signalled an alignment in values. Twitter can also be an excellent tool for finding out about agents, competitions and mentoring schemes.

I queried thirty agents in batches of six. I received twelve form rejections (which means a standard email), seven requests to see the full manuscript resulting in four offers, and five personal rejections which were the most helpful because they offered advice and encouragement. Such emails were generous and kind, making it clear that although my novel was not quite ready or to their taste, it would find representation soon. I have since thanked these agents because without them, early in the process, I may have given up. I contacted remaining agents to let them know I had accepted an offer of representation and withdraw my novel from their consideration. The world of publishing is a small one; courtesy is always the best policy.

Once invited to meet agents, I prepared a list of questions so I could compare their responses. I wanted to know what they liked about my novel and which publishers and commissioning editors they foresaw approaching and why. Our conversations went off on tangents – inevitably as I have now learned with publishing people – to a discussion of our favourite authors and writing influences. It was important for me, having written a story with social and political criticism at its heart, that the agency I chose understood and showed enthusiasm for the issues that are important to me.

I chose The Good Literary Agency (TGLA) because of its commitment to realising diversity in publishing. Uniquely, it is a social enterprise agency, founded by the novelist Nikesh Shukla and his agent Julia Kingsford, to develop and represent writers from under-represented groups; in particular, working class, BAME, disabled and LGBTQ+ writers. The agency was started with Arts Council funding so profits from sales will be reinvested in writer development. I'm proud to be a part of changes in the industry that will help real-life young people from my protagonist's background access mentoring schemes and development opportunities – offered not only by TGLA, but also by schemes such as Penguin's WriteNow and new imprint #MerkyBooks amongst others – to tell their own stories.

Nicola Garrard, author of contemporary YA novel, *Twenty-Nine Locks*, shortlisted for the Lucy Cavendish Prize 2019, and finalist in the Mslexia Children's Novel Award, 2018.

Prepare some questions for the agent(s) when you meet them and write down their answers so you can remember what they said as the experience may feel rather overwhelming. These might include the following; the responses you get should help you decide if you want to be represented by them.

- What is it you liked about my book?
- Which publishers and editors will you be looking to pitch my book to?

- How much input do I have in deciding if a publisher is right for my book?
- Could you describe what happens once I agree to sign with you?
- How will my book reach other markets, such as the US and foreign publishers?
- What opportunities are there for selling sub-rights in my work and who manages those aspects, does it take place within your agency or do you work with sister companies?
- What percentage do you keep of my earnings and what are the financial arrangements I would sign up to?
- What social media would you use to promote my work? Would I be responsible for this area of marketing or would it be led by you or a publisher?
- What recent deals have you struck for your existing authors?
- What approach do you take to managing an author's career?
- What happens next?

In turn, the agent(s) might be interested in hearing about other work you have written or ideas for future novels you have. They might want to know which other agents (you are not obliged to tell them) or how many are also interested in representing you and be keen to hear how you see your writing career develop.

If you are lucky enough to have agents fighting to represent you, then it might come down to your gut feeling as to who you click with best: is this someone I can get along with? Rely on a good mix of head and heart when signing up with an agent. Try to balance the rational and emotional aspects when making a decision. An agent should be someone you can trust to run your career in a business sense and who you can work with as a personality, someone whose opinions you trust and whose approach and manner you respect. Agents will be sussing you out too: is this an author I can work with and help achieve publishing success?

What do literary agents do?

> *Remember, it's not just about the one book you've written. You're looking for a long and fruitful career as an author, so take time to find the best possible ally and champion. . . It may prove to be one of the most important relationships of your life.*
>
> Jo Unwin, agent at her eponymous literary agency

THE THREE-HEADED AGENT

An agent wears several professional hats when executing their role as author representative. They need an eye for what sells, a head for finances, good judgement, fine communication skills and empathy.

1. The agent as business partner
Agents are rewarded financially through the work they do on behalf of their author-client. An agent typically takes 15 per cent commission of net receipts on authors' earnings; higher for translation rights and other subsidiary rights deals such as serialisation, film and TV. So, quite literally – economically speaking – agents are dependent on authors: authors provide them with their livelihood. That's good news for you! Agents need authors and are on the lookout for bankable writers (and illustrators) – not only creators of well-crafted works, but ones that will have a market.

UK-based agent Julia Churchill succinctly encapsulates the agent role: 'My role as a literary agent is to help my authors have successful careers. I endeavour to make money in as many rights streams as possible (with an eye on the long term), and enable an easier professional life for my clients so they can focus on writing. My job involves spotting talent, helping to develop it and selling it.'

You will notice how Julia frames her role: it is as a business manager first and foremost, someone who makes money for her author and in selling an author's talent. An agent's negotiation skills come to the fore when securing an initial deal, but they will also concern themselves with how an author gets their rights to publish back when a title stops selling above a certain number of copies. They worry about the long-term health of an author's revenue streams and in order to do this effectively, will have a very strong knowledge of the market – not only in their home environment but overseas too.

Some authors might sell better in translation and have a bigger following than in the country where they live. Agents with a good international reach – either through their own contacts or via colleagues in-house, talent scouts or in a partner agency overseas – are a real asset in this case. The agent's role is to be informed and be up to date: in short, know what's going on in the publishing business, so an author doesn't have to. In managing an author's career, an agent should not make unilateral decisions: her job is to offer the author choices and guide them in making good decisions when faced with opportunities. They are there to support in other ways too, beyond the transactional.

2. The agent as editor
Most agents enter the profession because they love books and reading. That's the first step to becoming a good professional reader too: to develop the necessary skills to provide sound editorial advice.

In chapter 2, we touched on editing from an author perspective when preparing a manuscript for submission. We'll look at it again in the next chapter when considering the multiple tasks and stages that your manuscript will pass through on its route to publication.

Editing covers a multitude of hands-on attention, from structural reworking through to detailed copy-editing. Copy-editing is, as the name suggests, close attention to the details of your 'copy', i.e. your writing. It's the dotting of i's and crossing of t's; checking for consistency; ensuring clarity and sense and readability; checking for spelling and grammatical errors. It's the final tidying up of your manuscript before it goes to be set to page layout in the printable font size and style.

Agents don't copy-edit. They worry about the overarching structure, focus, arc and tone of your novel. They are likely to give advice on characters (too many, too little developed, inconsistent in their behaviour?), setting, dialogue, length of chapters, order of events and much more.

All editing is part of a broad process to help improve text and make it more readable. It should be intervention not for its own sake, but sound and intelligent advice to burnish a text so it shines brighter and enhances the original further. Editing is seeing the wood *and* the trees. A good agent (and editor) should not impose or demand a change; but should raise a query when something doesn't work creatively so that the author can come up with their own solution as to how to put it right: to (re)*write it right*.

You might not always agree with your agent's editorial comments. Seeing your submitted work (the best you thought it could be after your own rounds of rewrites) adorned with dozens of track changes and marginal comments can be daunting. But, editing should not be demoralising. Any writer who thinks they don't need editing – in effect, doesn't require other sets of eyes to comment critically on their work – is misguided. Writing and editing are very different and complementary skills.

To recap, once you are signed to them, your agent becomes your professional guide and mentor. The most hands-on way in which they nurture your talent and help you grow as a writer is through their editing expertise. Publishing editors might do the same – it can be a hazy area as to who will interfere most editorially with your work. Assume that either your agent or your editor, or both, will in a positive way. They should know the market for your book and want to help shape your writing.

Your agent-as-editor is in effect your first true reader. Editing – like much of publishing – is subjective, so finding an agent you can trust and whose advice you'll be happy to take or fruitfully debate, will, for most authors, be a key requirement.

3. The agent as author champion

Your agent is proving to be a person of many talents: a likeable professional with business acumen and editorial acuity. And it doesn't end there.

Authors do sometimes change horses: they might move from one publishing stable to another through their career, and it is known for agents and authors to go their separate ways, but this is less common. One author I met recently was on his third agent and only his third novel too. To lose one agent smacks of misfortune, to lose two carelessness . . . You might infer that the author was a troublesome individual – not true. Agent One ceased to be an agent and returned to the role of commissioning editor in a publishing house from whence she'd originally come; Agent Two was her colleague and became the author's agent in a move of convenience he subsequently regretted. He was a newly published author and forgot to ask himself the crucial questions we suggested you ponder on pages 123–4. Their split was amicable. Third time lucky: the author is now with an agent who 'gets' him and his work, who is a passionate advocate for his writing and who speaks of him as both a client and a friend.

The point of this anecdote is twofold: to remind you of the personal touch that an agent brings to the relationship: is this someone I can work with, get on with and trust? And, secondly, to highlight the role of your agent as the primary champion for you and your work.

The agent as author-champion is of practical use. Should you disagree with your publisher over matters large or small (cover design, editorial approach) or you are frustrated that you are not getting the marketing or publicity support you think your work deserves, then your agent can discuss with the publisher as your proxy or professional representative. It leaves you free to write and to keep a positive relationship with your editor intact.

The agent acts as adviser and manager who builds an author's career and often their confidence. But, more importantly, an agent has a holistic view. They can see where their author fits in the wider publishing firmament and will keep a steely lookout on what's afoot in the industry. Their well-informed expertise is crucial for an author, particularly one new to the complex world of publishing. Your agent takes on the roles of PR, talent manager, confidante. A good agent should be working hard to keep their authors employed: working with them to pitch new ideas to their existing publisher or a new contact.

An agent will make time to foster a close working relationship: they have to, so an author – their paymaster – can trust them with their work. Remember to ask yourself what *you* want from your agent – to be a creative sounding board, to handle detailed negotiations on your behalf because you don't know how to or don't want to, to be there when you want and need them to allay your fears and insecurities, for them to be a positive force, an honest critical friend and an all-round fount of publishing knowledge? Any agent worth their salt will be a rich mix of all these attributes.

What happens next?

You have an agent and an understanding of how you will work together. But then what? Your agent will contact publishing editors to pitch your book to them. The next chapter describes what happens within publishers when an agent approaches them.

HOOKING AN AGENT – REMEMBER TO:

- Do your homework: research the right agents for you to submit to

- Know your market and readership by visiting bookshops, reading widely and understanding how publishing works

- Sell your idea: what's the hook? Why should an agent, publisher or reader take notice?

- Come up with an attention-grabbing title

- Be professional and courteous and think of your submission like applying for a job: highlight your credentials and suitability

- Don't get disheartened if you receive a wave of rejection emails (you probably will). Review your submission. Try another raft of agents. Remind yourself that your work is being turned down by a specific agent on a particular day and that the agent has not any personal animosity towards you.

CHAPTER 4

Contracts, legal matters and finances

The author-agent agreement

Authors should always sign a letter of agreement with an agent, which should at least cover the following aspects:

Exclusivity The agent will request sole representation of the author's works, unless otherwise mutually agreed, for the marketing and negotiation of publishing rights and any subsidiary rights, such as film, created during the term of the agreement.

Mutual interest The agent will make best efforts to advance and protect the interests of the author. In turn, the author will refer all enquiries to the agent.

Commission payable to the agent on gross income, usually 15 per cent on UK deals and 20 per cent where subsidiary agents are involved.

Payment will be made promptly.

Protection of commission The agent will continue to receive commission on any payments to an author until rights sold to a publisher revert to an author.

Liability The agent is not liable if manuscripts are lost.

When he first became a literary agent in 1985, Andrew Lownie says:

> letters of agreement between author and agent were rare. Authors were signed up on a handshake on the basis that everything could be sorted out amicably if anything went wrong. That is no longer the case. There is now more at stake and we live in more legalistic times with authors more prepared to

AGREEMENT BETWEEN ANDREW LOWNIE AND ....

1/ Andrew Lownie is appointed your sole and exclusive representative, unless otherwise mutually agreed, for the marketing and negotiation throughout the world of all rights including but not limited to book publishing and volume subsidiary rights, motion picture, television and radio rights.

2/ He shall make all best efforts to advance and to protect your interests, to negotiate the exploitation of rights to the best advantage and to advise you to the best of his ability. You will not be committed to any proposal or contract without prior authority in writing. All enquiries concerning the rights in such work will be referred directly to him.

3/ On all contracts he negotiates he will be entitled to a commission of 15% inclusive of any sub-agents' commission but exclusive of Vat on UK book rights and 20% on US, translation and film rights. These rates will not be changed without your consent and he agrees to give you prior written notice of any proposed change. Commission shall be calculated on the gross amounts payable to you before any deduction from or charges against these amounts.

4/ Andrew Lownie shall account for and promptly pay to you as far as possible within ten working days all amounts received by him on your behalf.

5/ This agreement will continue in force until it is cancelled by either party, giving to the other at least thirty days written notice of cancellation. Following cancellation or termination of this agreement it is agreed that Andrew Lownie shall continue to be entitled to commission on amounts receivable under each contract negotiated or in the course of negotiation by him while this agreement was in force. His entitlement shall continue for the life of each contract.

6/ While Andrew Lownie shall take every reasonable care of typescripts and other material while in his possession he cannot accept responsibility for any loss or damage to them while they are not on his premises.

7/ You confirm that no agreements exist which are inconsistent with this agreement and that no agreements, either oral or written, will be made by you which will interfere with or prevent the provisions of this agreement being carried out.

8/ This agreement shall be governed by and construed in accordance with English law.

....

....

The Andrew Lownie
Literacy Agency Limited

36 Great Smith Street
London SW1P 3BU
Tel: 020 7222 7574
Fax: 020 7222 7576
Email: lownie@globalnet.co.uk
www.andrewlownie.co.uk

Author-agent letter of agreement

move agents than in the past. Letters of agreement are almost universal. They provide certainty and clarity but vary in length. Some drawn-up by lawyers and contracts specialists cover every eventuality but can be rather intimidating – my agreement is a page and covers the most salient points. (A copy of his standard author-agent agreement appears opposite.)

You should *never* accept a verbal agreement only.

Negotiating a publishing contract

Being signed by an agent can seem like you've arrived. But, it's not time to uncork the champagne just yet. There are two main things an agent will do to try and secure a publishing deal for your book: pitch and negotiate.

PITCHING

Your agent will be a seasoned networker; with good links with the editors who publish the type of book and authors they represent. Both agents and editors (variously known as commissioning or acquiring editors) are on the lookout for great new writing. They keep a close eye on what's hot and what's not: Are vampires still in? Do dementia memoirs continue to sell? Are psychological thrillers flying off the bookshop shelves? Pitching a debut author is a challenge. Remember how taxing drafting your cover submission email to agents was and the number of drafts you went through to craft the killer elevator pitch? Your agent goes through a similar process and becomes indebted to your own pitch when trying to persuade editors that they should see your full manuscript. An agent who takes you on will believe your work is publishable, but they too may get rejected multiple times and it may take longer than you or they hope to find the right publisher.

Editors, planning a three- or five-year editorial programme, may be seeking a debut voice to fill a specific slot – say a YA romance in the style of John Green. However good *your* manuscript is, if it is similar to the work of an author already on their forward list (the titles they have scheduled to be published in the forthcoming twelve to eighteen months) or they don't have space for it, then they may not be able to offer you a deal.

The process runs something like this:

PROPOSAL

An agent sends in a proposal to the commissioning editor, who if interested will ask about the rights available (for example world English language or UK only, translation and audio) as this will make a difference to the sort of deal she might be able to offer. However much she might be entranced by your writing she will need in turn to 'pitch' your title to the wider publishing team. This is usually in a formal acquisitions meeting, where she will present her case for publishing your novel armed with details of competitor titles, sales analysis and why she thinks it would be a welcome addition to her list. She will complete and circulate a Publishing Proposal Form (PPF), such as the one opposite. Other publishers have different names for these documents. Sometimes a full draft **P&L** (profit & loss) will be worked at this stage or that might follow once the internal editorial meeting has given the green light to pursue discussions with the agent further (or with an author direct). Sales and marketing managers will assess the commercial merits of the proposed acquisition. It's possible for a title to fail to get through this stage and thus means the commissioning editor is not able to continue discussions with the agent.

The book's P&L is informed by costs (editorial, production and marketing expenses) which are themselves based on the format and extent and whether the book will be in colour or black and white; sales estimates, subject to market discounts; and the level of advance and royalty rates that the editor plugs in to their calculation system to see if the book is profitable. If it is, further discussion with the agent will ensue.

NEGOTIATING

Let's assume your novel or non-fiction work has made it through the acquisitions process, what happens next?

PUBLISHING PROPOSAL FORM

Title	Behind the Curtain: A memoir of life in East Berlin	*Pub date*	September 2021
Author	Dr Yvonne B. Schmidt	*Price*	£16.99
Format	Hardback year 1 (paperback year 2); Demy 138 x 216 cm	*Sales*	Hardback year 1 5,000; paperback year 2 10,000; backlisting 800 copies a year
Extent	75,000 words, 256 pp. Includes line drawings at head of each of the 10 chapters; line maps and 8-page colour plate section	*Rights available*	US and Commonwealth in addition to UK

SHORT DESCRIPTION

Yvonne Schmidt is a successful UK-based neurosurgeon who grew up in a divided Germany. Her candid and moving memoir of her childhood in East Berlin, secluded from the Western World, explores the impact of this experience on her and her wider family. She describes the privations that they endured but also looks back on the positive aspects of community. From childhood, her education in Germany and Russia, and her emerging as a young medic on the eve of the fall of the Berlin Wall, she weaves an engrossing story of what she sees as her two lives and how these have shaped her identity. In telling her own story and that of her family, including the death of her surgeon father in mysterious circumstances, she tries to reconcile these two lives.

AUTHOR CREDENTIALS

Yvonne Schmidt is a leading neurosurgeon, based at Liverpool University Hospital, and a Visiting Fellow at Harvard Medical School. She is a regular contributor to BBC Radio 4's *Mind Games* and is part of the UK Government's Improving Mental Health initiative. This is her first book.

- Social media – via Yvonne's 7k followers (would look at how to increase this following dramatically)
- Podcasting – Yvonne has been a host and guest on the *Science in Society* podcast that reaches 12.5k listeners each week
- Yvonne is an experienced public speaker, broadcaster and is used to media appearances. She has good contacts across the media; Radio 4 *Bedtime Reads* have already expressed an interest.

USPs

- Fascinating and beautifully written memoir of life behind the Berlin Wall
- Strong evocation of a 1960s–70s childhood and adolescence
- Explores the mystery around her father's premature death
- Marrying of personal, cultural and political aspects of a life
- Publication to coincide with the 60-year anniversary of the building of the Berlin Wall (13 August 1961) and of the author's 60th birthday (born 24 September 1961)

COMPETITION

No direct competition; there are other titles on life in East Germany, but this one is a unique exploration of life before and after the wall. Quality memoir is selling well, see for example Nielsen BookScan figures for *Growing up in Mao's China* (Baker Street Press, 2019), and *Mr President and Me* (Carnage, 2019). See also the recent success of politically themed fiction and non-fiction more generally.

The publisher will make an offer on your work – or indeed on several works, which you may not yet have written. And there begins a to and fro between agent and editor on money: royalty percentages and advances, schedules and rights so that a formal legal contract can be drawn up.

Sometimes, an agent's pitch will appeal to more than one editor. A bidding war results. Usually this will involve the author, who will get to meet all the interested editors. The publishers – and this is where the shoe really is on the other foot – will pitch *to you* in a bid to add you to their publishing list. A bid will consist of more than a financial offer. It will include a draft marketing and sales plan and possibly a quirky approach to entice you (cakes, limos, editors dressed as one of your characters). It's a chance too for the author to see which editor they respond to on a personal level: is this an editor and publishing house who gets my story?

DRAWING UP THE CONTRACT

Once your book has been accepted in principle by a publisher, your agent will start to negotiate with the commissioning editor on your behalf to secure the best deal for your book. What exactly is an agent agreeing to?

Publishing contracts can be lengthy documents. They will follow standard formats and might make use of an agent's boilerplate or one from the publisher. In either case, it's a good idea for you (the author) to become familiar with some of the terms and clauses that your agent will have negotiated on your behalf so you are aware of your obligations and those of the publisher. The **legal advice** from the Society of Authors (SoA) is particularly useful if you are an agent-less author. 'Membership of the Society of Authors is very beneficial. They have expert lawyers who will check contracts for you for no extra charge.' (Rachel Bladon, writer and editor for English Language Teaching resources). You don't need to go to the expense of consulting an expensive media lawyer and most provincial solicitors are unlikely to be well-grounded in copyright and book contract law.

A simple structure underlines all publishing agreements and it should be a legal contract that is fair to both parties: publisher and author. It covers practical matters, such as what your book is, how many words you will submit and by what date; finances: how much money you will receive as an advance and what percentage of the book's cover price or receipts from sales you will earn when a copy of each format (audio, hardback, paperback, ebook) is sold. The contract includes clauses covering copyright, moral rights, indemnity, *force majeure* and the like. The key clauses for authors relate to authors' obligations, rights sold and the payments linked to these as rights are exploited.

Legal definitions and clauses

WHAT IS COPYRIGHT?

Copyright is one aspect of intellectual property rights (IPR), relating to 'works of the mind' and it allows writers – the rights holders – to authorise the use of their work in various ways. It also allows authors to take action against *unauthorised* use. Your agent and publisher – as you should too – protect and police the valuable property that is your work, which is original and unique to you. You should not assign copyright to a publisher or to an agent. Copyright varies from country to country in how it is defined, enforced and protected. Copyright in the UK lasts for the life of the author plus seventy years.

Registering copyright Your publisher will usually do this, lodging a registration form and 'depositing' a copy of your book with the British Library on publication where it is then formally catalogued for posterity. You may notice that on book imprint pages it confirms that 'A catalogue record for this book is available from the British Library'. There are five libraries of legal deposit in the British Isles; they can each receive a free (or gratis) copy of your book if they request one. Publishers may choose to provide ebooks rather than print editions. It is a good idea to check with your publisher, especially if they are a small or new company, that they will be doing this on your behalf. If you are self-publishing, then you'll need to register your work yourself. In the US your book can be registered with the Library of Congress.

HOW RIGHTS WORK

Rights are many and sub-divisible, that means that they can be licensed to a third party (i.e. a publisher) outright or in part and for a set time period and territory (for example for publication in the UK and Commonwealth but not in North America). From an author's perspective, if you own the copyright in your work you then have a say over how it is licensed for use by others. Authors need control over their own content – their intellectual property – and need to earn a living (however meagre that might often be) by controlling the ways in which the content is published and released.

WHAT ARE THE RIGHTS THAT AN AGENT MIGHT NEGOTIATE ON YOUR BEHALF?

Apart from agreeing terms for the publication of your work in various markets and in primary formats, your agent will negotiate subsidiary (or secondary) rights and how much payment as a percentage you will receive as and when these rights are exploited. They may license some of these rights to your publisher (such as permissions, audio, book club or serialisation) or keep some of these back and license elsewhere, along with other rights such as TV, film or theatre adaptations and translations.

If this all seems a bit dry and theoretical, then it's a good reminder that publishing is a business and the key role that your agent has is to get you a good financial deal. For an example of how subsidiary rights might be exploited, let's take a really obvious example: Harry Potter. What started out as a series of novels in print mushroomed into a multi-platform industry of its very own. The core publisher rights (hardback, paperback, illustrated, ebook, US and UK editions), were followed by the licensing of subsidiary rights to produce movies, theme parks, merchandising (from chocolate frogs to socks, lunch boxes and wands), translation into over eighty languages, audio . . .

A good book is the start. But it can open up other possibilities and offer financial rewards far beyond its pages. Your agent, who negotiates the rights deals, gets a percentage cut each time a deal is struck.

A LEGAL LEXICON

Defamation To defame someone is to damage their reputation and can result in legal action taken against the author or publisher if the case is serious enough. Defamatory content might include mocking and ridicule or making a false statement about a person or company. In fiction a character could be considered defamatory if they bear resemblance to a real person or body of people. Defamation court cases can be extremely expensive, meaning that publishers will often cease publication if there is even a possibility of being sued and will include clauses in their contracts stating the author is responsible (legally and financially) for any defamatory content found in their work.

Libel Defamatory statements which are written or published. This can now include social media posts and comments – the authors of which have been successfully sued in court.

Slander Defamatory statements which are spoken aloud. For an author this could include statements made during a book tour or promotional interview.

Privacy and confidentiality A breach of privacy occurs when confidential information is shared beyond the person or people for whom it was intended and can be met with legal action. A duty of confidence exists between an author and their publisher which prevents confidential information such as ideas and manuscripts

---

as well as commercial information about the publisher from being shared. An author must also respect the right to privacy – in either fiction or non-fiction – if their work is inspired by real people or events. For example, if you are writing about your former line of work avoid sharing confidential or sensitive information, or if you are writing a romance novel avoid basing your lead character on an ex and sharing private details which might expose or embarrass them.

Data protection You have a duty to protect the privacy of your readers if they share their personal information (name, D.O.B., gender, email or home address, etc.) with you. This might be through a newsletter sign up, survey or book order on your website. The Data Protection Act 2018 insists that recipients of this kind of personal information must store it safely, use it only for the purpose communicated to the individual, and only store data for as long as is necessary.

Intellectual property (IP) An idea or creation which is not tangible or material but is sellable and ownable. This includes trademarks, copyrights, and patents of character names, plot devices and fictional places; text, photographs and illustrations; databases and software.

Trademark A sign, design or expression can be protected by a trademark which identifies the individuality of these symbols and their distinction from those used by others in a similar business and protects them from copying. For example, J.K. Rowling has copyrighted various character names and features of her Harry Potter series, such as Hogwarts School of Witchcraft and Wizardry and Gryffindor House.

Volume rights The rights for a publisher to publish a book in its main editions: print, audio and ebook.

Subsidiary rights Also known as ancillary rights, i.e. secondary to volume rights (see above), these are rights which are licensed to a publisher which then licenses them to a third party. These might be a foreign publisher with whom a translation is negotiated or a newspaper or magazine that wishes to print an extract from a book. A literary agent will often not assign copyright in some subsidiary rights to a publisher and will manage them for an author. These include those rights that might be exploited in areas beyond the page, such as film or TV and merchandising rights. See pages 143–4 for a list.

Moral rights There are two key moral rights which an author should be aware of, they apply even after an author has assigned their copyright to another party. The right to **paternity** gives an author the right to assert themselves as the creator of a work and prevents false attribution. The right to **integrity** prevents a work being edited or changed without the author's permission.

Permissions If someone wants to use part or the whole of your work, they must first receive your permission to do so (or the permission of the copyright or licence holder). As an author you must do the same if you want to use someone else's work, for example an illustration or quotation. Permissions are granted in a contract and usually in return for payment. Permissions must be cleared before publication to avoid contravening copyright.

CLAUSES STEP-BY-STEP

Definitions used throughout the contract will often be included at the beginning or in an appendix to avoid any ambiguity, and might include terms such as 'Net receipts', 'Hybrid Product', 'First Serial', 'Territory', and 'Electronic Book'.

Legal operation and enforcement of the contract is covered by a few standard clauses, such as those relating to 'Interpretation', 'Arbitration', 'Confidentiality', 'Notices' and 'Entire Agreement'. This also covers my favourite of all catch-all clauses on '*force majeure*', which will read something like this:

> The time for fulfilment by the Publishers of any of their obligations under this Agreement (including the obligation to publish the Work) shall be suspended during and delayed for such period of time in which the fulfilment of such obligation is prevented or delayed by reasons or circumstances beyond the Publishers' control, including but not limited to war strikes, lock-outs, fires, Acts of God, governmental restrictions or controls.

FREE TO PUBLISH

The author confirms that she is able to enter the agreement and that the book she is writing is a unique, new property, her own work and will not contain any legally compromising material. Note that the first example below indicates the style of legalese in which your contract is likely to be couched:

Exclusivity 'The Author hereby grants to the Publishers during the legal term of copyright the sole and exclusive licence to publish the said work in volume form.'

Warranty and indemnity are confirmed, meaning the author states that she is freely able to enter into the agreement, is the sole author, owns the rights in the 'work' and that it is unique, i.e. has not been published elsewhere previously and does not contain any libellous or defamatory material or content that isn't hers to include, i.e. that is someone else's copyright and that the author has cleared permissions with the copyright holder for any part of somebody else's work being reproduced in the book. The author agrees to cover any legal costs, other fees or losses if she is in any way in breach of the warranty.

TERRITORY

This is the geographical areas where the book can be sold, for example UK and Europe, or North American, or World territories.

RIGHTS

Legal Term is the period that the contract covers, from date of signature of the contract by both parties or until rights are reverted to the author.

Granting and Reversion An author agrees that the publisher is allowed to publish their Work during the legal term. Rights might revert (back to the author) automatically when sales dip below a minimum annual level, of say fifty copies. An author may negotiate to have rights in their book reverted and will be able to purchase any remaining stock. At that stage the contract is also formally terminated.

Termination might also occur if either party breaches any of the terms of the contract, for example if the author fails to deliver a manuscript of the quality expected on time and if it is found to be plagiarised. Late delivery alone would not usually be grounds for termination, but an author should always inform the agent or publisher if a contracted delivery date cannot be fulfilled.

Copyright Notice and Infringement
This covers how the author's name will appear in the book, i.e. © NAME OF AUTHOR, 2020. These clauses confirm that copyright in the Work is the property of the author. They will also make it clear that, if the publisher decides to protect the copyright of a book insofar as it threatens the value of the rights sold to a publisher, the author will assist the publisher (at the publisher's expense).

Subsidiary rights include:
1. Anthology and quotation rights
2. Broadcast reading and audiobook rights
3. Digital and electronic rights
4. Dramatisation, film, documentary, television sound broadcasting video or other mechanical reproduction rights
5. English language rights (royalty-exclusive)

6. First serial rights (first place e.g. in a magazine where an extract from an original Work is serialised or published)

7. Large print, educational, reprint or paperback rights licensed to a book club or to another publisher

8. Micrography reprography, merchandising and manufacturing rights

9. Second serial rights (rights sold subsequent to the first serial rights, see above)

10. Single-extract or digest or book condensation rights

11. Translation rights (royalty exclusive)

12. US rights (royalty exclusive)

Each set of rights will be subject to a royalty percentage, payable to the author when these rights have been exercised. Some rights are held back or retained by an agent or author, so they might be exploited at another time and be subject to negotiation with a third party after publication. These tend to be the potentially more lucrative rights if exploited, such as dramatisation and film, translation or audio. Some 'hybrid' authors will license print rights to a publisher but retain digital book rights to allow them to self-publish in that format; a contract would make clear in which territories each edition might be sold.

PRACTICALITIES

Delivery – this will include a realistic delivery date and the specifications as to what will be delivered in what format (complete digital manuscript), to what extent (70,000 words including any end matter) and accompanied by any material (extracts, quotations) for which copyright might need to be cleared.

PAYMENTS

Advances The advance is an example of financial goodwill, a pact that author and editor have cemented through the contract to agree to work together and to make money from the activity. It is usually paid in two or three equal tranches, payable on signature of the contract, on delivery and approval of the final manuscript, and on first publication. The advance against royalties means a payment made before any actual revenue from sales of your book have been received.

Royalties are the fees paid to an author on the sale of copies of their book and are subject to sliding scales, so that as a book becomes more successful an author benefits more. As more and more copies are sold the investment the publisher made in producing the first print run will be recouped; subsequent runs might become very profitable for the publisher and rightly an agent will argue for an author to profit from this success too. Such rising royalty rates for a published price contract might look something like this:

1. on home sales: 7.5 per cent of the published price on the first ten thousand (10,000) copies sold; 10 per cent of the published price up to twenty thousand (20,000) copies sold and 12.5 per cent of the published price on all copies sold thereafter, such royalty not to be deemed a precedent between the Publishers and Author or agent;

2. on home sales where the discount is 52.5 per cent or more: four-fifths (4/5ths) of the prevailing royalty; on home sales where the discount is 60 per cent or more: three-fifths (3/5ths) of the prevailing rate

Free and presentation copies will be provided to the author (anywhere between six and fifteen free copies) on publication and to potential reviewers as part of a promotional campaign; royalty payments are not made against these gratis copies. Authors may purchase copies of their own book at discount.

Payment process, accounting periods and other details about how and when the publisher will remunerate the author (or their agent on the author's behalf) will be included.

PUBLISHING PROCESS

Author corrections and their proofreading responsibilities might be clearly laid out, covering what checking tasks an author will be expected to undertake and when and which might be carried out and paid for by the publisher, such as having an index prepared or clearing permissions for images or quotations. It might also include a clause in which the publisher 'reserves the right to charge the Author' for the cost of author corrections to page proofs if these are over and above the usual level of alterations. Such costs might be debited against the author's royalty account.

Promotion clauses advise that a publisher shall advertise, promote and market the Work as they deem appropriate 'in their sole discretion'. If you feel strongly as an author that you wish to be consulted about any aspect of promotion or cover design you could ask for such clauses to be modified. The most you are likely to get is an amendment that agrees an author will be 'consulted' and asked to 'agree' to the publisher's plan and that their agreement 'will not be unreasonably withheld'.

Publication date might not be firmly set when the contract is signed but the publisher's commissioning editor should have a clear idea of what quarter they would like the book to appear in. An agreement would usually stipulate that the book should be published within twelve months of date of delivery and acceptance 'unless prevented by circumstances over which they have no control or unless mutually agreed'.

New and updated editions for non-fiction titles might be referred to, defining what would constitute a 'new' rather than a 'revised' edition and how much new content it might include, say at least 10 per cent new material. The author would be offered first refusal on preparing a new edition, but the publisher would want to include a clause to allow them to ask another writer to complete such a project if they perceived there was a market for it, but the original author was unable or unwilling to take on the commission.

The contract should not daunt an author. It is supposed to be a joint declaration and not biased in favour of one party or the other.

OTHER TYPES OF CONTRACT

Joint authors will be named in the contract as 'Author' and are governed by all clauses in a contract equally, unless different financial provision is indicated in the payment of advances and royalties, for example if one author is the senior party receiving two-thirds of any total royalties payable. One of the joint authors – who have elected to work together and who put together the joint proposal to an author or publisher – may agree to be nominated as the representative author and will thus be subject to all contract clauses on both their behalf.

Where an **author and an illustrator** have been brought together by the publisher, they are subject to their own separate contractual agreements. The total royalty percentages payable might be equally shared or be weighted in favour of the more successful party; though neither the illustrator nor the writer would know what the terms of the other's agreement are. On the book cover they are likely to get equal billing unless one party is a complete unknown.

Editor contracts for a collection of articles, essays, short stories or poems might also be subject to royalty payments, but the percentage would be much lower than for an authored work. The writers of the articles or stories within the collection (**contributors**) would most likely receive a fee for their work if an original piece or a re-use fee (subject to their own agreements) if it is anthologised from a pre-existing piece.

Work-for-hire contracts offer writers a flat fee (though a further payment may be made for any re-use). These are standard for educational, reading scheme stories and for new titles in series fiction produced to order (e.g. for an established packaged series such as *Rainbow Fairies* whose titles are authored by a group of writers working to a tight brief).

If you want to self-publish and want to work with individual freelance experts, they may not have a formal contract, but do ask for details of what services they will be providing to what timetable and what fee in writing. Larger, long-established **self-publishing provider services** should have a straightforward set of clauses that you can sign up to before engaging their services. These are likely to include clauses covering an author's granting and retaining of copyright, author's warranty, and from the service provider's side an agreement to publish on receipt of a manuscript. Such a contract might be sketchy in places; where it refers to 'an acceptable' manuscript it would be a good idea to ask the provider to define what that means and why might a manuscript not conform to such a definition. It's always good to know what you are and are not signing up to. One service agreement I saw recently made clear that 'The author assumes sole responsibility for decisions concerning the advertising, distribution, and promotion of the Work.' No ambiguity there.

If you publish an ebook with **Kindle Direct Publishing** (and with other platforms) you'll be asked to sign a lengthy agreement, downloadable from their site. This includes the type of clauses that a traditional publisher's agreement includes, such as royalty rates (considerably higher than those from a mainstream publisher), and payment periods (ditto, reconciled and reported regularly compared to bi-annual or annual reporting by a publisher). Do be aware of this clause in the KDP contract though and look out for updates (the clauses affected are referenced on the site): 'Agreement Amendment. The Programme will change over time and the terms of this Agreement will need to change over time as well. We reserve the right to change the terms of this Agreement at any time in our sole discretion.'

Whatever type of contract you enter into as an author, once a contract has been drawn up, discussed, amended to the publisher's and author / agent's mutual satisfaction, two final copies are produced that both parties will date and sign, each retaining a copy.

With a signed contract on her desk, the commissioning editor is ready to start planning for the new addition to her list. The first task to legitimise its existence is to arrange for an ISBN to be allocated.

ISBNS

ISBN stands for International Standard Book Number and is a thirteen-digit identification code unique to each book. Each format (paperback, hardback, ebook etc.) and edition of a book is assigned its own ISBN. You can find an ISBN on the back cover of a print book next to the barcode or on the inside imprint page in the book's prelims (see page 186). In an ebook the imprint page and ISBN might be listed at the end of the book instead. The ISBN will also be listed on all online stores as part of the product information alongside the publisher and publication date.

An ISBN consists of five parts or groups of numbers, each section separated by spaces or hyphens: 978-1-4729-4751-2

They are the:

- **Prefix**, always 3 digits, either 978 or 979.

- **Registration group**, which identifies the country, region, or language area participating in the ISBN system; it is between 1 and 5 digits in length. 1 indicates the ISBN above is for a title in English.

- **Registrant**, which identifies the publisher or imprint and can be up to 7 digits. 4729 is Bloomsbury Publishers.

- **Publication**, which represents a specific title and can be up to 6 digits. 4751 is the *Writers' & Artists' Yearbook 2020* edition.

- **Check digit**, always the final single digit that mathematically validates the rest of the number.

ISBNs are used by publishers, book retailers and libraries to identify a title and its various formats and editions for the purposes of ordering, monitoring sales, listings and reference. This data is held by the Nielsen Book Database whose listings are organised by ISBN. In the UK and Ireland ISBNs are sold through the Nielsen ISBN store (www.nielsenisbnstore.com). They must be purchased from the ISBN agency in the country where the publisher or self-publisher is based and not from the agency in the country where you intend to publish (if these are different). If you are signed to a publisher they will obtain an ISBN for you. Bulk-buying ISBNs is more cost-effective than buying individually but this might only benefit traditional publishers who are publishing dozens or hundreds of titles every year. Currently a single ISBN is priced at £89.00, 10 will cost you £164.00, 100 cost £369.00 and 1,000 cost £949.00.

There is no legal requirement to have an ISBN but you will need one if you intend to sell your book in bookshops (both bricks and mortar and online) or have your book made available in libraries. Without an

ISBN your book will not be included on the Nielsen Book Database meaning it will not be visible to book retailers. Not having an ISBN therefore limits your book's discoverability and the avenues through which you can sell it.

ISSN stands for International Standard Serial Number. It fulfils the same purpose as an ISBN but is used for newspapers, magazines, journals, periodicals and other works which are serialised and regularly released and updated. ISBNs are only for whole works which have been completed and reached a definite end. **ASIN** stands for Amazon Standard Identification Number and is used by and within Amazon for the same purposes as an ISBN.

CLASSIFYING YOUR BOOK

The UK Cataloguing-in-Publication (CIP) programme creates a record for every new book that is registered and includes this in the British National Bibliography (BNB); this is a useful link into the library market. Libraries can identify books that might be of interest to their readers. BNB requires details to be sent at least four months prior to publication date to produce a CIP record that is in line with British Library requirements and will include subject codes and library classification similar to other bibliographical codes that are used online to group titles by subject, such as THEMA codes or BISAC.

The costs of publishing a book

There are several parties in the publishing fraternity that are looking to make money from the selling of the book and whose profits increase the more copies sold:

- **The author**
- **The author's agent** – who takes a cut of their author's earnings, typically between 12 and 15 per cent in the domestic market, more for overseas and other exploited rights.

- **The publisher**
- **The bookseller / online vendor**

To illustrate the cost of producing a book and the thin margins that can be earned this is a simplified profit and loss calculation for a single title.

COSTS

The costs to create a book fall into two types: **fixed costs**, also called upfront costs. These expenses are the same irrespective of the number of copies that are produced. They are the start-up fees that are a minimal requirement to getting a book into print or published as an ebook or audio file and as such they tend to be service rather than material costs.

They include the fees for:

- content: one-off contributor or image permission fees for example;
- editorial work: copy-editing, proofreading, indexing;
- design and production: cover illustration, text layout, typesetting, recording.

They also incorporate other activities such as marketing and promotion in the form of materials (adverts, launch costs), which may be assigned (as a percentage of overall costs) to an individual title or set of titles or a list.

These costs are title-specific and will typically be included in a publishing editor's P&L calculations for each book. In addition, a publisher may apportion a percentage of staffing costs against each title to give a more realistic picture of how much it truly costs to prepare a book for publication and present it to the market.

As well as direct overheads (for example, assigning a fixed £3,000 to each book to cover editorial management or adding 4 per cent on overall costs to cover marketing activity), the publisher has a whole host of other staffing, management and business costs that are part and parcel of running an organisation. These tend not to be apportioned to a specific ISBN, but the finance team would factor these in when reviewing the profitability of a full publishing list.

EXAMPLE

75,000-word adult thriller, standard royal format
Fees and costs might look something like this:

Cost	e.g. £	Notes
Author advance	£5,000	payable in three tranches prior to publication
Editorial fees		
Copy-editing	£1,000	round figures used in the example
Proofreading	£500	
Design fees		
Cover	£0	designed in-house
Text design	£100	publisher uses a standard template
Typesetting	£1,000	setting text to page
Marketing	£2,500	% of total editorial and design fees
Overhead	£2,000	standard business overhead fee
TOTAL FIXED COSTS	£12,100	

These are the costs the publisher incurs before they have sold a single copy and as it can take up to twelve months to prepare a book, from handover to publication, that is money tied-up in the product before it can see any return.

Variable costs as the name suggests are dependent on the number of copies that are produced of a title and are on a scale of charges based on the amount of material used and number of copies that are sold. As such they cover paper, printing and binding, shipping and warehousing and sales costs. You can see how these costs fluctuate and profits likewise in this example:

The thriller referred to above, has a cover price of £16.99 but will be discounted, on average by 55 per cent. It's a new author, but he is a well-known journalist, so the first printing is costed on two possible print runs of 2,000 copies and a more bullish 5,000 copies.

	2,000 copies	5,000 copies
Printing & binding @ £3.00 a copy	£6,000	£15,000

The overall costs and profits for this thriller now look like this for the two print runs:

	2,000 copies	5,000 copies
Fixed costs	£12,100	£12,100
Printing costs	£6,000	£15,000
TOTAL COSTS	£18,100	£27,100

Income received from sales assuming they all sell (remember discount on the cover price is on average 55 per cent) for 2,000 copies is rounded up to £18,700 and for 5,000 copies is £46,750 [copies × price × discount % / 100]. Some of the copies will be gratis (free, for publicity use, author's and editorial copies) and won't have a royalty payment, but for this example let's keep things simple.

Profit will look like this:

	2,000 copies	5,000 copies
Total costs	£18,100	£27,100
Income	£18,700	£46,750
Other deductions		
Royalties earned	£100	£7,750
(@ 15% of the cover price		
or £2.55 a copy) in		
excess of advance		
OVERALL PROFIT	£500	£11,900

The lower run is more realistic for a debut hardback, but the publisher makes next to no profit; they could print higher but might get stuck with copies they can't then shift.

Getting co-edition deals in order to make printing a highly illustrated book a viable option for a publisher is usually essential. This is particularly necessary for high-quality low-priced children's titles, where having a sizeable print run will be necessary to make a credible return on the investment in the project. Children's publishers gather at the Bologna Book Fair each March or April to sign up new authors and to ink deals with international partners. They are looking to recoup the initial (fixed) costs they have invested in an author and illustrator and will usually try and pre-sell a book idea or project well in advance of publication, on the strength of some sample page designs or spreads or a convincing pitch. An author's agent might do the negotiation by selling the individual rights for each market rather than handing these over to the publisher to negotiate, but the practical side of working with other global publishers to have a combined print run to allow multi-version / language printing (with a separate black plate for the text of the story) to be run at the same time at a single printer is part of a wider business transaction. The books will then get shipped or airfreighted to the different markets for selling.

An author's income

AUTHOR EARNINGS

Surveys of author earnings tell the same story from one year or decade to the next: the average annual income for an author is well below the living wage if an hourly rate is calculated from the hours spent researching, writing, promoting and dealing with admin and other writing-associated tasks such as reading. As in previous surveys, the 2018 Author Licensing and Copyright Society (ALCS) survey of authors' earnings found that a minority of stellar-earning authors represent a high proportion of the total income earned: the top 10 per cent of writers earn around 70 per cent of overall earnings. You don't need to be a maths genius to work out that that doesn't leave much for the other 90 per cent to share between themselves. ALCS found that there was a drop in average and median earnings and a stagnation in mean earnings: £16,531 in 2006; £16,809 in 2014 and £16,096 in 2018. Taking inflation into account, the survey showed a real-time drop across those twelve years of 42 per cent in median earnings from an equivalent of £18,013 in 2006 to £10,497 in 2018 and even when factoring out part-time and occasional writers (i.e. those not earning exclusively from their pen), the take-home message is that the writing life is a precarious one. Simultaneously the industry has witnessed a rise in profits for publishers. The Society of Authors has been vociferous in its lobbying to try and redress this and argues for a more equitable balance of payments. Perhaps this is another reason why self-publishing can seem an attractive option for new authors? The survey also found that those who had an agent (40 per cent of respondents) were decidedly better off than those (primary occupation writers) who did not, to the tune of tens of thousands of pounds (£46,879 compared to £17,780 a year).

The decline in earnings doesn't appear to have put writers off. There are more of you than ever. Yet the survey makes clear that being a full-time writer is tough: only 28 per cent of those surveyed who described themselves as 'primary occupation writers' (i.e. those who earn 50 per cent or more of their income from writing and writing-related activities) are able to live as writers without recourse to other income streams, such as having a second job. Not surprisingly authors look for additional ways to supplement their main publishing income (see table below).

Sources of earnings among primary occupation writers (2018)

Source of Earnings	Mean (£)	Median (£)	#Respondents
Publishers	21,495 (73%)	3,720	1,172
Lectures	2,714 (9%)	250	696
Self-publication	2,613 (9%)	0	583
Creative writing classes	1,297 (4%)	0	552
Public Lending	766 (3%)	100	863
Grants and Bursaries	730 (3%)	0	484
ALCS	727 (3%)	196	1,100
Awards and Prizes	435 (1%)	0	469

Source: Data from UK Authors' Licensing and Collecting Society (ALCS) 2018 survey in table from *UK Authors' Earnings and Contracts 2018: A Survey of 50,000 Writers* © CREATe www.create.ac.uk May 2019.

Hot on the heels of the ALCS results came recommendations (in June 2019) from the UK All Party Parliamentary Writers Group in its report *Supporting the Writers of Tomorrow*, informed by evidence from professional writers and industry bodies such as the Society of Authors, Writers' Guild of Great Britain, the Publishers Association and the ALCS. It highlights key areas for improvement, such as widening participation through the setting-up of a Creators' Council to look at diversity, amongst other aspects; a review of tax and benefits for authors; a reduction of rate of VAT on ebooks (currently the standard rate of 20 per cent); the protection and promotion of the existing UK copyright system; and the levelling of the playing field for online bookstores and their bricks-and-mortar competitors.

Why is it so difficult to become rich or mildly comfortably off as an author? Books are expensive to produce. Each title is an individual product line and as such each one has its needs to be promoted and marketed in its own right. Books fall into standard formats and types and can follow established processes in how they are physically created in order to maximise economies of scale and follow repeatable procedures. But the actual *content* of a title is what makes it unique, and it's that difference that publishers are selling: something that will enrich the lives of the reader, whether it be a piece of writing or illustration that the purchaser didn't know they needed or wanted. Blanket campaigns entreating us to 'read more books' are laudable of course, but such marketing activity is so broad that it might be deemed akin to 'eat more greens' – any greens – i.e. read more books, any books, and that will be good for you. That's not much help to the struggling author trying to get his or her title in front of the buying public.

ADVANCES AND ROYALTIES

Once a publishing contract has been signed, the commissioning editor or the contracts department, depending on who negotiated the deal, will trigger payment by the publisher's accounts department of any advance due to an author on signature. If you have an agent this will be paid to them and they will forward to you, minus their percentage commission.

The publisher will have set up some way to track subsequent author payments (the additional staged advances) in line with the contracted terms and will report, once a book is published and starts to sell, on monies earned against this advance payment. In the short-term, at least in the first or first two years of publication, an author may not receive any royalties, or rather the author percentage of revenue collected by the publisher will be offset against the advance on royalties. Only when this advance has been earned out will an author start to see additional payments trickling through by BACS payment and reflected on their royalty statements. These are emailed (via your agent if you have one) twice a year to tie in with the publisher's accounting periods, though sometimes only annually. It's a good idea to check what your publisher's standard payment schedules are.

Most companies will have a default minimum royalty payment threshold, which might be £50. Any amount below this figure would be retained by the publisher and paid in the next accounting period assuming that it had then reached or exceeded the threshold. VAT is payable on advances and royalties if an author is registered for VAT; the publisher would need the registration number and signature of a Self-Billing Agreement (SBA) authorising the publisher to attach VAT to any payment. Authors who are not resident in the UK have 20 per cent Withholding Tax (WHT) deducted from their advance and royalties; but authors can apply to HMRC for an Exemption Certificate to avoid these deductions. It is the publisher's responsibility to keep on track with payment schedules and authors or agents do not need to send invoices in to request they get made.

Sometimes a publisher will agree to set production or editorial costs that the author is asked to bear against royalties, which will also need to be earned out. This is more usual for academic titles than for other genres. These fees might include paying for an index to be created for a book or for additional fact checks or to cover illustration fees that exceed the total fee budget stipulated that the publisher will bear. Authors only get royalties on new books sold – so one time only not on second-hand book sales.

Royalties can be calculated on a book's **published price** (PP) – a simple calculation where the author receives a percentage of the cover price irrespective of any discounting on that price, so for example 10 per cent of £20 for every copy sold even if most copies retailed at nearer £15. If 500 copies are sold in an accounting period, the author would receive payment of £1,000. An agent commission of 15 per cent would reduce this to £850. That might seem like a pleasant amount; but if you consider the hours put into planning and writing your book and the additional pitching and administration you will have put in, it is a derisory amount. If you want more robust earnings you need to hope you have a surefire bestseller or a title that will backlist over the long term to furnish you with a regular bi-annual windfall. **Net receipt** (NR) payments are even less remarkable: this is based on a percentage of the actual revenue the publisher receives on sales (minus costs) for the period in which it is being calculated. Your royalties would be paid, in the example above, on the £15 selling price and not the £20 RRP.

Royalties on sub-rights income received during an accounting period are also included as a separate line on the royalty statements. If it is not clear how to read the royalty statements you receive, you should ask for clarification from your agent in the first instance or your editor.

MANAGING FINANCES

If you are a part-time writer, then your income from writing is likely to be well below the average salary. If you are receiving 'freelance' income from your writing – as an advance, royalty or a one-off fee (for writing a guest blog or newspaper comment piece, an author talk or school visit) – it is your responsibility to register this with HMRC and declare this in your annual self-assessment form as you would for any other income additional to your day job. If you are classed as self-employed, you need to be officially registered as such and pay on account to the inland revenue. If your total self-employed earnings (including that not from writing) exceeds revenue of £85,000 a year you are obliged to be registered to pay VAT and pay it on all earnings every quarter.

Authors who earn well from their writing may find it advantageous to be registered as a limited company and should consult an accountant on the pros and cons of this as there are fewer tax incentives to operate in this way than there once were.

Authors can claim for allowable expenses and capital allowances to be deducted from their income if they are incurred exclusively for business purposes, these may include writing materials, computer equipment, travel to see your agent or publisher. Some grants, notably those awarded by the Arts Council are chargeable to tax, but winnings from literary prizes are not deemed to be part of an author's professional income and thus not taxable, at least at present.

As with anyone who is self-employed, authors are responsible for their own pension provision and will not receive sick pay.

REGISTERING WITH ALCS AND PLR

The Authors' Licensing and Collecting Society (ALCS) collects and distributes monies due to authors for 'secondary uses' of their work. This includes payments made when schools photocopy pages. They can provide a small amount of regular income. Registration with ALCS is easy; life membership is only £36 and free if you are a member of the Society of Authors, the Writers' Guild of Great Britain or National Union of Journalists. In 2019, ALCS paid out a total of £34.8 million to writers.

If you register your books with the Public Lending Right (PLR) scheme administered by the British Library, you will be eligible for payments each time your book is borrowed from a public library. These payments from government funds put aside for the purpose are made annually based on sample loan data collected from selected libraries across the UK. Around 22,000 creatives: writers, illustrators, photographers, translators and editors who have contributed to books lent out by public libraries in the UK receive PLR payments each year.

FINANCIAL SUPPORT

Authors experiencing financial hardship or who would welcome assistance with a writing project can apply to one of the Society of

Authors trust funds, such as the Authors' Contingency Fund. The K. Blundell Trust provides grants to published writers under forty to help them with their next book. Travel scholarships, funded residencies and other bursaries and fellowships are worth investigating. A list can be found on regional development agency Literature Works' site: https:// literatureworks.org.uk/resources/bursaries-and-grants-available-for-writers-in-the-uk/. Crowdfunding might offer a more secure option to fund your work if you want to bypass the traditional publishing route. Look out for small writing commissions to tide you over when writing your novel (it's good writing practice too) and avoid working for free or for work-in-kind.

Entering writing competitions might lead to wider exposure for your work and with luck some prize money or possibly the promise of a publishing deal. There have been efforts to foster debut writers across the book publishing industry more generally, with prizes inaugurated to encourage this talent. Recent launches include the Paul Torbay Memorial Prize for Debut Novelists over 60 (established in 2019). Other awards for unpublished works include the well-established Betty Trask Prize for novelists under thirty-five (set up in 1984, published and unpublished novels are eligible), which like the Torbay prize is administered by the Society of Authors and funded by other writers; the Costa First Book Award (first awarded in 1971 as the Whitbread Awards); and the Authors' Club Best First Novel Award (1954), which helped launch the careers of Brian Moore and Alan Sillitoe in its early years.

Research specific literary societies for prizes relevant for particular genres, such as the US-based Horror Writers Association who award the Bram Stoker Award for Best First Novel annually and have done so since 1987; the UK's Crime Writers Association New Blood Dagger (since 1973) for the first crime novel by a hitherto unpublished author; and the Katie Fforde Debut Romantic Novel Award for the best romantic novel by a first-time author, administered by the Romantic Novelists' Association and first awarded in 2019. Keep a look out for other competitions for which you might be eligible.

As the ALCS survey on author earnings indicates (see pages 154–5), making money from your writing is difficult. The legal stages can also be drawn-out. Professor Sara Haslam, academic with the Open University and author, highlights the frustrations authors might have as they start to climb the first few rungs of the publishing ladder:

> One frustrating part of the process can occur when there can be a long time wasted in the run-up to securing a contract, followed by deadlines for the completion or return of material with what can seem too tight a turn-around. Early and clear communication is always key I find: what is possible and why.

Asking your agent and your publisher to explain processes, contractual clauses and other publishing mysteries to you is not something you should shy from. Seeking advice from independent sources, such as the SoA is also encouraged.

CHAPTER 5

From final manuscript to published book

After signing your contract

Once you have a signed contract and have punched the air with passion or high-fived your best friend, you will soon realise that you have become slave to a series of scheduled dates and deadlines. Your publishing contract will list some key dates: the date you will deliver the very final version of your manuscript to your editor and may include the (provisional) date that your book will be published. There will be a clause that indicates that your book will be published within so many months of delivery. This is usually a generous twelve to eighteen months, to allow flexibility in where it will fit in the publishing programme alongside other titles and seasonal considerations. Once delivered your manuscript will be accepted by the publisher, as long as it does not contravene any clauses in the contract with regard to plagiarism and libel and it conforms to the specifications on word length, supply of images and any other details the contract stipulates. It is very unlikely that a publisher will reject your book at this stage, but they do remain legally within their rights to do so if it falls well short of the quality they were expecting or if it is not the book they commissioned. It would be unlikely to get as far as final delivery for an editor to be surprised in this way. A dedicated editor will have agreed in advance with both author and agent on what rewriting and enhancements to the manuscript they first fell in love with might be needed to produce a final, publishable version.

For fiction – which, as discussed in chapter 3, usually reaches a publisher via an agent – the agent may take a very hands-on role in working with an author to improve their manuscript. There may be several manuscript drafts which take on board suggested restructures, plot reassessments and stylistic improvements. Agents spend a considerable amount of their time helping an author to prepare the manuscript they will be happy to deliver to their publisher. It depends on the agent and the editor and the particular needs of each author and the state of their originally submitted manuscript on how much input is needed and what working relationship will be most effective for all parties. Good, frequent and honest communication between the three – agent, editor and author – is thus important to manage each party's expectations. If an agent and author are expecting the publishing editor to devote weeks and months to a close editorial review of the final manuscript, but the editor has other ideas and plans to do only a more cursory read because she has a stable of over thirty books to juggle at any one time and has assumed that close editorial work will already have been done by the agent, then this needs to be addressed. When you are first approached by an agent and subsequently meet an editor keen to sign you up, it is a good idea to ask how much editorial hand-holding each will be offering you. The final manuscript delivery date will have been arrived at based on the perceived amount of extra refinement all parties agree will be needed to reach that status. This might be only weeks or months, or it could be years.

For some books, such as narrative non-fiction or the second title from an author which may not yet have been written when a multi-book deal was signed, then there may be a few years between contract to delivery. For a travel guide, memoir, popular history or other non-fiction that entails significant original research and which has been contracted based on a convincing pitch and sample, the author is likely to be looking for an advance to help cover some of their research time. Except for very established and bestselling authors, the advance won't stretch to cover an author's costs in any meaningful way, though it might help to mitigate against some of the time taken off from a day job as unpaid leave in which to write.

The different editing interventions that take place within the publishing house when the final manuscript is delivered, usually electronically (the contract will stipulate the required format), will depend on the publisher, the type of book (educational, reference, adult novel, picture book) and the author's needs. Editing is the first stage in a long set of processes that your manuscript will travel through on its way to becoming a final, ready-to-be published book.

Publishing workflow, schedules and planning

The bare bones of the process of converting a manuscript – the raw material – into a professionally produced book – the product – is straightforward. It's something publishers are very used to doing: turning words on a page (a piece of text in a Word file) into a presentable document that is appropriate in style, tone and length for the readership for which it is intended.

When they prepare to publish a book, publishers will consider its look, feel, style, promotion and delivery and make sure they reflect the book's content, the profile of the author and that it reaches the intended market within a pre-set budget and to a pre-agreed schedule. Publishers will have expert staff in-house or freelancers who will manage and advise at each stage of the process. Each of the distinctive parts of a book's journey from idea to purchasable product is itself divided into numerous stages. Take 'editing' – that alone might encompass structural editing, fact-checking, clearance of copyright material if used, critical review, self-editing and rewriting – usually across many rounds, and copy-editing to check for sense, typos and grammatical errors. After design and setting comes proofreading of text and designed layouts, checking not only that the text is all there and correct but it looks well-presented too. It may sometimes feel that once your book has been handed over that you lose control. An agent will help support you through the process and intervene on your behalf when or if you disagree with your editor.

Stage	Action	Protagonist
WRITING	Idea Manuscript	Author
SUBMISSION	Literary agent Publisher	Agent / Editor / Author
PRODUCTION	Editing Text design Typesetting Blurb Cover	Editorial / Author Designer Typesetter / Production Editor / Marketing Designer
PROMOTION	Publicity PR Marketing	Marketing / Publicity departments
SALES	Booksellers Publisher website Distributors Rights	Sales department, including reps Co-editions or rights manger

Typical stages in the publishing process

Self-published authors are advised to review these stages, so they have a clearer idea of what is involved in publishing a book and so they can decide where and when to seek professional, paid-for support.

SCHEDULES

A sizeable amount of any editor's role is to plan, manage and keep several balls in the air at any one time. I used to liken my role when I was a junior desk editor and later a development editor to that of a spider, sitting at the centre of a large and intricate web of activity, with my fingers (legs!) in several places all at the same time. Simultaneously, an editor has to be concerned with the bigger picture and think about how their list will develop, what new titles will be signed up from agents or commissioned direct from authors, how to keep it viable with a full publishing programme and healthy profit & loss (P&L) for three or five years ahead. She also needs to worry about the specifics of individual titles.

I needed to be efficient, organised and rather insistent sometimes with colleagues in other departments to ensure that the thirty or so titles I had entrusted to me would be properly cared for, given the attention that they and their authors deserved. The books would each be at a different stage in the publishing workflow, from newly delivered to final proofread and each step in-between: index commissioning, peer review, cover briefings, blurb drafting, marketing strategising, and sales figure estimating.

A managing, commissioning or acquisitions editor, responsible for a list of titles and probably an editor or assistant editor too, will be planning their publishing schedule for years ahead. This will involve consulting with sales and marketing and other editorial colleagues to decide which titles should slot into the publishing schedule across the company to give them the best chance of being reviewed, noticed and bought. Where a title gets slotted in will depend on purely practical arrangements for books that are not time sensitive: on when the final manuscript is contracted to be delivered and thus when publication can be expected, usually ten or so months after manuscript delivery. For lead titles or titles that tie in with a significant anniversary or relate to a breaking news story or craze, then publication might be fixed to an immovable date around which marketing and publicity activity will be generated well in advance of publication. Some titles might have their publication brought forward to link to external events and others might be slowed down if there are concerns about some contentious material that requires sensitive treatment or additional libel or defamation reads for example. Some books are kept secret or embargoed so no one except for a few key members of staff at the publisher and at the printers (all sworn to secrecy) will know what it looks like or how the text reads before publication date. This became the norm for publication of each Harry Potter title and helped create a huge buzz and anticipation on the part of both professional book buyers (the trade, booksellers and distributors) and the book-buying public.

There will be schedules to cover all books in the company, all books on a list and schedules for each title. Editors and production staff will live by these schedules; a simple outline is given opposite. This might be kept as a spreadsheet or in a company-wide content management database that is the backbone of the publishing business: where all forms, calculations, materials and tracking associated with a title are stored to give a full and traceable picture of all stages in the book's development. Larger publishers will certainly have one of these, smaller ones are likely to be much more manual in their approach. In both cases, having a version of the schedule is helpful to an author and editors will usually consult you when drawing this up to take account of your personal circumstances where they can, rather than imposing it upon you. You should be mindful that any changes in schedules caused by author-imposed delays will mean changes not just to your book but will have a knock-on effect more widely on other books in the system. They will impact on freelance editors commissioned to take on your manuscript or a production controller who has booked a slot on a printing press, so do try and stick to dates that you have previously agreed to; it makes things more efficient and happier for all those along the line of activity in and outside the publisher.

A sample production schedule. This will vary depending on the length and complexity of your book and if there is an urgency to get it fast tracked to publication.

Scheduled tasks	Key dates
MS delivery date	28/03/2019
MS to copy-editor	25/04/2019
Copy-edited MS in	23/05/2019
Handover to production	06/06/2019
1st proofs in, index commissioned	13/06/2019
1st proofs back to production	27/06/2019
2nd proofs in	11/07/2019
2nd proofs back to production	25/07/2019
Final page proofs in	01/08/2019
Pass for press	08/08/2019
Advances in	03/10/2019
Stock in	03/10/2019
Publication	28/11/2019

If a book is fully illustrated or has some other non-text content these need to be factored in too and allocated dates in the schedule for when they will be commissioned, delivered, reviewed and amended so that they are ready to be handed over to production with the text.

Working with your publisher

Authors expect to build up a strong working relationship with their editors; they want to be able to trust and understand the decisions an editor makes about their book. I like to involve an author in all stages of the publishing journey and to make sure I manage their expectations as to my availability, what I will (and won't) be doing editing-wise to their manuscript and to be transparent about the whole process. Editors are not all the same and it's a good idea from the moment you are contracted

EDITORIAL DIRECTOR	DESIGN DEPARTMENT
Plans overall direction of list	Cover design
Supports Editor in their role	In-text design and layouts
Makes sure the list is financially viable	Commission illustrations, maps, photos
Helps resolve problems when they arise	Liaises with freelance designers, picture researchers etc

PRODUCTION DEPARTMENT	EDITOR	MARKETING & PUBLICITY DEPARTMENTS
Makes the book a reality	Negotiates with agent	Creates promotional materials
Costs, schedules, brokers and manages	Works with author	Manages social media and website
print and ebook stages from 'handover' to final copies	Takes receipt of final MS	Handles publicity and author events
Arranges reprints	Oversees the full process	Books advertising space
	Liaises with publishing colleagues	Options extract rights
	Commissions freelance editorial work	Provides advance information to Sales

RIGHTS & CONTRACTS DEPARTMENT	SALES DEPARTMENT
Draws-up contracts	Negotiates discounts on bulk selling to:
Identifies and negotiates rights deal (e.g. translations)	Bookshops, Distributors / Wholesalers, Book clubs
Represents the publisher at rights fairs	Manages stock and reprints

The role of the editor and her publishing colleagues

to try and get a sense of the nature of the relationship you might enjoy together. It should go without saying that the relationship needs to always be professional and balanced, but sometimes it can be much more than that: when author and editor really get on and have things in common beyond a book, it can be a very rewarding and long-lasting relationship. Just as editors are different (and as we shall see below, under Editing, their roles and responsibilities are too) so authors will have different needs and expectations based on any previous publishing experience or knowledge they might have. I like to assume that most authors want to know about the process and I try to elicit how much they already know so I can judge where I need to add detail and where to avoid being patronising. As an author you need to be honest with your agent or publisher about the limitations of your knowledge and comfortable enough to ask questions.

Authors can often feel let down by publishers. They complain that they and their book did not get the attention they expected. Sometimes an editor may be exceptionally neglectful, but in the lion's share of cases, authors will feel this way because their editor hasn't been regularly in touch or has failed to carefully manage their expectations.

In the worst of circumstances, authors can fall out with their editor – or their agent – or not work well with the illustrator with whom they have been paired. This is regrettable but will usually stem from a creative disagreement rather than a personal slight. It is best if all parties can remind themselves that publishing is a business, that it is covered by legal agreement and that publishers are professionals who not only want the best for their authors and their book but also have a track record in how to deliver published titles to market.

Editing

WHY IS CONSISTENCY IMPORTANT?

The publishing process is a single continuous line of professionals working on your manuscript, passing the editorial baton from commissioning editor to desk editor, copy-editor and proofreader, via a designer and typesetter. By having style guides, a coherent, clear and consistent approach, there is an efficiency and continuity that makes economic and practical sense and reminds each member of the editorial chain(gang) that they are not working in self-contained isolation. Publishing a book successfully involves teamwork. Each person in the publishing house takes on temporary responsibility for your manuscript under the overall eagle management eye of your designated editor – usually the editor who will have commissioned and signed up your book in the first place or an editor who reports to her and who is your publishing champion within the publisher. With any luck they will be with you throughout the whole process from gestation to the birth of your book into the market, and your subsequent books too. Editors do move around a fair amount – but don't worry; if this happens, as long as there is a clear sense of what your book is about, who it is for and how it will look, and how it will be marketed and sold, and this is backed up by clear documentation and regular communication, then your experience of being published should be a positive one.

The **commissioning** or acquisitions editor will take receipt of the full manuscript, review this and feed back suggestions for any further rewrites to the author if necessary. An editor shouldn't tell an author how to amend their text, but they *should* point out where it is working well and not so well so an author can decide how best to adjust their own work. Authors tell me they are always very appreciative of positive commentary on their manuscript; otherwise, it can be very demoralising to receive a manuscript covered in marginal notes and a heavy dose of track changes. I feel strongly that an author should stand up for their text where they believe a change is *not* needed and I should be able to justify why I've indicated that a sentence might not be working or the text is best served if a paragraph is moved or dropped altogether. This makes for a genuinely creative working process and should result in a better manuscript. At this stage, if needed, a libel check, close fact-check or sensitivity read might be done. As an author you have signed a contract to confirm that what you deliver to your publisher is free from inaccurate, defamatory or libellous material. At best such errors undermine the credibility of your text, at worst unproven allegations, exaggeration or repetition of unfounded hearsay or quotations could land the author and publisher in the libel courts. Fortunately, this is very unlikely. Medical or legal titles that include advice, dosage information and such like will need close scrutiny and a publisher may ask an author to reconfirm that all facts have been fully checked at their own expense; they may arrange for a checker if necessary themselves and pay for this or charge it to the author's advance. I've known some publishers appoint freelance writers or editors to support an author in their final text rewrites where they think the author needs it; also at the author's expense.

A sensitivity or inclusivity reading of a text – for books for children or Young Adults – is becoming more common. A reader will check for inclusive language or areas which might cause unnecessary offence to certain readers or where a plot line is particularly sensitive (abuse, mental health, same-sex relationship) to see that it has been appropriately handled. Such reads are not about censoring an author's ideas or writing, or at least they shouldn't be.

For academic or educational books, manuscripts are frequently sent out for independent peer review, usually to at least two readers, to satisfy the publisher that the author has produced a well-argued, convincing work or one which conforms to the requirements of the curriculum for which it has been commissioned to support. The commissioning editor needs to ensure the content or subject reviewer – a fellow scholar or teacher – is able to give a balanced opinion.

When the commissioning editor is satisfied that the manuscript is ready for publication, she hands this over to her **desk editor** if she is not seeing the book through herself. The desk editor's role is to oversee and coordinate all the stages up to final copies. She will appoint and liaise with freelance editors to copy-edit and proofread text and will ensure each book keeps on schedule and within budget and is prepared to the quality that the publisher expects for all its books.

Copy-editing is when your final manuscript is gone through with a fine-tooth comb and checked for sense, grammatical, spelling and punctuation errors. The text will be made consistent in style and format. Additional materials such as tables, images and end and footnotes will be checked to see that they have all been delivered and are numbered or labelled to match the text and are correctly cued to it. The copy-editor will also mark text that doesn't make sense or is confusing, suggesting slight rewrites. The amount of time it takes to copy-edit a text depends on the word count, its complexity, how well it is written and if the author has adhered to a publisher's style or spelling guide. The copy-editor will add notes on spelling, punctuation or capitalisation that they have imposed on the text as this will be useful at the proofreading stage and will highlight any special characters, including accents or other symbols, that the typesetter should be aware of. The desk editor may ask the copy-editor to work directly with an author to resolve any queries raised at the copy-editing stage or may sort these out herself with the author direct once the copy-edited manuscript has been returned in-house. Whichever route is followed, once queries are resolved and the track changes all accepted, you should have a clean manuscript with the headings marked up in line with a design specification. I like to highlight headings and other styles clearly in different colours and provide the setter with the corresponding key. It avoids adding in text around headings such as [A HEAD] which might get set in error.

Armed with the 'clean' manuscript, the copy-editor will hand it over to her production colleague who manages an external typesetter who prepares the page proofs. The manuscript is usually accompanied by a standard form with a checklist that will have prompted the editor to make sure they are providing all the essential details about the setting requirements for the text.

Proofreading takes place when page proofs are received. There may be several rounds. For more detail about the proof stages, see page 196.

MISTAKES TO LOOK OUT FOR WHEN COPY-EDITING AND PROOFREADING

These are some of the things that professional editors are trained to spot. It's a useful checklist, especially for self-published authors.

- Incomplete punctuation, such as missing brackets and speech marks
- Inaccurate use of the possessive apostrophe and in contractions, such as its /it's
- Consistency in spelling: US / UK, -ize / -ise
- Consistent style and spacing for measurements, numbers, ages and dates
- Words that have similar spellings or sounds but variant meanings, such as cue or queue, effect and affect
- Missing words, duplicated text or transposed text, for example 1948 when 1984 is meant
- Missing bullet points or inaccurate numbering sequences in lists, pages, sections
- Capitalisation for proper nouns, places, trademarks and specialist terms in line with the style guide
- No explanation for acronyms or abbreviations; other than for really obvious ones (BBC); give the terms in full on first use
- Incorrect and mixed use of tenses, singular and plural

In addition, proofreaders will make sure that:

- Layout is consistent and correct across each page or spread
- Pagination and running heads have been included correctly
- All content including prelims and end matter has been incorporated
- Cross-references from one part of the text to another are accurate

- Heading styles have been implemented to match the type specification
- Text that should be in italic type, such as book titles, has been correctly styled
- Text, margins and columns are all aligned
- No text has been set in error or duplicated
- All illustrations, maps or tables have correct captions

PROOFREADING SYMBOLS

The industry standard (BSI or British Standard Institution) proof correction marks were used universally by copy-editors and proofreaders for correcting manuscripts and proofs in hard copy. It was a form of 'shorthand' code with which designers and typesetters were also familiar. These days, when nearly all scripts and proofs are read and annotated on screen, the symbols are less necessary. A working knowledge of them is very useful though and they remain an accurate and quick way to mark text changes coherently. I like my editors to still use them where they can when marking up proofs in PDF; the alternative is simply highlighting something to be amended and providing an inserted comment which can be ambiguous or unclear to the setter who then takes in the correction. The proof correction marks you are most likely to come across are shown in the tables below.

I'm a big fan of these marks as they remind me of when I started out as a publishing trainee: one of my first tasks was to learn the symbols. I still use them. I like their elegant usefulness and they remind me of my dad, who worked for BSI, employing them as he proofread International Electrical Standards in his study.

Most non-fiction titles will have an **index** which will be created by a freelance indexer at first proof stage once it is known on which page text will come. If for any reason the first proofs are predicted to have a substantial number of layout changes where text might move, then it is advisable to hold off getting an index prepared until a second round

Proof-correction marks

These marks conform to BS 5261C: 2005. In the tables below, 'character' means a letter or individual mark in the text; 'matter' means the content and could be text, a table or a picture.

Marks/symbols for general instructions

INSTRUCTIONS	MARGIN	TEXT
Leave the text in its original state and ignore any marks that have been made: stet (Latin for 'let it stand')	⊘	_ _ _ _ under the characters to be left as they were
Query for the author/typesetter/printer/publisher	?	A circle should be placed around matter to be queried
Remove non-textual marks	X	A circle should be placed around marks to be removed
End of change	/	None

Marks/symbols for inserting, deleting and replacing text

INSTRUCTIONS	MARGIN	TEXT
Matter to be inserted	New matter, followed by ⋋	⋋
Additional matter supplied separately	⋋ followed by a letter in a diamond which identifies ⟨A⟩ additional matter	⋋
Delete a character (and close up)	⌀	/ through the character
Delete text (and close up)	⌀	⊢⊣ through text
Character to replace marked character	New character, followed by /	/ through the character
Text to replace marked text	New text, followed by /	⊢⊣ through text

Marks/symbols for grammar and punctuation

INSTRUCTIONS	MARGIN	TEXT
Full stop	⊙	⋋ at insertion point or / through character
Comma	⸓	As above
Semi-colon	;	As above
Colon	⊙	As above
Hyphen	⊢⊣	As above
Single quote marks	⸜ or ⸝	As above
Double quote marks	⸌⸌ or ⸍⸍	As above
Apostrophe	⸍	As above
Ellipses or leader dots	⸛ ⋯ ⸛	As above
Insert/replace dash	Ⓝ Size of dash to be stated between uprights	As above

Marks/symbols for altering the look/style/layout of text

INSTRUCTIONS	MARGIN	TEXT
Put text in italics	⌐⌐	___ under text to be changed
Remove italics, replace with roman text	⌐⊥⌐	Circle text to be changed
Put text in bold	⌁⌁⌁	⌁⌁⌁ under text to be changed
Remove bold	⌁⌁⌁	Circle text to be changed
Put text in capitals	≡	≡ under text to be changed
Put text in small capitals	=	= under text to be changed
Put text in lower case	⫢ or ⊥	Circle text to be changed
Change character to superscript	⋎ under character	| through character to be changed
Insert a superscript character	⋎ under character	⋌ at point of insertion
Change character to subscript	⋏ above character	| through character to be changed
Insert a subscript character	⋏ above character	⋌ at point of insertion
Remove bold and italics	⌐⊥⌐	Circle text to be changed
Paragraph break	⌐⌐	⌐⌐
Remove paragraph break, run on text	⌒	⌒
Indent text	⊐	⊐
Remove indent	⊃	⊃
Insert or replace space between characters or words	Y	⋌ at relevant point of insertion or | through character
Reduce space between characters or words	⋏	/
Insert space between lines or paragraphs	Mark extends into margin	—(or)—
Reduce space between lines or paragraphs	Mark extends into margin	→ or ←
Transpose lines	⊆	⊆
Transpose characters or words	⊔⊓	⊔⊓
Close space between characters	⌢	character ⌢ character
Underline words	(underline)	� circle words
Take over character(s) or word(s) to next line/column/page	Mark extends into margin	⊏
Take back character(s) or word(s) to previous line/column/page	Mark extends into margin	⊐

of proofs ('first revises'). The index is commissioned by the publisher, prepared in Word, typeset, and checked at proof before it gets added to the main text proofs. The Society of Indexers has a Directory of Professional Indexers on their website (www.indexers.org.uk) with rates. In 2019 the recommended fee for the index for a straightforward title was £25.50 an hour, £2.85 a page or £7.70 per 1,000 words. For indexes to be effective in ebooks, each index entry has to be anchored within the text at a precise location via a hyperlink.

FINAL PROOF CHECKING

When each round of proofs have been checked and the index proofs incorporated, a final set of checks and balances are usually done by the desk editor to make sure nothing has been missed. She will check once again that all text is present, that the chapter headings and numbers given on the contents page match the text pages and that the overall number of pages (called the extent, see page 185) is an even working, meaning it can be divisible by 16; this is important for printing.

Design

THE COVER

A cover design is important for saleability and discoverability, especially for trade (general reader) titles which are usually discretionary rather that must-have buys. Cover images and the designs for professional, reference and educational titles are less important as they are unlikely to affect purchase as much as reviews, recommendations and being a set text. The covers should still be clear, well-designed and indicate what the title is about with an image, if it has one, appropriate to subject matter and the age of the reader. Bookshop browsers – in person or online – will be more susceptible to cover designs and are likely to be drawn instinctively to some books and not to others. The cover can be a quick indicator of the genre a book falls into and will conform to the prevailing look that readers have become accustomed to. It should convey a clear message which could reflect how you want a reader to feel or that highlights a theme from a novel. Is the designer being asked to present a sunny, fun summer read or create a darker, sinister mood through their design? There is a cross-publisher look or style for thrillers which distinguish them from cosy detective fiction, literary writing or from the different types of work that fall within romance. What might seem a copy-cat style of cover design is really a shorthand for informing readers of the kind of story they should expect to find between its covers. Text or typography is just as important for a cover as images, and the combination of these is what creates an overall design; this look is provided by a cover designer who understands how text and image can work together. Authors should be consulted on covers but it's rarely the case that they have power of veto over a publisher's choice.

If you want to self-publish you can find cover templates online, inviting you to create a design in a few easy steps. These may be helpful in considering the key elements that you will need to include on your cover, but just putting all the necessary pieces together will not produce a design that has artistic flair. It is usually easy to spot covers that have not had creative input from a professional designer who understands layout, including how much space to leave around text and the outside edges of a cover. A designer will consider what balance should be struck between a title, subtitle or strapline and how different typefaces can work together as well as which typefaces can be used for free and for which a fee will be payable. In the same way that self-published authors are advised to pay for expert editorial input into their writing, I suggest you seek professional design help too.

Most books do not get displayed in bookshops with the cover facing outwards, unless it is part of a 3-for-2 or other promotion on a table at the front of the store, and online each book's cover is on show, but initially only as a small thumbnail. That means it is important for a cover design to work well whatever its dimensions and for cover text to be clearly seen and read. The back cover and spine are also important.

In a bookshop the spine is what readers will usually see. It needs to include the book's title and author name clearly and allude to the genre through the style of lettering. The publisher's colophon will also be included. The back cover or jacket copy includes an ISBN bar code, the blurb or selling copy (see page 182) and should highlight (in a subtle, persuasive way) why a reader should buy and read the book.

Having sat in innumerable cover meetings in my career, I can report that choosing a cover by committee is not a very satisfying experience. As an editor, I know if a cover reflects the contents of the book and evokes an emotion in the bookshop browser that I'm hoping for: alarm, humour, delight, curiosity . . . I'm pleased. I'm happy to leave cover decision making to a sales manager who is out in the market and can advise what else is selling, and say if a cover can be seen clearly from a distance (or not) or if it looks too closely like a rival's recent title on a similar subject.

YOUR BOOK'S TITLE

For most non-fiction, the title is used as practical shorthand for clearly indicating what the book is about: *Vegetarian Cookery, Guide to Polar Exploration, Betsie's Motorcycle Manual* and might be accompanied by a subtitle that gives a little more detail or highlights a unique selling feature of the book: *Vegetarian Cookery: Healthy Meals in under 30 Minutes*; *Guide to Polar Exploration: When to Go, What to Take, What to See*; *Betsie's Motorcycle Manual: A Woman's Guide to Fixing Your Bike*. Discursive, narrative non-fiction tends to take more liberties and might adopt a more creative title; subtitles then become essential if a purchaser wants to know what subject matter the book is covering and so it can be quickly found via Google and Amazon searches. Examples include *Prisoners of Geography: Ten Maps That Tell You Everything You Need to Know About Global Politics* by Tim Marshall (Elliott & Thompson, 2015) and Yuval Noah Harari's *Homo Deus: A Brief History of Tomorrow* (Harper, 2017).

Titles for novels tend to follow well-tested styles: single-word punchy titles for doorstop popular fiction or fantasy tales: *Dune, Apocalyse, Wool, Popcorn* and something rather more ruminative for a literary work: *The Unbearable Lightness of Being, The Strange Incident of the Dog in the Nighttime, The Hundred-Year-Old-Man Who Climbed Out the Window and Disappeared.* Both can be effective. As the title is not a description of the book's content but just an oblique reference to something in the story you can have fun deciding what will work best. Often the final decision will be based on making sure it does not duplicate a title already on the market and how it works on the cover. Does it look right? Is it too long or too short to work in the typography or overall cover design? Once an author's brand starts to get established the title might help in developing a consistent identity for that writer. Victoria Hislop's debut novel is called *The Island* (Headline Review, 2005), which was an international bestseller, three of her follow-up novels are called *The Thread, The Sunrise* and *The Return.*

It's always good to have a working title when you are writing and submitting, but you and your publisher may go through several iterations until the final, publishable one is arrived at. It's as much a marketing, sales and design decision as it is an editorial one.

THE BLURB AND OTHER COVER COPY

Remember how tricky it was to write your pitch to an agent? The boot is now on the editor's foot. Drafting selling copy that accurately captures the themes, tone and essence of a book in an engaging way and declares 'buy me' is an art. The best way to write a successful blurb is to critically appraise copy on the back of existing titles to see what works and to emulate them. Most blurbs conform to existing formulae. For fiction, that means making clear the situation that the main protagonist finds herself in and hinting at the difficulties she needs to overcome. A blurb shouldn't give the ending away; it should provide just enough detail to hook a reader. It can embrace hyperbole, praising the book and the author to the skies. That said, less is always more when it comes to length as far as blurbs are concerned. Concise, punchy copy in short sentences with plenty of space for the words to breathe rather than tightly packed lines of text is best. Think about the key words that encapsulate the story or the benefits to the reader of a non-fiction title. What essential information or idea do you want to get across? Strap lines or, if you have one, an endorsement or review quote work well on front or back covers. Hardbacks will have flaps too but avoid the tendency to fill up all the space these afford.

Blurbs have become increasingly important in promoting books and as vehicles for them to be discovered online. Once an editor has drafted the blurb copy, they should run it past the author to check there are no inaccuracies included and that they are happy with the short author biographical description if one is being included on the back cover. I like to pass my blurbs via the marketing and publicity departments too in case they have some enhancements – they usually do as their heads are more naturally attuned to how to attract a reader through selling copy. The blurb is also used as the basis for catalogue copy and online bookstore descriptions. That means it is worth spending time getting it right; drafting and redrafting until it reads like effective copy and will encourage any browser to purchase the book.

Pricing The price on the back of a book (the cover price) will be what the publisher thinks the book can bear; it will be pegged against similar or direct competitor books in the same genre in the market. The actual price a book is sold for depends on the type of book, its intended readership and where and how it is sold. Price is a significant factor in purchaser decision-making. Given how much time I've spent in publishing and around books, I know how much work goes into each book's creation and they are cheap compared with other hobbies and experiences that can be bought: compare the pleasure and hours spent engrossed in a story with the cost of three hours at the theatre, two at the cinema or 90 minutes at a football match.

There is no VAT on books purchased in the UK, but ebooks carry the standard 20 per cent. They tend to be cheaper than print and are often heavily discounted in promotional campaigns, sometimes for short periods to stimulate high-volume sales. Publishers may start out with price parity for their print and ebook editions of the same title (including any VAT payable), but discounting is the norm in countries like the UK and US not controlled by fixed price books (such as Germany and France).

TEXT DESIGN

Your publisher will need to decide what your book will physically look like inside. Even if it is in ebook only it is important that the text is easily navigated and in a font that is pleasing to read. The editor will have advised her colleagues when presenting the publishing proposal form to an inhouse editorial meeting (an example of which is given in chapter 4) as to the likely format of the book she has commissioned. A text designer will prepare the look and feel for the inside of your book, which will sometimes follow a standard template. Often a designer will prepare a sample chapter or a few spreads, design samples for the prelims and endmatter and a handover guide for a typesetter. For illustration-led titles and children's picture books, where it matters exactly what text appears on which page and text and images are fully integrated, pages are laid out spread-by-spread by a designer.

The following have to be considered and decisions are made on practical, economic as well as creative and aesthetic grounds.

Format (also sometimes referred to as the '**binding**' type for print editions): will your book be issued as a hardback or paperback on first publication, will there be a simultaneous ebook in Mobi and ePub formats, will an audio edition appear at the same time or follow later for scheduling reasons or to test the market as to its suitability and likely sales uptake in that format?

Page dimensions: what size will your book be? This is also confusingly referred to as the book's format. It is likely to be a standard size. It might follow an existing series or template design and the dimensions of other books on the publisher's list. The production department will encourage editors to select a page trim that is a fit for the press on which they plan to print it. The common dimensions for trimmed page size in mm are:

Crown 8vo 186 × 123
Crown 4vo 246 × 189
Large crown 8vo 198 × 129

Demy 8vo 216 × 138
Demy 4to 276 × 219
Royal 8vo 234 × 156
Royal 4to 312 × 237
Mass market A format paperback 178 × 111
Mass market B format paperback 198 × 129

Extent is the number of final actual pages for your book (the prelim pages plus the chapters and endmatter) which will be printed and bound. Printing is done in combinations of 16 or 32, or depending on the press used, up to 64-page sections or **signatures**. A signature is a group of pages that are printed on both sides of a single sheet of paper of various dimensions, which once folded and trimmed become a total set of pages based on the original sheet size. Extent becomes irrelevant for ebooks from the binding perspective but will remain a consideration from an editorial one. Is the book the *right* length for the subject matter and for the market for which it is intended and is the cover price the right one based on that extent?

Colour or **black and white (b&w) printing** will be dictated by the subject and readership of the book and how illustrated it is. The options are mono (i.e. black and white) printing, printing in two colours or in four (the printing colours are black, cyan (blue), yellow and magenta (pinky-red)).

Before a book is edited (and for picture books or other illustrated titles even before the writing is completed), an editor will have decided with a designer and production colleague all of the above if they have a direct impact on how the book will be laid out or structured. Paper provenance, shade (white, off-white or cream), grammage (how thick each sheet is) and binding styles (sewn or stuck, with or without ribbons or headbands) and their impact on a book's spine width all have to be agreed prior to printing.

A third use of the term 'format' is to describe the way text is formatted – and will refer to how it is rendered in digital files and how that might then translate to what text looks like on the page. It includes layout dimensions, styling of type (for example, in bold, italic or small capitals), line spacing and typefaces.

The parts of a book

Although you will be very familiar with what a book looks like, you may not have stopped to consider its constituent parts. They differ for the type of book you have created. If you have written an adult, YA or middle grade genre or literary fiction, which will be text-only, then your book will have a straightforward structure. It will have a standard set of **preliminary pages** ('prelims') that appear in all books (though sometimes in a different order or location) and a series of chapters, each of which is roughly the same number of pages in length. As the author, you will deliver the main text or chapters and don't need to worry about the prelim pages. Your editor will pull these together and add them to the manuscript before she hands it over for copy-editing or she may ask the copy-editor to prepare these pages prior to handing the complete, edited manuscript over to the production department for typesetting.

Prelims are traditionally 'numbered' with roman numerals (i, ii, iii), though these are not usually printed on all of the actual prelim pages such as the title or half-title pages (see below). That means page one in Arabic numbering (1, 2, 3) printed in the book will be page one of the actual narrative. The prelims (those pages that are 'before' the main text) are the information pages about your book – the pages about the pages that follow them – and include:

(i) **Half-title page:** which is usually just the main title for the book set in smaller type than on the main title page. If the extent does not allow for this page when the final proofs have been received because it tips the extent into an extra signature, then it can be dropped.

(ii) Blank page: or it could be where a **frontispiece** – an illustration, usually in black and white for a standard title and not common in novels – appears. It might also be used for review quotes in a paperback edition of a previously published work, a list of other titles in a series, or the author biography (if this is not included at the back of the book, inside the front or back cover, on a hardback jacket flap or on the back of the book).

(iii) **Title page**, which includes the main title, any subtitle as well as the author and publisher name with publication date and the publisher logo or colophon.

(iv) **Imprint** or **title verso page**: which includes all the legal and production information about the book, such as who the publisher is, their address and where they are located; copyright lines with dates; edition numbers if relevant; impression number – which printing the particular book is from; the book's ISBN; and details about the typesetter and printer. It might also include the roles and names of the individuals who worked on the text, layout and other aspects of the book. This is common in books with complicated layouts or highly illustrated titles, series or travel books and those that have involved a fair amount of project management. It's not usual to name the editors and publicists for novels in the prelims: that's a courtesy that is sometimes afforded them by the author in their acknowledgements, which come at the back or in the opening pages of the book.

Copyright lines read something like this:

Copyright © A. Writer, 2019

A. Writer has asserted her right to be identified as the author of this Work in accordance with the Copyright, Designs and Parents Act 1988

It is also where information to protect the author from any accusation of defamation is included, such as:

This is a work of fiction. While, as in all fiction, the literary perceptions and insights are based on experience, all names, characters, places and incidents are either products of the author's imagination or are used fictitiously.

And to remind readers that the content of the book is subject to copyright law and thus can't be reproduced without permission.

Impressions (or reprints) are shown like this, the lowest number indicating which printing it is (in this example, the third impression of the title):

$$4\ 6\ 8\ 10\ 9\ 7\ 5\ 3$$

The **main text** will then start on the following recto or right-hand, odd-numbered page: page 1. Fiction prelims sometimes include a black and white map that is essential to the text, an **epigram** (a short, usually witty or satirical phrase), **dedication** or an **Author's Note**. These can either be numbered as if they are prelim pages (in roman numerals) or as the first page of main text (Arabic numbers). For example, on page 1 of *War Horse* (Egmont, 2006) in his 'Author's Note', Michael Morpurgo describes the painting that inspired his novel. Memoirists will often include a Note to indicate that their recollections are just that – their own and not subject to other perspectives and to indicate if any individuals referred to have had names or distinguishing details changed.

Some novels open with a **Prologue**, or short introductory chapter that sets out a backstory for the ensuing narrative. That's what Ransom Rigg does at the beginning of *Miss Peregrine's School for Peculiar Children* (Quirk Books, 2013), where he establishes the voice of his narrator and the tone of the book; it concludes 'Then a few years later . . . an extraordinary and terrible thing happened, and there was only Before and After'. It can be a useful framing device, such as that used by Yann

Martel (entitled 'Author's Note') in the *Life of Pi* (Canongate Books, 2003) when a character who is not the narrator of the main narrative introduces how the story that is then related came about. Try not to get too exercised about a prologue: if your book needs one then write one but consider what its purpose is and if the text that you include in it might be just as well contained in chapter one. If you deleted it, would it be detrimental to the reader's understanding of your story or can you afford creatively to jettison it?

A picture book of 24 or 32 pages will often have the copyright details that would usually come on the imprint page in a book's prelims at the very back of the book or even on the back cover, snuck away to allow more room for the story and illustrations: it would be wasteful to give over a whole page to legal details. These are important, but they can be pared back to the essentials: copyright line, publication date and publisher contacts. There may be line illustrations at the head of each chapter or on separate pages for middle grade books (books for eight to twelve-year-olds), but these will not need to be fully integrated with the text and are not subject to detailed design instructions to the typesetter who will be running the text to page. In ebooks, the copyright page appears at the end.

A NON-FICTION book will also include some of the following in the prelims after the imprint page and are numbered in roman numerals: **Contents page; Foreword, Preface** or **Introduction; Illustration lists, list of abbreviations and key terms.**

For both fiction and non-fiction, there may be **parts** as well as **chapters**. Non-fiction chapters will always have an actual title rather than just a number to make clear to the reader what topic it will cover. They are a good way to make what might be quite a dry subject more enticing. Some novelists or memoirists include epigrams or relevant quotations to introduce each chapter.

For non-fiction, notably practical, how-to and education books or academic titles, which benefit from a clear breakdown of the text into discreet, easily navigable sections, there will be a range of heading levels, main and subsidiary (sub) shorthanded to A, B and C headings in publishing mark-up lingo where A is the top of the hierarchy. These books might also include footnotes, other navigation devices to aid the reader, such as numbered lists, bullet points, tables, diagrams and non-textual content like maps, line drawings, illustrations and photographs. Photographs can be integrated or in their own plate section tipped into the binding on a superior paper to enhance the reproduction quality of the images; this is also useful for practical i.e. economic reasons if you want to include a few colour images in an otherwise text-only book. There will also be captions accompanying the images.

Endmatter is, as the name suggests, all the stuff that doesn't come in the main text and was not needed to clutter up the prelims. It tends to be material that is in addition to the main work but which adds context, extension or additional navigation of the chapters that precede it. They are also known as **Appendices** and sometimes named as such.

For novels, there may be no endmatter, or just a page or two with acknowledgements which include authorial thank yous (to an agent, publisher, readers, family members) and more formal, legal ones for use of any material subject to copyright used in the book, such as lines of poetry or song lyrics. Both fiction and non-fiction sometimes include an **Afterword**: in fiction it is usually of the what-happened-next variety, which may help tie up any loose ends at the end of a novel or to conclude a series. They are not typical in fiction. In non-fiction they might be included in the paperback edition to a previously published hardback. For example, in the paperback to *Why I'm No Longer Talking to White People About Race* (Bloomsbury, 2018), Reni Eddo-Lodge has written an additional essay 'Aftermath' in which she reflects on events that took place since she wrote the hardback and the political climate that greeted its publication.

If a book includes illustrations or photographs, the copyright holder for each will be included here. It's where, if there is one, you'll find a **Glossary**, list of **Further reading** (or a **Bibliography** – a list of all the books referred to in a book). These will conform to international industry standards in the way they are edited or laid out. You'll see in the Further reading section in the endmatter of this book (page 259), I've diverged slightly. The more technical books follow convention; for the books where I provide personal recommendations, I've adopted a more informal style. Publishing is packed full of processes and rules, but they are there to be broken when it makes sense to do so.

End notes which relate to numbers inserted at points in the text will come in the endmatter too, usually as a list for each chapter with the page number and note number given. The most familiar end material is the **Index** in non-fiction.

ANATOMY OF A PAGE

The **structure** or **layout** of the actual pages of the book also follow some well-worn formats.

Double-page spread (DPS) is the area across two facing pages; what you would see if you had a book open in front of you. A DPS is particularly relevant when picture books are being designed as these are seen as a single entity across which an image might stretch.

1. **Verso page** is the left-hand, even-numbered page of the book.

2. **A running head** appears at the top of all sections, such as chapters, that are more than one page in length but not on pages that are section openers, such as the first page of a chapter, part, index or contents page. We are so used to seeing them frame a page that one without them looks bare. For fiction, especially novels, with chapters that have no names and only numbers, the running head throughout is simply the book title or an abbreviated form if that is very long. Running heads look best if they fill no more than two thirds of the page width. For non-fiction the running head is a useful navigational tool and the usual rule is that a book's title or a main section title (i.e. chapter) appears on the left-hand page and the chapter or heading for a section within a chapter appears on the right. Ebooks (other than fixed format PDF ebooks) dispense with running heads.

USEFUL DEFINITIONS ③ Boxed text

SEQUELS, TRILOGIES AND SERIES A *series* consists of several books about a particular character or group of characters, or based in a certain place or world. A second book with the same characters/world is a *sequel*; while three books make up a *trilogy*.

PACKAGERS will invent an idea and will normally have the responsibility of editing, designing, hiring writers, getting approvals, and finding artwork for a book. They will then approach a publisher with a project and sell them the rights to it.

EXERCISE 1: PLOT AND SUBPLOT ④ Text area

Look at a children's book that you have enjoyed and is of similar length to the one you are writing. See if you can take apart the layout of the plot (this can be useful practice for getting to grips with writing a synopsis and analysing your own writing structure). Where does the story begin? What are the main plot points? Here is a very simple example using Cinderella and a subplot of the ugly sisters' story. The plot is in roman type and the subplot in italics.

⑤
Bullet points

- Cinderella's father dies and she is miserable; her wicked stepmother takes over the house, making her a servant.

  - *Her stepsisters look for ways to make her life a misery, taking her things and making her work for them in the house.*

⑥
Outside margin

- Cinderella meets the prince by chance, they are drawn to each other.

  - *The stepsisters hear the prince is looking for a bride and squabble over which of them will marry him.*

- Her stepmother tells Cinderella she is not allowed to go to the ball and has to work in the kitchen.

  ⑦ Gutter

  - *The stepsisters tell Cinderella to make them dresses for the ball so she has no time to make one for herself, even if she could go.*

⑧ Crop marks

CHAPTER 7

Non-fiction
⑪ Chapter title

*'I hate describing anything by what it is not. We don't tell a boy
he is a 'non-girl' so why do we say 'non-fiction'? It is so much more.'*[1]

Some writers are naturally drawn to non-fiction. It is certainly a wide
and varied arena, well worth considering and as creative an endeavour
as writing fiction. Non-fiction can take almost any form with books
for all ages in a wide variety of formats, from short board books for
the youngest children in highly illustrated and often quite beautiful
books on a wide range of subjects – machines, nature, science, history,
space, the human body, mental health and so on. Narrative non-fiction
is where facts are presented within a narrative or storyline in a creative
imagining of the information, while fact/fiction mixes both fact and
narrative non-fiction.

Approach and subject matter ⑫ A (main) heading

WHERE DO YOU BEGIN? ⑬ B (sub) heading

With non-fiction, you still need to think about the age level you are
targeting, although the age range may be wider than when writing fiction because it is not accessed the same way. In non-fiction, not every
word needs to be read in the same way as in fiction; children might
skip to the sections that interest them most and read only some parts
of each double-page spread, especially if the information is scattered
throughout the illustrations. They are more likely to come back again
and again, to re-read and sample other facts. When considering what

[1] Stewart Ross ⑭ Footnote

⑮
Trim area

145

3. **Boxed text** is a useful way to draw attention to a piece of content or to include material that is additional to the main flow or argument of the main text.

4. **Text area** is the area inside the page's margins where text will appear. The text font can be centred, justified or with a ragged right edge. The space between text lines is known as **leading**, and like fonts or typefaces is measured in points. A designer will consider the best font and size for text to be readable. We are used to reading no more than ten to twelve words on average across a line.

5. **Bullet points** and numbered points or other devices can be used to break up text into smaller chunks to add variety and emphasis to the text being displayed.

6. **Outside margin** is the area from the outer edge of the paper for a print book to the text area and is usually 1.5 times wider than the gutter or can be the same width. If you want the inner and outer margins to appear the same width the inner margin needs to be slightly wider (usually 2 mm) to allow for the gutter and the book not opening flat as the gutter gets reduced after binding.

7. **Gutter** is the inside margin of the page from the printed text area and disappears into the binding.

8. **Crop marks** or trim marks are marks in the corners of page proofs and final pass-for-press PDFs to indicate to the printer where she should trim the printed pages. They should be removed from ebook files.

9. **Page number** can appear at the top or bottom of the page and sometimes in the outer margin. For novels they don't much matter to the reader so often are set in the centre of the bottom margin of the page. For non-fiction they are much more useful as they cross-relate to numbering in the contents page, in cross-references or in the index, and therefore should be easily seen: which might mean putting them on the outside margin. Ebooks (other than fixed format PDFs) do not include page numbers.

10. **Recto page** is the right-hand, odd-numbered page of the book.

11. **Chapter title and number** is the main title for a section or part in a book and is an opportunity for a designer to display some creative flair and link its style to the genre or content of the book.

12. **A heading** is the main heading in a section or chapter and will usually have a line to itself, with text starting ranged left (not indented) below.

13. **B & C headings** are sub-headings which are smaller than A heads and may have text run-on without a line space.

14. **Footnotes** are keyed to text with superscript numbers and can appear on the page where the annotated text appears or as endnotes at the end of a chapter or all gathered together in the book's endmatter. They are used to reference bibliographical or other primary sources that support an author's argument and which would slow up the flow of the text if referenced in full in the body text.

15. **Trim area** is the area that will be in the printed (and trimmed) book. Ebooks don't have trim sizes; the text area and type can be altered to suit the device that it is read on and the needs of the reader (see note 8).

Bled illustration is one that extends to the edge of the page and when the book is printed will have no white space around it and thus will usually be designed to be slightly larger than the trim size; 3 mm extra on the bled edges is standard. The bleed is the area that sits outside the trim area and will be trimmed off prior to binding.

Production

A design specification is produced to inform the typesetter on what layout, formats and styles the edited manuscript text should be converted into. This technical specification will include details on all the elements shown in the spreads on pages 192–3 in addition to any other design requirements. Most books will be written in Word.

For text-only or text-heavy books, a manuscript will be handed over with its design specification to the publisher's production department from where it gets forwarded to a typesetter. A production controller will typically work over a list of books or lists of books and become expert in a particular format, building up strong links with the third-party setters, ebook conversion houses and printers with whom they work. A production director or manager will oversee the complete production team (sometimes known as the content management department) and will be negotiating with these third-party businesses on behalf of all the publisher's lists to get competitive deals. Many of the companies who perform the conversion and layout-to-proof functions are based overseas. India in particular has huge expertise in this area and can offer competitive rates. Production controllers usually manage print and ebooks though some publishers may have separate ebook departments who manage that side of the operation. Highly illustrated or design-led titles are likely to be laid out using a publishing software package such as Adobe InDesign (by a designer in-house or working freelance). Either way, what results is a set of first page proofs, or page spreads in the case of InDesign.

PAGE PROOFS

At first proofs stage, production, editorial and the author will see the book as it will appear in its final printed form. It is an opportunity to check that the layout works well, to adjust it slightly, to move text to another page if a single line is stranded at the top (widow) or bottom (orphan) on a page and check for wordbreaks, turn lines or other layout issues that might impact on an unambiguous flow in the text. It is also when the text is looked at one more time to check for any typos that have slipped through or is amended to reflect anything a libel or sensitivity read might have highlighted. Ideally such reads will have taken place before the manuscript is sent to the copy-editor, but schedules don't always allow for that.

Page proofs stage is not the time to be rewriting the text; authors may be tempted to tweak and revise, but they are asked not to unless there is inaccurate or malicious material or factual errors in their book not picked up before, or a sentence or two that might be difficult for a reader to follow. The proofreader (usually a freelance, self-employed editor) has a brief to check that the text that was supplied to the typesetter is correctly formatted, appears in the correct location in the book, and that no text or other non-textual material is missing or still needs to be provided as well as ensuring that the text all makes sense. The proofreader is a second set of expert editorial eyes who might pick up an inconsistency the copy-editor let through. Most proofreading will be 'done by eye'; that's to say that the text is read without reference to the manuscript. A close line-by-line comparison read when a proof is checked against the manuscript edits would be very time-consuming for a full-length book but is used when checking shorter texts such as blurbs or indexes. I also like the proofreaders who work on books for me to have the manuscript alongside them so they can refer to it if they think some text looks out of place, or there seems to be a paragraph or even a whole section missing from the proofs, so they are able to resolve such queries as they go along. Proofs, like manuscripts are nearly always provided, read and corrected in PDF files. Some authors might need or want to see paper proofs, perhaps to an enlarged print size; most publishers arrange for these to be prepared and mailed out to the author.

Responsibility for making sure page proofs are professionally checked and marked with any corrections is that of the publisher, overseen by the author's desk editor. Authors are always invited to read their book in proof and to provide any updates to tie in with the scheduled date for the page proofs to go back to the setter (via production) for the corrections to be implemented. Then follows further rounds of proofs as needed. Each time the corrections marked on the previous round are checked to make sure they have been properly implemented and have not caused any inadvertent knock-on effect to another part of the text. When all corrections have been made to the satisfaction of editor and author, a final press-ready or pass-for-press PDF complete with trim marks will be signed off by the editor and forwarded to the printer by the production controller with a confirmation of the print instructions which will already have been agreed: print run, cost, schedule and where stock will be delivered. A final cover PDF and files for any colour plates will accompany the main text to the printer if they are able to offer the complete process, or the cover and plates will be sent to a colour-printing specialist and when printed these will be delivered to the first, text-only printer, where they will be reunited and bound, stuck or sewn together. Hardback books tend to be bound, covered in protective board which gives the books its 'hard' structure, and wrapped in a dust jacket containing all of the information also found on a paperback front and back cover and spine.

EBOOK

Once your manuscript has been perfected it is time to convert it into the various formats it is going to be published in. Ebook conversion will be done in-house or outsourced by the publisher – either way it is not something the author has to worry about unless they are taking the self-publishing route. There are two ebook formats, Mobi for Amazon Kindle and ePub for all other providers including Apple Books and Kobo. If you are self-publishing there are various companies you can pay to convert your manuscript for you or you can learn to manage the conversion process yourself using programmes such as Vellum or Scrivener – there are lots of resources online which talk you through the process. If your ebook contains lots of images or in-text hyperlinks you might want to consider paying an experienced service provider to carry out the process because hyperlinks can be tricky to manage. Only undertake the process yourself if you are confident you can create a professional product – you don't want to damage your book's chances of success because of poor design, layout or readability. After your manuscript has been converted it is up to you to decide whether to publish solely on Amazon – which you can do through their Kindle Create service and for which they offer you benefits including 90-day

THE WHOLE PROCESS – FROM DELIVERY TO SIGN-OFF

As a commissioning editor, I offer all authors as much or as little assistance as they would like during the writing process. Authors are asked to deliver the manuscript in one non-formatted Word document (not separate ones for each chapter), with no embedded illustrations. Most authors are expected to clear permissions for any extracts they include. With some authors I will have seen every chapter a number of times, and fed back during the process, for others the submission date will be the first time I have seen the text.

Once I am happy with the manuscript (this will often involve a round of queries or suggestions back to the author to resolve), it is handed over to my desk editor, usually around two months after submission. She is then responsible for taking the book through to publication, based on a schedule and budget I have outlined and I might suggest an illustrator or reference a particular style of layout I favour, or flag any concerns in terms of permissions needed or particular problems for the copy-editor to unpick.

Before the manuscript is submitted, we brief the cover – this involves filling in a 'Cover Briefing Form' and discussing this with the in-house senior designer, publicity, sales and other colleagues. We work on covers very far in advance to ensure our sales reps have these when they present the books to the trade. Most covers are freelanced out; some are designed in-house. The author is always consulted. Our vision for a cover will always be based on a deep dive into what else is out there, what's coming out, what has worked or what hasn't, and how we want to best represent the tone and pitch of the book to the audience. Our design standards are extremely high.

Most one-colour books print in the UK and have a shorter turn-around time. If the book is four-colour it will print in the

Far East most likely, which involves a longer production schedule (mainly for shipping). We still have schedules of around a year – from submission to publication. It takes a month once stock is in for the warehouse to process the book. If we're publishing simultaneously with the US we might be working on a slightly different schedule and occasionally the US will have a different cover or might Americanise the text.

The ebook publishes on the same day as the print edition. We also take a view on whether a project would benefit from an audiobook if we have the rights; we produce these in-house too. We do sometimes ask the author to narrate but we use professional narrators in the majority of cases.

Charlotte Croft, Publisher at Bloomsbury; her responsibilities include commissioning new titles, list building and managing a team of editors.

I prefer to build a relationship with an author rather than through their agent. I have some lovely agents I work with too, but I dread the call or email from the agent asking for a 'chat' – it usually means the author you were speaking to just before has something they're worried about but couldn't ask you – which can make everything feel combative. Agents are really useful in the financial negotiations and most are brilliant communicators – but ultimately the publisher wants to get the best from the book too. I like authors to let me know when they disagree with me. I'll always explain my reasoning; I want to make sure my authors are happy with everything too.

Commissioning Editor for UK consumer publisher.

inclusion in their Kindle Unlimited service which increases your visibility – or to publish across platforms. You can upload your ePub file directly to publishing platforms or use a service such as Draft2Digital which will manage multi-platform uploads on your behalf. If you self-publish you are in control of pricing – consider pricing low (or giving away for free) to attract readers and then increasing the price once you have gained some traction. It is also important to remember that Amazon offer different royalty percentages dependent on the price you charge for your ebook. If you are being traditionally published your ebook will usually be released at the same time as your print book and may be sold at a slightly lower price to reflect the money saved on printing, storage and distribution.

AUDIO

As with ebooks, audiobook publication will be overseen by the publisher, unless of course you are self-publishing. The author rarely narrates their own audiobook – narration is a professional skill and much more difficult to master than it appears: a narrator has to be able to build suspense, convey emotion, and evoke the tone of the title. Instead a narrator must be found, if you are self-publishing there are services online which match authors and their texts with suitable narrators and facilitate auditions and manuscript reads. It is important to choose a narrator who is right for your title: consider gender, tone, pitch, age, and experience. Services include Audiobook Creation Exchange, Draft2Digital, Troubador and Authors Republic. Using an online service to record your audiobook can be far more cost effective than recording in a studio which can cost hundreds and even thousands of pounds. You also have to decide how you will pay your narrator – either upfront or on a royalty basis. For the latter you might expect to split royalties 50:50. An audiobook requires the same level of editing as your original manuscript (which might need tweaks and changes before it is read aloud) and you will also have to decide whether to include additional sounds or music. Once you are happy with your finished recording and have checked the sound quality as well as the sequencing, pronunciation, and delivery of your title you can upload it to audiobook providers including Amazon, Audible and iTunes. Audiobooks might be published at the same time as a print or ebook, or created and released at a later date if demand is found to be great enough.

Self-publishing

The web is rife with sites and companies that will offer to publish your book, promising that the process will be free and that they can make you rich and famous overnight.

CHOOSING A SELF-PUBLISHING SERVICES PROVIDER

When self-publishing, you can choose to do all the hands-on editing, design and production work described above yourself; you might prefer to commission a series of individual experts for each stage who you will manage and pay as they complete the tasks on a one-by-one basis; or you may opt for the all-in-one package that self-publishing service providers offer. These are also sometimes known as author services companies or author-assisted services. They will provide a complete package of services for a set fee, from manuscript editing through to delivery of finished books, or some of the discrete stages in the overall workflow. In effect, they perform the functions of a traditional publisher, but unlike in mainstream publishing, you pay for the work. The cost is a one-off amount and the provider should not take a cut of any royalties you receive on sales of copies of your book. After the production stages, are distribution and selling (covered in the next chapter) and some end-to-end service providers do offer help with these too. Check the small print and details of any agreement you enter into and be open-eyed when deciding what support you think you need.

Self-publishing companies such as Lulu and BookBaby, Grosvenor House, Authoright, Blurb and IngramSpark provide services including cover design, editing, and print-on-demand publishing. The author is responsible for registering the copyright and ISBN, production management, and marketing. When authors are their own publishers, they also have more control over the final price of the book, which is a major selling point to prospective readers. However, the self-publishing company will usually help the author determine a price for the book by providing a calculator for printing options. This allows the author to see plainly what their portion of the profits will be for each book sold.

Consider the experience, expertise and professionalism of the companies you look at. Compare quotations from different suppliers, take soundings from other self-published authors via their blogs and at conferences, such as the annual Self-Publishing Conference held in Leicester by Troubadour Publishing each Spring. You may not always be comparing like with like when judging the value for money of services, so take your time to make a decision and ask as many questions as you can to allay any concerns you might have. You may have specific requirements based on the type of book you want to self-publish, so make sure you work with individuals or companies that have experience with illustrations and colour reproduction if you want to publish a large format four- or five-colour picture book in print. Reputable companies will always be happy to help and guide you.

For independent advice on self-publishing providers, consult the Alliance of Independent Authors (ALLi) – or even better, sign up as a member so you can receive candid, regular information and be part of a supportive network. They have an advice centre and their Watchdog Desk keeps up to date on which providers are reputable and which should be avoided. Details of their three levels of membership are given in the Professional and membership bodies list in the Resources section on page 265.

The quality of self-publishing services is improving, but it is an unregulated sector. It's easy to set up as a consultant, advisor, editor or broader services provider in this area with very little prior experience or knowledge. There are a huge number of people interested in getting their book in print or ebook. Try to avoid being one of those who falls for a scam. As you'll have noted above, publishing production takes time, involves many people with particular skills and these individuals, if they offer quality service, will not and should not be cheap to hire. Be prepared to pay professional rates for professional-standard work.

You can find what these are on the Society for Editors and Proofreaders (SfEP) site; they publish a free-to-search directory of its members listing their skills and the editorial services they offer. SfEP membership confirms that an editor or proofreader meets a minimum standard. The freelance editors that work regularly with publishers are likely to be accredited to them. You could take their free proofreading test to see how able you are to spot typos in your own manuscript: it might help confirm that having professional support to get your manuscript to a publishable level is a sound investment. Who wants to release a book for sale that has spelling, grammatical or layout errors?

Avoid reputational damage by treating self-publishing with as much business-like professionalism as traditional publishers. It will mean that you incur costs, though if you can become part of a cooperative of creatives, you might be able to trade skills with each other. If you have marketing skills and are a whizz at blurb-writing, you could exchange those with a contact who has strong design skills or another who can pass on social media expertise to support the promotion of your book. You can find an extensive international directory of sole traders who offer help to authors – everything from text and cover design, editing, marketing and publicity to web design – through www.reedsy.com who are passionate about making sure self-publishers make books as good and as beautiful (i.e. as professional) as those established publishers produce. Reedsy's mission is to try and help you assemble the team who will bring your book to fruition, which allows you to take on the management of these tasks to your own requirements and to negotiate payments direct and so bypass the packaged services referred to above.

You don't have to seek help with your self-publishing project – if you think you have the requisite skills then you can literally do-it-all-yourself. Kindle Direct Publishing (KDP) will allow you to upload your manuscript in less than five minutes; it will appear on their bookstore within 24–48 hours. If your book has been through the necessary editorial and design stages first then fine, if not, then you might want to hold fire until it has been through some of the checks and review stages that this chapter has been championing. Full do-it-yourself publishing might be a challenge you relish, but pretty soon you'll work out that keeping all the stages in the publishing process on track, making sensible judgements on what margins, book format, heading style, illustration resolution, jacket layout and much more might just show you how full-time an operation it is creating a quality book. These days there is little to stop you producing a product you can be proud of, finances and time aside, which makes it all the more perplexing that so many self-published books are badly produced. There is an avalanche of information and guidance available for the newbie authorpreneur so spend time reading up on what pitfalls to avoid.

A SELF-PUBLISHER'S TOP TEN CHECKLIST

Have you...?

1. Edited and re-edited your book to its highest standard
2. Sought professional advice where necessary
3. Checked the rights for use of images or text you have included
4. Chosen a format for your book (print and/or digital)
5. Chosen a striking, memorable title, blurb and cover
6. Obtained an ISBN
7. Created a marketing plan for promoting your book
8. Decided where your book will be sold
9. Set up an author webpage
10. Assigned good search keywords

The best way to prepare a well-produced book is to see what is already in the marketplace: what looks good and sells well. On the Kindle store, if you scroll down to 'Product details' and the publisher is listed as 'Amazon Digital Services' or the name of the author is given, that will suggest that the book was self-published. Take a look at a genre you are writing in to see some examples of authors who have taken time and effort to produce a quality product and those who are wide of the mark. You'll also notice, if you are writing for a niche area – which might have a large potential market, but which publishers have traditionally shied away from – how many books there are to satisfy different readers' appetites: gay and lesbian erotic fiction, paranormal romances or low fantasy for example. Self-publishing might be the best or only way to reach these readers.

How much might self-publishing cost? It depends on the format you will publish in, the length of the text, if it includes special formatting or illustrations and if you want print or ebook or audio editions or all three. Reputable provider Matador who (rightly) believes each book is different and thus provide a written quotation in response to each request they receive from an author based on the specific requirements that they provide, gives an example on their site (July 2019 pricing). For a 192-page manuscript supplied in Microsoft Word they will charge around £725 (excluding any VAT) to cover all pre-press tasks (including typesetting, design, ISBN, barcode and cover). But that doesn't include any editorial fees, or costs for printing – which would be an additional £340 for 100 copies. These are reasonable and competitive prices and it is good to have such transparency, but don't be fooled into imagining that quoted costs cover everything you would like them to: check what exactly you will be getting for the fee you agree to and what the payment plans will be: do you pay up-front or some in advance and the rest when the book is complete and ready for publication?

SELF-PUBLISHING YOUR AUDIOBOOK

It is becoming an increasingly competitive field and so authors should shop around to find a good deal and to find the company that is best suited to providing the appropriate product for their work. You should ask yourself similar questions to those listed above when assessing the value and merits of any self-publishing service and not get too enthusiastically swayed by the sales pitch of a supplier. Amazon's Audible Audiobook Creation Exchange (ACX) has allowed self-published authors to enter the field and for a few hundred pounds it's possible to produce a credible product if you are prepared to narrate and edit your own book. You get to keep 40 per cent of the Audible cover price.

Whether a book is traditionally or self-published, once typesetting is completed and final print-ready proofs are signed off, the files are sent to the printer or digital conversion house to create an ebook. The author – and the editor – can sit back and wait for advance copies and stock to reach the publisher's warehouse, which will these days be on the same day. In the past advance copies might have been produced and sent to the editor by the printer for checking and okaying before the full run was printed. This could still happen for small-run printing or print-on-demand, when a single copy can be created, checked, and adjusted if necessary, before having a larger print run produced and distributed. This is a cost-effective way for self-published authors to check that they have prepared a book to a sensible design and format.

CHAPTER 6

Reaching your readers: marketing, publicity and selling

Definitions

This chapter should really have come at the beginning of this guide if their order is any indication of a chapter's importance. It doesn't because this book is arranged to reflect the logical chronology of book publishing: from writing all the way through to distribution and sales. It is this latter part of the process that is the most important – and the most challenging. As noted several times already, publishing is (usually) a commercial enterprise and publishing companies exist to make money for their owners or shareholders, for their authors and for their staff so that they remain in employment. We have seen how tight (or non-existent) margins can be on individual titles (chapter 4) and that the upfront costs of creating a book ready for sale are significant. Reaching readers is the last stage in the process, but they are the reason that the process exists. Finding effective ways to reach purchasers is a key aspiration of any sales team. Having a clear, efficient, timely-to-market distribution strategy and network is vital for any publisher. Making sure this is backed up by promotional and publicity activity is important too. Tying these two strands together into a sales and marketing strategy that supports the publishing programme that editorial directors and commissioning editors have mapped out is crucial for the long-term sustainability of any publishing house.

The marketing activities that publishers use increasingly involve establishing a direct relationship with individual readers and are no longer reliant on third-party intermediaries (bookshops, reviewers, media) to get their message across. Most publishers will have dedicated marketing and publicity teams, which often fall within a wider sales and marketing department – that might also bring together staff who sell rights. If you are lucky, you will have dedicated marketing and PR executives assigned to you and your book.

MARKETING

Successful marketing is the simplest approach for the maximum effect. A marketer's aim is to draw attention to a book through clear messaging in the way that is most cost-effective and successfully translates a reader's interest into a sale. Publishing is peculiar in that it has a huge number of individual product lines (the books), each demanding to be marketed and sold according to its specific needs. You can see that this would be challenging to any business trying to devise and implement a company-wide marketing strategy. A publisher's ambition is to sell as many of each product / title as they can. Historically this has been by transactional marketing via third-party sellers (i.e. a book is 'sold' to a bookshop by the publisher who in turn sells to their customer accompanied by marketing information: what the book is about and who it is for). This approach might work for some titles – where there is a compelling, newsworthy or topical hook with which to promote their qualities through a PR campaign – but as a way of building a loyal customer base that will want to buy other product lines (titles) in the future it is not an efficient form of engagement. Titles can be grouped by subject matter, or genre, or form (poetry, fiction, non-fiction) or by author, age range or publisher, and can be marketed to readers based on such groupings and crucially can be promoted to them via social media which can reach hundreds and thousands of potential customers simultaneously. Publishers can now build up a loyal readership not just for one book and one author but can develop wider relationships with customers beyond an individual sale.

PUBLICITY

In most publishing companies there will be two very distinct departments: one for marketing, the other for PR or publicity. There may not be a huge amount of overlap in terms of the day-to-day promotional opportunities they arrange for authors. Marketing encompasses the paid-for materials that are produced to support a title, such as adverts, promotional posts, printed leaflets. Publicity is promotion for a book that is not paid for by the publisher (in some cases, the publisher might themselves receive payment, for a serialised extract for example). Publicity includes reviews, interviews, features written by the authors and events. An author is more likely to have an assigned publicist than an assigned marketer. For less high-profile titles the marketing executive might offer support *after* the PR and publicity seems to be taking off by producing banners or placing adverts with some particularly good quotes from reviews that have been secured by her publicist colleague.

It's a good idea to find out who will be the main point of contact for the publicity of your book so you can discuss potential leads, opportunities and activities with them. Will you deal with publicity or marketing and sales through your editor or with someone in that department directly? If you are lucky enough to be invited into your publisher to suggest your own ideas and have a one-to-one with a publicist or marketeer (and most authors are not) then use it as an opportunity to highlight all the selling points of your book and to demonstrate how articulate and engaging you are. Displaying a spark, a wit and a willingness to discuss the craft of writing or a topical subject that you tackle in your book, might just persuade the publicist to get you a local radio interview or bookshop reading.

PR (public relations) is about building an author brand and reputation. Publishers may employ in-house PRs or publicists or bring in external contacts to manage campaigns for major authors. These campaigns are about creating a clear message around a book and an author. Good publicists will have an excellent and extensive set of contacts that they will mine to try and get substantial coverage across the media such as newspapers, magazines, blogs and online magazines, radio and TV at national or regional level, as well as events at bookshops, literary festivals or other relevant organisations.

Marketing or promotional materials might be a sales leaflet, catalogue or order form that are part of a sales kit created for the trade (bookshops and wholesalers), or a flyer with an incentivising discount code to be handed out at an academic conference or writing workshop to promote the titles of a professor or novelist speaking there. E-versions of these can be distributed more widely and are cheap to create, as are images that can be added to the footer of a publisher's or author's email. A JPEG file designed by your publisher will look much more dramatic and professional than just incorporating the title of your book into your email signature. It also avoids having to hard-sell your book to your friends, family, business associates and acquaintances: they won't be able to avoid it – every time they receive an email from you it will be staring them in the face! They can be shared on Twitter and Facebook too. Other promotional materials include giveaways such as pens, linen tote bags, mouse mats, notepads and bookmarks. To be worth the outlay, these are best reserved for a series or for publishers or lists which are trying to build a strong brand identity within a market segment. Teachers, academics and medics love to pick up freebies at the conferences they attend and in these sectors company recognition is likely to be high: publishers want to sell to the market but also are keen to invite proposals for new titles. Banners on and off-line, posters for distribution to libraries and bookshops and activity packs for parents and schools to download from publisher and author websites can also be useful ways to place your product.

Promotion can be done by the publisher, by the author – most of it will be up to an author to generate, and by third-party bloggers, endorsers and contacts who are happy to recommend your book to their own lists of contacts or to tweet an endorsement. Authors tend to have a collegiate spirit and will usually be willing to mention a fellow author's work if they are similarly supported.

Marketing and PR campaigns

A marketing strategy or campaign for your book will be developed based on what's considered appropriate for the title. Your views on this might diverge considerably from those of your publisher. Every author wants to have as much marketing attention as they can get, but the harsh reality is that most books may only get a standard treatment. Publishers will consider if a fiction or non-fiction title will be one of its lead titles in a season, one that they will get behind with all their marketing clout, attention and funding and more modest, mid-list titles will inevitably receive less attention. When considering what support your book should get, the marketing department will factor in the following:

- Author profile, track record and brand.
- Access to target market, existing contacts and channels.
- Key selling points of the book: is it original, topical, sensational, newsworthy, or of human interest?
- Timing – the time of year when your book is being published and if it can be linked to an anniversary or seasonal event.
- How many copies of your book the publisher has budgeted to sell. The more an author has been paid, the more copies the publisher needs to sell to make that book profitable and therefore the more likely you are to get a substantial PR and marketing campaign.

Contemplating what aspects of a book or an author's biography or lifestyle might appeal to specific communities of consumers and finding where these potential customers might be actively engaging with one another and with book-related material is a necessary part of a marketing executive's research. Knowing what makes readers buy books is helpful. Publishers are not famed for spending on quantitative market research, though it can be an effective way to find out where best to deploy resources. In her 2017 survey of the readers on her own mailing list (12,000 at the time), indie author and professional researcher Maggie Lynch found that the top ten reasons for purchasing a book were as follows (the percentages are for respondents who agreed that the reasons were either 'very important' or 'extremely' important):

1. Author is well known to me (68%)

2. Book cover (53%)

3. Book recommended by a friend (38%)

4. Book description (36%)

5. Book is part of a series with more than one book in the series available (35%) with only one book available in the series (29%)

6. A Preview or the Look Inside feature (29%)

7. Price (21%)

8. Reviews (20%)

9. Social media recommendations through Facebook, Twitter, Instagram or Pinterest (17%)

10. Online advertising prompt (14%)

The full survey findings, analysis and results from other similar surveys can be found on the ALLi site: https://selfpublishingadvice.org/opinion-what-makes-readers-buy-books/ © Maggie Lynch 2018.

Such results suggest that promoting a new author, unless they have an existing online fanbase, is a difficult proposition, but they also highlight how important it is to get the *publishing* of a book right. The book's cover, its selling copy or blurb and its content all rank high. This implies that quality is what readers want. Getting them to find it is the marketer's task. When preparing another title in this *Writers' & Artists' Guide to* series on self-publishing we invited the 35,000 subscribers to our site to take a short survey to tell us what advice they needed to self-publish successfully, what other resources they already had available to them on the subject, and how they would like to access more information. Their responses have helped shape the book my colleague Eden subsequently commissioned. It proved to us that there was an existing market for the title, has provided a customer base we can promote the book to, both of which helped to attract the self-publishing service providers we invited to pay for advertising space (which will underwrite some of the book's production costs).

How to reach readers effectively

You know your book better than anyone else. Publishers need your help in telling them (and your readers) what it is about and in sharing your passion for it. You don't need to be an outgoing, loquacious type with a strong online presence, but undoubtedly this would help and makes marketing your book easier.

If you are published by a publishing house (rather than opting for the self-publishing route), you will have had contact with someone in your publisher's PR department. You would usually have completed an Author Publicity Form or Author Questionnaire several months prior to publication – where you will have been asked to share any contacts you have in the market that could be useful for helping to promote or enhance the profile of you or your book. These might be contacts you have in local media or specialist organisations: this is particularly beneficial for non-fiction books. If you know of websites, bloggers, or influencers that appeal to groups that might be interested in your book or if you already have an online following via a website, Instagram, Facebook or Twitter account, the publisher's publicity team would like to know. They will help you develop your online profile further and garner more followers. Overt hard sell via your personal site or feeds is generally a no-no (in contrast to what a publisher might offer via their own, commercial digital shop window), but you can offer your followers details about yourself, your interests, and the writing process; anything that is relevant and helps build an interest in what you have created. Creating a buzz around your book, thinking about what might benefit your reader if they get hold of a copy (again, relevant mainly for practical non-fiction), offering incentives to purchase: discounted copies, free e-samples (for example part of a chapter of your novel to whet a reader's literary appetite), or donating copies via competitions can all be worthwhile and cheap publicity options.

The information supplied in the **Author Questionnaire** is very useful for publishers when deciding what will be the best approach to launch a title. Authors should conjure up all the contacts that they have; it is a useful exercise as authors will be expected to do self-publicity and not just rely on what their publisher initiates. If you are a self-published author then you will need to put together a publicity plan of sorts, so the discipline of gathering details such as those listed in the questionnaire will help you do that. If you decide to employ a freelance marketer to support you in reaching your readers, then it will be a useful tool for them too.

The questionnaire will typically ask you for the following:

Personal details: how you would like to be contacted, where you live, and who your agent or other representative is. You may be asked for your date of birth, which is needed to register copyright (covered in chapter 4) and also if your book is likely to be submitted for any prizes.

Newsworthy features: what distinguishes your book from competitor titles on the market. This can draw on the USPs you articulated way back when you started to send your manuscript out to agents. It may seem odd to be providing a publisher with information they should already know, but this form might be the first contact you have with the publisher's publicity department. If your book involved extensive research, travel or resulted from a particular obsession: let them know. Even if it appears incidental to you it might engender some interesting publicity.

Previous publishing record: the other books or articles you have had published or media appearances you have made in the past. Do you have any contacts resulting from these that might be useful to follow up for your new book?

Potential reviewers: do you have contacts in your professional field or in any organisations you are affiliated to who would be interested in receiving an advance copy of your book (or a set of uncorrected proofs) with a view to reviewing it, mentioning it, sharing it, or linking to it from their blog? Do you have contacts in the media or with book bloggers in the UK and overseas that you are happy to share?

Marketing: who do you see as the main market for your book – who might it appeal to and why? List any professional, religious or age groups or regional associations. For fiction, it is unlikely you would be asked this.

Sales: if you have written non-fiction you might be asked if there are any groups or associations interested in buying a quantity of copies, for example to be included as a textbook for a course or a giveaway at a conference, business event or festival.

The **social media** that you use and are regularly active on and the number of subscribers or followers you have, will be very useful. Provide the URLs for your website, author Facebook and Twitter pages.

HOW AN AUTHOR CONTRIBUTES TO THE MARKETING PROCESS

Our editorial team prepare an AI (Advanced Information) form on Biblio – which is our in-house publishing tracking system – early on in the publishing process. Parts of this feed out automatically to Amazon and to our own website. This includes reviews, author biography, keynotes and other information about the book including crucial metadata and keywords to help optimise searches.

We liaise with marketing and publicity colleagues throughout, from pre-contract all the way through to post-publication of each title. Marketing and publicity will flag if they would like bound proofs to be produced (this often impacts on schedules for us as they will need the text in good shape earlier than we would usually have it ready) and we will work with them to make sure text is ready on time.

My marketing and publicity colleagues will often want to meet with the author or agent to discuss plans and will send out an author questionnaire asking for contacts and ideas that can feed into their marketing plan.

Our US marketing team will be in contact with the author separately; US editions tend to publish two–three months after the UK one. Our UK-based authors don't usually travel to the US, so most interviews will be by telephone or social media.

Depending on the rights available our rights team will be working alongside us to sell co-edition, licensing or serial rights. We sometimes produce blads (a sample booklet with content from the book – it stands for Basic Layout And Design) for our four-colour titles to show to foreign publishers in advance of publication at London or Frankfurt foreign rights fairs. These are either printed spreads or shown on an iPad. Sample spreads are also useful when selling serial rights to newspapers and magazines.

I think the key for us is not to see the book as the first rung on a promotional ladder – it should be the cherry on the cake, or at least the filling. We will be looking for an author who probably already has a public profile in their field. We check social media profiles, writing experience and previous publicising of their brand to see how we can build on those.

Charlotte Croft is a Publisher at Bloomsbury.

There is sadly sometimes a mismatch between an author's expectation and the actual, realistic opportunities for publicity – which we work hard to manage to avoid disappointments. But it's worth saying that if the author doesn't have a profile already our marketing and publicity teams will struggle to get them interviews with the media. Two other elements that also need sensitive handling are anticipated sales numbers (sometimes the reality is markedly different to the author's notion of what 'good' sales are), and the lack of a launch party. For my list we will only have one or two launches a year, if we think there's a good publicity reason. Authors sometimes organise their own celebrations, and we might be able to contribute, but I think a common publishing misconception that still hasn't gone away is that there's a launch party for every book.

Commissioning editor at publisher of consumer books

PROMOTIONAL TOOLS

> *Be social-media savvy. The publisher will support you as far as*
> *publication and then you are on your own, unless you are a lead*
> *title or a famous face. The stronger you are on Twitter/Instagram*
> *(the two best platforms for writers), the more likely you*
> *are to stay afloat and visible.*
>
> Lucy Courtenay, author of books series for children
> and romantic teen comedies

The promotional tools available to a publisher (and author) are extensive. Getting your title to stand out in a hugely crowded market is a challenge. In this section are some of the ways that might be effective for your book. It's advisable to be selective and concentrate initially, in agreement with your publisher – see your publicist as an ally, on a few activities and to do these well rather than adopt too scattergun an approach. Be creative, try new ideas, be positive and proactive.

- A **press release** is a promotional document sent to media outlets – print and online – to announce that a book is about to be published. Its task is to generate interest. It should have a purpose and a clear hook and it should be no more than one side of A4. What in the press release might invite a magazine or books editor to ask for a radio or print interview or a review copy?

- **Review copies** are sent to book bloggers and literary editors in advance of publication with the hope that it will lead to a mention or full-blown review. A four-star review in a magazine or paper with a wide circulation is a great way to feed a promotional campaign. Endorsements from other readers via Amazon or Goodreads are useful when trying to 'sell' an idea for a feature or an author for a literary event after publication. A positive response in one area is likely to stimulate interest elsewhere. Sometimes bound, uncorrected proofs of a title might be sent out to other authors from whom a publisher is seeking an endorsement that might adorn the front cover of the book. They will also be sent to magazines that have a long lead-time (over two months) who would therefore be less likely to cover the book after its publication.

- **Print advertising** is rare for books. Stellar, lead titles from well-known, prize-winning authors with a strong track record or a paperback film tie-in might get a mention on a bus shelter or station hoarding, but as a debut author you might warrant a targeted Facebook or Twitter ad if you are lucky. The book pages of national papers and glossy magazines do carry ads, but a review or comment piece, serialisation or feature packs a greater punch and is free.

- **Competitions** run by publishers or by authors themselves can generate good will and reader engagement. Winning a mentoring session or a copy of each of the author's backlist titles show that an author has a willingness to share their experiences and the fruits of their success.

- **Newsletter mailings** can be an inexpensive and targeted way to reach customers. Newsletters should engage and offer a benefit not just sell. They are likely to highlight several frontlist titles and be a regular feature of the marketing team's activities. They might include an extract from a soon-to-be-published title, an interview with an author, a link to an author blog on the publisher's website, an offer of free books or details of a competition in which to win tickets to a literary event.

- **Events** to promote a new author may be difficult to arrange before publication, unless it is one local to where the author lives. Should the book garner praise, possibly a longlisting for a prize, then bookshop readings and signings, interviews and invitations to speak at literary festivals may follow. If you are a children's author you could arrange to visit schools either direct or more likely through an author speaking agency who will manage the fee and format of the talk, reading or workshop.

WHAT DOES A PUBLICIST DO?

The role of a publicist will vary from publisher to publisher and from campaign to campaign, but essentially the job of a PR is to secure coverage of your book, with the aim of engaging readers and securing sales. It's not paid-for advertising or promotion, it's persuading journalists, writers, bloggers, producers, events organisers to review, feature, interview, host an event with your author.

Normally starting a few months ahead of the publication date, the PR will read the book, chat to the author and have a clear idea of what makes this book original and interesting (the USP). What are the most newsworthy points? Are you uniquely qualified as an author on this particular subject? Is it a debut novel which has sold in twenty-five territories and had film rights optioned? The answer to these questions should appear on the press release.

A publicist also needs to identify the target audience for the book. This is crucial in order to create a relevant targeted campaign, which results in book sales.

Once those things are done a press release will be written and a hit list of media contacts drawn up. This next bit might be when it seems to the author that it's all going a bit quiet, but it's the period when all the pitching is being done. Your publicist will be sending targeting pitches (probably via email) to all those they would like to cover the book in some way. This is when it is so important you've had a meeting about the book, and you have shared any interesting angles and stories that they might then be able to pitch for you. You publicist will be offering you up for interview; sending ideas for pieces that you could write that relate to the book; persuading literary editors and reviewers to review the book on publication; maybe setting up events or a book tour. Gradually these things fall into place, things are negotiated (will paper X follow paper Y, with the story you're pitching) and a schedule is drawn up.

When I'm organising a PR campaign I'm very aware of how important timing can be. If we're aiming for a book to hit the *Sunday Times* bestseller lists for example, having media and key events running in the week of publication is so important. The surge of interest and awareness generated should result in book sales which, coupled with pre-orders being released, will immediately contribute to that all important 'first week of sales'.

A good publicist will be creative, strategic, assiduous and have fantastic contacts within, and knowledge of, the media. They will communicate brilliantly with you and the rest of the publishing team so that everyone is working to the same goal and all opportunities are maximised.

Emma Finnigan has been promoting books for twenty years, at the Orion Publishing Group, Penguin Random House and for the last three years as Director of Emma Finnigan PR.

- **Serialisation** is when an extract or a series of extracts from your book are licensed for a fee to a newspaper or magazine. Are there aspects of your book and how it came to be written – a great hardship or illness that you overcame, perhaps – that would be worthy of a feature in a special-interest magazine or society newsletter? This would normally be arranged by your publicist or someone in the publisher's rights team.

The experience of Kirsten Cozens, a press officer at Walker Books who won the Publishers' Publicity Circle Children's Book award for her campaign for *Julian is a Mermaid* (2018), is a good example of successful publicity developing from small beginnings. She had no budget assigned for the title, but persuaded her manager to provide £150 which she used to create an eye-catching mailing and promotional bookmarks. Because the book features a transgender protagonist, she sent review copies to LGBT influencers and secured a quotation from RuPaul for the paperback back cover – which Kirsten credits as generating the initial wave of attention. This led to wider media interest, the book's inclusion on the Waterstones Children's Book Prize shortlist and Klaus Flugge longlist. Waterstones Piccadilly hosted a reading by the author (Jessica Love) which was attended by drag artist Alyssa Van Delle, and Love hosted a storytelling and headband-making workshop at Tate Modern. It suggests that a big name publisher (Walker Books) does not always guarantee a large marketing budget, but implies that if you are creative you don't need one. *Julian is a Mermaid* went on to win the Waterstones Children's Book Prize (2019) and 2019 Stonewall Book Award.

MAKING THE MOST OF SOCIAL MEDIA

Before you start

Think about which platforms are most suitable for you and your book. Think about where your audience is, where you feel most comfortable, and go there. Use free tools like Hootsuite (www. hootsuite.com) and Tweetdeck (www.tweetdeck.com) to post outside of working hours. An active author can make a big difference to the number of users reached and titles sold. Ross Morrison McGill (author of *Teacher Toolkit*) tweeted regularly to his 10k followers and turned his book into a bestseller.

Plan your campaign, as you would any other element of your marketing. Social media, like publicity and PR, can be used to respond to customer enquiries and build an immediate rapport. Feedback is quick and within days you can see what is working and what is not.

General rules

Being active on social media could fill your whole day. It's better to do fewer things well, with more followers and higher engagement on fewer platforms, than low numbers across many. You may find that one platform outperforms all others, in which case, focus all your energies there.

Avoid the hard-sell. Social media is a place where people exchange views and opinions. They like to see products and may follow brands, but you are influencing their decision making, entertaining them, not selling directly. It's fine to post '25% off all books today!', but most of your output should be more general. Think about what people who like your books are interested in. Military-history publisher Osprey's top tweet was a photo of a tank and the words 'Happy Monday morning!'. Insights, funny clips, beautiful images, interesting facts or nuggets – this is what individuals respond to.

Remember that platforms are global, so be sensitive to other countries' climate, time zones and pricing. For example, state if a sale ends at 12 midnight GMT.

Where is your audience?*

For books, it's likely to be on one of the big four:

- **Facebook** is still the largest platform, with 2.27bn monthly active users. The largest age group (24 per cent) is 25–34. You can find anyone and everyone, so if you do take out targeted adverts, then you should be able to match these with your desired audience.

- **Instagram** is the fastest-growing platform, with 1bn users, with ages 13–17 the biggest group.

- **Twitter** now has 126m daily users, of which the largest group is 18–29 year olds (40 per cent). It's often used for customer service, as response times are so quick.

- **LinkedIn** is the predominant business network, for professional and older users, with 590m currently.

Pinterest and **Snapchat** are less likely to appeal to book lovers, but Pinterest may be worth a look if you publish interior design books, for example.

* Source for statistics: Pew Research Center 2019

YouTube is now bigger than Facebook and beloved of the younger generations. If you do have the wherewithal to produce videos and upload them to a channel, then do so.

What and how often to post?
Post regularly and as often as you can. Once a day on most platforms is the minimum. Post about interesting topics, not purely about your book, your author or your story. Use an engaging voice, don't force yourself to be funny if you're not a natural comic. Posts with images have better engagement that those without. If you are on Instagram, it's worth buying or using some simple props or backgrounds to create good images. Remember to size images correctly and follow the platform's uploading rules.

Engage your followers and treat them as equals. Try and involve them as much as possible through interaction, so that exchanges are a dialogue, not a monologue. Run polls and quizzes. Ask them which jacket design, book title or subtitle they prefer or even which book they'd like you to publish first.

If you run offers, samples and sales, be careful with your audience's data to avoid falling foul of GDPR (www.gdpr.org).

Amplifying your presence
Make sure you have prominent links to your social media account on your website and blog, on your email footers and signature, as well as promotional newsletters and emails. Put your social account details on printed materials and collateral – posters, business cards, banners, catalogues and leaflets. On social media, you get out what you put in. Make alliances, reference other people when appropriate, use hashtags when relevant. Don't jump on a hashtag bandwagon – it looks obvious and fake. Do follow influencers and people in the industry, and hopefully they will follow you too. Having a few high-profile followers who can repost your comments is very worthwhile.

Make sure your **branding** (logos, colours, typeface) is consistent across all platforms. Use Canva – www.canva.com to get started or pay a designer to create a suite of reusable templates.

Results and effectiveness
How do you know your social-media marketing is working?

- Your followers will grow

- Your engagements will increase

- You will be reposted and quoted by others

- You may be able to see sales spikes on Amazon or your own website

- If advertising, you can track conversion rates and see how much each interaction (and hopefully sales conversion) costs

- People will contact you because they found you on social media

Social media has a slow build, but it's worth it over time. It's an easy, fun and immediate way to communicate with your audience.

Petra Green is a freelance marketing and publishing consultant. She was previously Marketing Director – Data, Digital & Systems at Bloomsbury where she worked on brands such as Harry Potter and *Who's Who*.

HOW DO YOU KNOW WHAT WORKS?

How does a publisher know where to target their time and resources? How do they know what tools and activities are going to be most profitable? Using online **tracking tools** and **data analytics**, such as Google and Twitter analytics, allow you to see how effective a marketing approach or a particular software tool has been and thus build an evidence-based plan around future marketing for a title or for a list. However, what works for one title and author may not be replicable for another. A publicist will always keep an eye on the Amazon rankings when a key piece of media or interview runs – often you'll see the book jump straight up, thereby illustrating the tangible impact of PR on sales. Each book does have to be recognised on its own merits but knowing what can work and what is a waste of time is useful when persuading colleagues, agents and authors where energies could be most effectively directed.

The basic principles of monitoring a marketing and PR campaign are to track sales data and spikes (as well as social media mentions and engagement) and attempt to isolate the marketing activity which caused the spike. Maintaining a spreadsheet or database detailing timings and the cost of marketing and promotional activities is useful; and something authors can do too. Monitoring the impact of online and social media marketing is easier because there are so many tools which can be used to track engagement with these activities and track where website or retail visitors come from. Once it is known which activities generate the most sales and the highest return on investment (ROI), marketing spend can be reallocated or increased.

OptinMonster breaks down the elements of an email marketing campaign that should be monitored, including open, click-through, unsubscribe, complaint, conversion, growth, bounce and forward rates as well as ROI. They also offer solutions to problems such as cart abandonment. Mailchimp collects data on your newsletter subscribers, monitors their engagement, and segments them accordingly. It will calculate the optimum time to send emails, the appropriate tone to use and the frequency at which you should send emails for each segment and demographic. There are similar automated services which monitor traffic, user activity, user type and user origin including Kissmetrics, Mixpanel and Marketo.

There is clear evidence that **endorsements** from well-known brands or high-profile individuals can significantly improve sales of a book. Gloria Steinem's *My Life on the Road* (2015) jumped over a 100 per cent in volume sales after it was selected as the first title for actress Emma Watson's book club, Our Shared Shelf. Almost a third of the book's sales came after the book club announcement spurred the publisher Oneworld into fast-tracking two reprints totalling 6,000 copies.

The first batch of books featured on YouTuber Zoella's book club (June 2016) with WH Smith flew up Amazon's bestseller chart with one title, Amy Alward's *The Potion Diaries* (Simon & Schuster, 2015), moving from a ranking of 35,595 to 316 and seeing a 11,164 per cent increase in sales in just twenty-four hours. Six of the other books included also experienced sales spikes in their thousands. After Bill Gates named John Brooks' *Business Adventures* as one of the greatest books he had ever read, the out-of-print 1969 title was bought by Open Road Media and went on to sell 77,000 print copies and 126,000 ebooks.

In 2015, the *Harvard Business Review* conducted a study of the sales impact of a *New York Times* review on nearly 250 books published between 2001 and 2003. They found that a positive book **review** could increase sales by between 32 and 52 per cent; and a negative review would decrease sales for an established author by up to 15 per cent but increase sales for an unknown author by an average of 45 per cent.

After being shortlisted for the Man Booker Prize in 2018, sales of Anna Burns' *Milkman* increased by 1,103 per cent. After winning the award, publisher Faber & Faber scheduled another 100,000 copies to be printed.

The power of metadata

For customers to buy your book they need to be able to find it. Online, that means making it easily discoverable and able to stand out amongst the millions of other books in the market. The key to discoverability is metadata. This 'data about data' or information that describes your book is indexed by search engines such as Google, Bing and Yahoo! and, importantly for bookselling, by online retailers. The metadata that's needed and which feeds online book records includes the title, subtitle, author, and ISBN. Key words and phrases included in the book's blurb or description will also be searchable and the classifications (subject categories) assigned to the book will dictate where it will be categorised in online store subject taxonomies. There isn't space here to detail the wonders of search engine optimisation and how to improve a title's ranking, but spending time selecting meaningful keywords for your book is time well spent. Whether you are a self-published author or if your publisher is managing your print and ebook creation, it's not enough simply for the text file and cover of a book to be uploaded to Amazon or other book retail sites and to assume that readers will find and buy it.

TITLES, CATEGORIES AND KEYWORDS: EXPLOITING YOUR AMAZON METADATA

Sorting out your metadata isn't hard. It isn't especially technical. So scoot over to your KDP dashboard, then add your data following the rules below.

Categories

The bigger the bookshelf, the greater its need for categorisation, so it's no surprise that Amazon has the most finely grained set of book categories ever developed. So there is, for example, a category not just for Romance, but for Romance > Historical Romance > Regency. These can be further refined by theme (Amnesia, Beaches, Gambling) or hero (Cowboys, Doctors, Firefighters), and so on. The same is true in non-fiction. A large bricks-and-mortar bookstore might have a single set of shelves for Cookery, Amazon will add a bewildering variety of sub-categories on top, for example, Cooking > Health + Healing > Allergy, or Cooking > Beverages > Bartending.

Your task in choosing categories for your work is simple. You get to pick a maximum of two categories – bookshelves, in effect – and you want to pick the two categories where you think your readers are most likely to congregate. If you write Regency Romance, that's your category. Don't be tempted sideways. You might think, 'Ooh, but there are lots of people who browse the Romantic Comedy shelves, so maybe I should put my book there too'. If your book truly is a rom-com, then fine. If it isn't, don't be tempted.

Keywords
Think of keywords as additional ways to label your book for likely users. You get to pick seven keywords in total and the best way to choose them is to navigate to your core categories (let's say Romance > Historical Romance > Regency), then start picking out themes and heroes that work for your book. In other words, you are using keywords almost as a way to sub-categorise your categories even further. If you have keywords to spare, try to think how a browser might search for a book like yours. If you think someone might search 'Regency Romance Duke', then you could add the word 'duke' as a keyword.

Don't overthink all this. Your categories really matter a lot, and picking up obvious additional sub-divisions is helpful. Anything else you may do probably won't add all that much to your sales. Adding search terms such as 'gripping thriller' won't do you any good at all, because the competition around such terms is so intense, you'd have to have a skyscraper-high position on the bestseller lists to benefit.

Title structure
Choose the best title for your book.

Amazon provides you with the option of having a subtitle and a series title too. So book #1 in Angela Marsons's bestselling *Kim Stone* series has, as its full title: *Silent Scream: An edge of your seat serial killer thriller (Detective Kim Stone Crime Thriller Series Book 1)*. The first two words, *Silent Scream*, form the title. The bit about the edge of your seat serial killer thriller is the subtitle. The bit in brackets – *Detective Kim Stone Crime Thriller Series* – is the series title.

Adding a subtitle is generally a good idea: it's an extra way to advertise to readers and incentivise that clickthrough from a search page to your own book page. If you can naturally load that subtitle with search-friendly keywords (e.g. 'serial killer thriller') then do. But don't do anything that feels forced; you want something that is fluid and inviting.

If you are writing a series, the series title should simply capture the way your readers think about your books. In the Angela Marsons example, that is likely to be the central character, so that's what defines the name of the series.

All that sounds easy, and it is. Remember that your title and subtitle have to appear on your cover, so while it's fine to dream up any subtitle you like, you do need to make sure it's included in your cover design too.

Book description

This is the blurb for your book as it appears on your Amazon book page. There are two primary models to follow. The first is the one adopted by Amazon Publishing itself. You can see the basic model by looking at the likes of *The Magpies, Never Stop Walking*, or *The Rule of One*. You'll see that the book description has a line or two of bold text followed by a fairly short blurb. The blurb often sets up a mini-storyline in itself with a hook to get you reading, a setup, a twist, then a what-if or what-then question to lure purchase. In these blurbs, the total text often runs to as little as 120-150 words, so clarity and brevity are your watchwords.

An alternative model has been evolved by firms such as Bookouture, the force behind Angela Marsons's *Kim Stone* books. If you look at the full descriptions for those books on Amazon (making sure you're looking at the Kindle version, not the paperback), you'll see a whole 650-word extravaganza, with a ton of reviews and comments, as well as invitations to explore the whole series.

I like both of these basic models, primarily because I know that both Amazon and Bookouture test relentlessly and effectively to see what approach actually delivers sales. I prefer the Bookouture approach myself, but I certainly wouldn't quarrel with anyone taking the Amazonian route – and either way, a terrific blurb matters a lot. Amazon (characteristically) makes it needlessly hard for you to add the formatting elements of your blurb (things like bold and italics.) Your best bet is to Google 'Book Description Generator' or 'Book Description Tool' and you'll find free online ways to format your book description as you want it, then generate the HTML code to give to Amazon.

This is a very compressed tour, so think of it as a first guide to these topics, not a final one. Have fun. Publish well. And sell some books.

Harry Bingham is author of the *Fiona Griffiths* crime series and the Chairman of Jericho Writers, a membership club for writers.

Distribution and sales

The market gets to know about new books through the pre-publication information and activities that are described above. There are three main selling channels that publishers use to get books into the market. The main distribution routes are:

- **Business-to-business**: a publisher sells to bookshops – physical and online varieties – direct via the publishers' sales representatives (reps). Sales terms, including discount rates and returns policy are usually negotiated at a company level rather than at list or title level (other than for very high-selling titles) between the publisher's sales director and the bookshop manager (for independent bookshops) or with a head office manager (for the chains or online stores). The bookshops will know several months in advance of publication which titles are coming and when so they can plan their stock and any publicity activities that might be arranged to coincide. This sell-in timetable is based on a well-established calendar which can seem rather generous to authors, especially those used to businesses that move at a faster pace. Smaller publishers may not have their own selling team or reps and will pay (usually a percentage on deals made) another larger publisher or freelance rep to sell their titles for them. Overseas sales to markets where a publisher has no physical presence, contacts or expertise will invariably be handled by a sales agent in those territories or by an independent UK-based sales manager who travels overseas to represent numerous publishers in a market whose cultural and business differences she is well versed in navigating.

- **Wholesaler distribution**: the publisher uses a third-party 'middle-man' to sell to retailers on their behalf. They will buy in bulk and get a cut from any sale. The two main book wholesalers in the UK are Bertrams and Gardners. Easons and Argosy operate in the Republic of Ireland. Some retailers will buy only via wholesalers.

- **Direct-to-consumer**: This is the most profitable channel for the publisher. It is not necessarily where they will make most sales, but per copy income is greater because they don't share profits (i.e. do not have to offer discounts) to third-party bookshops or wholesalers. It means that the publisher can pass on an attractive discount to their individual consumers via their website, at the same time building up a list of customers who they can market other titles to. Instead of allowing the likes of Amazon to amass this valuable data about their readers, publishers can do it themselves. Armed with this information (making sure they have permission to do so by asking customers to tick the requisite box agreeing that they can be sent online promotions, electronic newsletters or special offers), the publisher can engage directly with their purchasers. They can ask them what their book interests are, share sample chapters to create pre-publication excitement and have control over the message they wish to share about their titles and brand.

In addition, there may be one-off sales deals, often referred to as **'special' sales** via book clubs and institutional or business-to-business sales subject to one-off negotiation when copies will be ordered in bulk. For example, if you have written a book that you think would be perfect as an unofficial textbook for a course and you are in contact with the course tutor, there might be a deal to be struck for a copy to be provided to each student and paid for from their course fee. A business might be interested in having their logo stamped on a book cover related to their commercial activities in some way and which can be used as a calling card when approaching new clients. If the quantity and revenue warrant the printing of a separate cover (possible these days with competitively priced short-run printing) then it's something your publisher might contemplate. The main blocker for such deals is usually time and if the publisher has a lack of staff to oversee them.

Book clubs are a way to reach an audience who might not go to bookshops often or conversely to create an opportunity for a passionate book-buyer to receive titles and special deals direct to their door or inbox. Franchise-style clubs include those run by children's publishers Scholastic, Red Fox or Usborne and depend on individuals who sign up with them to be 'seller' to target titles direct to readers (children) and purchasers (their parents or teachers) in return for a percentage of the book's cover price. They might do this through schools, playgroups, stalls at local fairs, word-of-mouth and catalogues. Book club selling can be good news for publishers as well as parents: all club books are discounted and have free delivery. Scholastic donate 25 pence for every £1 spent to schools who collect orders on their behalf, that's likely to be a better profit on these titles than selling through a retailer – particularly since they will be selling large quantities.

The Book People is a well-established club that sells titles at very high discount direct to individuals via their workplace through a series of local reps. Publishers will choose to supply them if they are guaranteed a large print quantity on fixed sale (no returns) if this helps the economics of their printing. As the example in chapter 4 showed, the more copies of a book you print in a run the lower the price per copy is to produce. You might be thinking that selling through the likes of the Book People will cannibalise the publisher's sales through its retail channels; but these are perceived to be additional to their core customer base.

Faber & Faber and Penguin Random House, among other publishers, also offer free sign-ups to their **reader clubs**: it's a way to build up an email list and community that they can target with future books (usually with a 'special' club discount), services and event information.

Mail-order subscription clubs still exist for books but are not as common as they once were. When I started in publishing nearly thirty years ago, a large order of several thousand copies for the Folio Society, BCA (Book Club Associates) or TSP (The Softback Preview book club) would be a familiar sight on a print order. Such clubs have been replaced by online retailers who can deliver any title of your choice quickly and at discounted rates. The Folio Society does still exist to provide limited edition, beautifully bound and illustrated gift versions of classic and contemporary titles.

Audiobooks and **ebooks** can be sold and downloaded direct from a publisher's website and an author's site (if they offer e-commerce) or via a link to the main e-tailers, such as Amazon, Kobo and Apple Books. Other alternatives to the big players, for those who want a more curated experience, are Wordery.com, Hive.co.uk – a national network of independent bookshops, and the online offerings from Waterstones and WH Smith. Subscriber services, such as Amazon's Kindle Unlimited, allow users to download as many titles as they like onto multiple devices for a monthly fee. A criticism of Kindle Unlimited is the small range of titles and the paucity of popular titles and bestsellers. That said, it's a good place to see which self-published books are in the market if you want to compare your own offering in terms of price, cover design and marketability.

RETAILERS

Bookshops There has been a dramatic erosion in the number of bricks-and-mortar bookshops on the British high street over the years. Over the same period that the chains have consolidated (the same company – Elliot Advisors – that owns the UK's largest bookshop chain

Waterstones also have Hatchards and Foyles within their stable), there has been a surprising number of new independent bookshops opened by passionate and optimistic individuals each year; though an equal number go to the wall year-on-year too. According to the Booksellers Association the number of independent bookshops rose for the second year in a row – from 868 in 2017 to 883 in 2018. To keep in business, bookshops, particularly the smaller, indie stores which don't have the clout to negotiate favourable discounts with publishers or the shelf space to offer the same choice of titles as the chains, will offer book-buyers experiences beyond that of simply purchasing a book. They entice browsers in with displays, competitions, author events and readings (which might carry a small entrance fee), beanbags and comfortable seating to allow reading before you buy, not to mention coffee. As well as diversifying in what they offer book-lovers – experiences and services as well as products – bookshops can provide personalised recommendations for their shoppers and for publishers they provide an actual shop window where they can show off their latest releases. Bookshops remain an important part of the publishing operation as well as contributing to the cultural enrichment of the towns and communities in which they are located. Bookshops will sell a wide range of book-related products, stationery and other merchandise which are more profitable than books and not subject to sale or return. Physical shops can't offer the same breadth of choice as an online store, but they can be places of excellence, expertise and specialisms. There are several bookshops that sell children's books only (everything from baby board books through to YA dystopian series). Stanford's in London specialises in maps and travel titles; Books for Cooks in Notting Hill is crammed with recipe books and gives demonstrations, runs cookery classes and produces its own cookbooks too. The Atlantis Bookshop in London's Bloomsbury sells books on magic and the occult; Book-ish in the Brecon Beacons combines bookselling with cards, toys and gifts and Belfast is host to crime-specialist No Alibis.

Other physical outlets, supermarkets, discount stores (such as The Works), garden centres and other specialist 'destination' stores sell books that might appeal to their clientele. Shops within the museum and culture sector are targeted by reps where a book has a particular link to an area through the book's subject matter or where an author lives. There may be opportunities to sell stock through other non-conventional book outlets too. For example a book on the exploits of the Royal Navy might be sold into military and history museums and historical sites, to bookshops in naval towns such as those in the south west and sold direct to veteran clubs or through magazines and newsletters for members of military associations, re-enactment groups etc.

Self-published authors will find it tough to get their books into bookshops without the backup of a publisher's marketing and sales teams, but it's not impossible to make inroads if you put a good proposition together to a local store. Think about what you are offering – why would they want to stock your book, is there a local-interest or topical angle? You should make sure you have a well edited and produced book and that all your dealings with the shop's manager are professional; you'll need an invoicing system. The bookshop would need to receive an email (don't arrive unannounced and assume you will be able to speak to staff) with similar information to that which the publisher would provide several months prior to publication. This would be an Advance Information sheet or catalogue copy which would include a thumbnail of your cover, a brief description, key selling points and the basic specifications such as format, price, ISBN, title, subtitle and author details. It would be useful to include a link to your website if you have one, but never include one to Amazon: that's a sure-fire guarantee that a bookseller will *not* stock your book. Booksellers are fighting hard to keep afloat; the disparity in business rates (at time of going to press) for physical shops and e-tailers has long been a bone of contention. A shop will also need to know how you will supply books to them – via one of the distributors mentioned above? – and what publicity you will do to direct readers to their shop.

Second-hand and antiquarian bookshops benefit the charities that run them or their private owners, but they don't provide any income for publishers or authors: there are no royalties payable on a resold book.

Online retailers are increasingly influential; the key ones are Amazon, Apple Books and Indiebound. Authors who have their own sites are encouraged to include links to these; the publisher will provide the relevant URLs. Offering customers many ways to buy a book across multiple platforms is key to opening up your writing to as wide a market as possible. Publishers have cottoned on to the fact that purchasers want to be able to access books in the format they want at whatever time they want it and from the online stores they shop at. Amazon is particularly adept at hosting multiple formats together so a reader can see the price and delivery options available to them (audio download or CD, print paperback, hardback edition or Kindle ebook). I know several bibliophiles who will invest in more than one format: an audio version for the car or the gym and a Kindle edition for the daily commute or as a holiday read.

RETURNS

Publishers provide book stock to retailers by a process known as 'sale or return'; they place an order and pay according to the payment terms and time the shop agrees to have the book for sale. The bookshop will know how well a title is selling through its EPOS (Electronic Point of Sale) system and will return titles to the publisher to receive a full refund on copies purchased that it thinks it can no longer sell. Effective stock management or inventory control is an important aspect of bookselling as well as publishing. Money tied up in stock – whether in a publisher's warehouse or the warehousing space it rents from a third party or in a bookshop's tiny stockroom – is money that can't be used to actively generate sales elsewhere. The shelf-life for a frontlist title is short, so keeping a book selling through publicity is a significant way to keep it in-store. Physical booksellers will have a huge number of titles queuing up to take the limited retail space they have available: they need to have fast turnover of stock to keep their offering fresh and attractive to customers.

Self-published books are usually supplied to bookshops on 'consignment terms' which means the bookshop only pays you for stock when copies are sold and will return unsold copies when you choose or ask you to collect them.

Publication date

With the publication of your book, you have reached a major milestone and realised your ambition. Congratulations in getting there and defying statistical odds. But what happens next? Authors say that after the to and fro of the publishing process, not to mention the constant attention from your agent, editor and publicist, publication itself can be rather an anti-climax. One of my authors (Linda Strachan, since you ask, who has written the excellent *Writers' & Artists' Guide to Writing for Children and YA*) includes a line in her book which has pricked my conscience. Authors, she says, love to receive some acknowledgement from their publisher on publication: a call, bottle of something or a bouquet of flowers doesn't cost the publisher much but will make an author feel loved and appreciated. As you wait for publication date to come into view, you may feel huge trepidation: how will the outside world respond to your book? Will reviewers take it up? Will bloggers recommend it? Might another author or high-profile individual champion it? Will readers want to read it? Will anyone part with money to get hold of it? You will not be alone in nervously wondering and asking such questions. Your agent and certainly your editor will be having similar thoughts. They believe that your book is worthy of dissemination and is something that readers will want to read. Remember their professional reputation depends on backing winners.

A DOSE OF REALITY

How do you manage your expectations for your book? It is unlikely that your debut will storm into the bestseller charts – although it might, particularly if it has the good fortune to be longlisted or shortlisted or best of all chosen as a winner for a high-profile national or regional writing prize. That's the sort of profile a new writer dreams of and the stuff of rags-to-riches success that the broadsheets love to celebrate. The reality for most authors is somewhat more prosaic. It's probably impossible to be emotionally ready should your book suddenly 'take off', but if it does, your publisher's publicity machine will expect you to be available for interviews at the drop of a hat. You might be asked to attend events, signings or to pen articles or blogs to keep your name and book in the spotlight. In short, you'll need to do anything to maintain its currency: it may only stay there for a few days or weeks before another new title or award-winning work hits the headlines and nudges you out of pole position.

But hold fire on your daydreams about a front-page exclusive in the *Sunday Times* Culture section, a promotional billboard on the London Underground or a new life of champagne and hobnobbing with the Rankins, Grishams, Rowlings and Wilsons of the writing world. Or at least temper them with a sensible dose of practical reality. The bald fact is that your book will most likely sell in hundreds, or a few thousands if you are lucky, especially if appearing first in hardback. Some – many – brilliant books just don't make it. Others tap into the zeitgeist and fly off the shelves.

WHAT AUTHORS THINK

Unsurprisingly authors can feel a sense of disappointment when publication day comes and then goes by with barely a mention.

I think the period immediately after publication is pretty hairy. You feel a sense of anti-climax, guilt at not immediately being nominated for big prizes (unless you are, which must be very pleasant, but this has yet to happen to me) and a general feeling that things should be happening but don't seem to be. I'm not sure that either agents or publisher can do much about this, but perhaps they could warn writers that the usual experience is that this period is rather quiet. And tell them not to look on Amazon, where there are bound to be some less

than fulsome reviews. Often, the advice is 'write the next book'.
I think indulging in some sort of extreme sport might be an idea.

Author of three novels for adults and short stories

Writers are keen to hear from publicity as to what is being done about
their book (no point overlapping) but also what is asked of them
and what they can do to help. There is not enough communication on
this kind of thing; it often feels like a vacuum. I wonder if publicity
departments worry writers will have too great expectations – perhaps
some do – or if they sometimes promise too much then go silent.

Linda Strachan, author of over seventy books
for children from picture books up to YA

CHAPTER 7

Life after publication

This book is about how to get published. It could have concluded at the of the end of chapter 6. But being a published author, as we have seen, entails more – much more – than putting words on a page, finding an agent and being contracted to a publisher. As an author, as well as being a storyteller, poet, memoirist or expert who has something interesting or entertaining or important to share, there are other valuable attributes that it is useful to hone. Writers are required to be competent negotiators, good time and money managers (if they want to make some income from their endeavours), a team player when working with the various departments of a publishing company, a self-publicist. You don't have to be well-versed in all of these aspects, but it does help if you are aware of their importance or know when to seek advice. As an author how do you continue to foster your skills, make time for your writing and keep at it?

Don't give up

This book is here to help you shape your expectations and realise your ambition. It should give you hope that you too might have a punt at being a published author and that the book in you might see the light of day. Take advice from authors who have made it – and which they have shared over the years across the bulging pages of the *Writers' & Artists' Yearbook*. They understand the disappointments you may experience in your quest to get your work into print and their insights might buoy you up when you are feeling particularly despondent or uninspired. Chapter 2 invited you to consider what sort of writer you want to be, and chapter 4 highlighted the financial challenges of being an author. These are there to help you question how you want to shape your writing life and how that might dovetail with all the other pieces of your day-to-day existence. It's important to remain realistic about the publishing process and how significant your own contacts, energies and input are to ensure that your book gets noticed amongst the many thousands that are published every year.

As we have seen in chapter 6, it can sometimes seem that, once the excitement of publication day has passed, that as an author, you are left to your own devices. You have been used to a stream of individuals at your agency or publisher getting in touch to shape the text and discuss marketing plans for your book. If you are fortunate you may have had a book tour, some media interviews, a review here or there and even possibly a (self-funded) launch event to welcome your book into the market. So, what happens next?

In large part that is up to you. Here are some of the ways you can maintain the momentum that spurred you on when writing and collaborating with your publisher in the weeks and months after publication.

Savour the moment Getting a first book published *is* a great achievement. You should be proud of what you have done: it will have been the culmination of much hard work and periods of self-doubt.

Reward yourself Once the excitement of post-publication PR activity – if you were lucky enough to get some – has subsided, take time off. Make use of the final stage advance due on publication to treat yourself. Encourage moments of idleness: it will remind you that life before writing and adhering to publishing schedules could be calming and rewarding too. Allow your mind time to rest and to wander – who knows what new plotlines, characters or lines of dialogue might get drafted. After a period of introspective concentration on your book as well as the multiple rounds of draft scripts and proofs, it's time to reacquaint yourself with the outside world. Catch up with other people's books you wanted to read but had scant time to devote to. Get re-involved with the community around you: it's where inspiration for your next book or the one after might come from.

Stay positive You've reached a significant milestone by being published. Keep in mind the warm glow you experienced when you first held an advance copy of your book; it's particularly important to do this when you get demoralised if sales are sluggish and below what you and your publisher had hoped for. Continue to aim high with your writing and your submissions: they will be better as a result.

> *Writing has to be a passion, a labour of love. The reward comes in the feedback from readers and speaking engagements where you meet an array of people who you might never otherwise have come across. It is really hard to find an agent, it's hard to get published, and it's hard to sell books. But don't give up. There is nothing like seeing your book on a shelf – or receiving an email from a reader.*
>
> Emma Sky, author of *The Unravelling: High Hopes and Missed Opportunities in Iraq* (Atlantic, 2015) and *In A Time Of Monsters: Travels Through a Middle East in Revolt* (Atlantic, 2019).

Don't spend your post-publication waking hours worrying about what you can't control, such as:

Poor sales It's not your job to sell your book: that's what your publisher does. Unless they have been particularly indolent, your book will have been launched with all the sales, marketing and PR activity that they think your book warrants, and that their often slim resources allow. If your debut has not flown off the shelves at Waterstones or been picked up by BBC Radio 4's *Book At Bedtime* then that's normal. You have to remind yourself that it would be exceptional if it had. It doesn't mean your book isn't a good one or that you should hang up your writing boots, it's merely a reminder that most books sell in small quantities and debuts from a complete unknown are even harder to sell. Celebrate when you get some good news and hold firm to your belief that writing is what you can and want to do.

Bad reviews Don't expect everyone who reads your book to love it. Avoid trawling the web for mentions of your title or taking twice-daily peeks at Amazon rankings and reader ratings if you think you won't be able to cope with any negative commentary you see there. You might be surprised by how enthusiastic and encouraging readers, book bloggers and other writers can be. If you think it will help your mental well-being, nominate a friend or ask your publisher or agent to forward reviews and mentions. These reviews are important to help promote your title immediately after publication and can be added to the book's description and metadata that feeds through to your publisher's website, Amazon and other online stores.

One of the delights of being an editor is seeing how well an author's book is received: it proves they were right to back it. Your editor would usually pass on a good review and help to contextualise or make a less favourable one more palatable. Your agent is likely to include them on their site alongside a mini profile of you and your book. You have suddenly become an important asset to them: they too backed a winner. You may find yourself sitting digitally alongside well-established, prolific writers held in high regard: which can be a positive boost to any new author's ego.

Don't give up your day job is a much-vaunted piece of advice. For obvious reasons, even if your first book sells well beyond anyone's expectations, it's a good idea not to jettison the regular and reliable income stream that your 'real' job brings in. You could start to think about how you might adapt your working life to accommodate more writing time – for example switching from full to part-time, if that's what you want to do – and plan how you might make proper money from a life in books (if that's something you think you would find fulfilling). See below under Networking for more ideas on how you might start developing such a strategy.

Be proactive Do you remember how self-motivated you had to be to write your first book, the research you had to do about which agents to approach, the numerous rewrites of the submission pitch you put together? You may now have a publisher, an agent and readers, but they

My first novel, *Tony Hogan Bought Me an Ice-cream Float Before He Stole My Ma,* was published seven years ago when I was thirty-two (in 2012). It received a very modest advance and was expected to be well under the radar but I made firm friends with my publicist at Random House and together we collaborated on a really creative publicity plan including a live reading of the entire book in Stoke Newington Bookshop and me touring independent bookshops on an 80s bicycle to hand out retro sweets to booksellers.

That book went on to be shortlisted for seven literary prizes, including the *Guardian* First Book and Southbank Sky Arts Awards, and won the Scottish First Book Prize. I gave up my day job a year later, published another two books, won another literary prize and have since built a career as a writer, workshop leader, public speaker and journalist. I'm far from rich but I pay my bills while doing what I love, and I can ask for nothing more.

To say all this came as a surprise to me, a woman who left school at fifteen, is an understatement. In fact, I realise now that my entire lack of expectation is what served me so well in that early part of my career. I had no concept of what my publication *should* be like, no idea what prizes I might be eligible for or what would count as 'good' sales figures. I had focused on the writing and then reaching readers and I approached the professional aspect of being published just like I had my in my career as a NGO project manager. I was, and strive to remain, reliable and hardworking, creative and intent on forging good relationships.

I'm an anxious person and publication might have been challenging for me, but I learned early on that most things in the industry, the giddy highs and the inevitable disappointing days, are fairly arbitrary. My biggest tip? Focus on the writing rather than the reception, acknowledge all kindnesses that are offered (there will be many) and try to enjoy every single second.

Kerry Hudson is the author of two novels and a memoir: Lowborn: Growing Up, Getting Away and Returning to Britain's Poorest Towns (Chatto & Windus, 2019).

are busily supporting other authors and will be distracted by the next raft of debut novels queued up behind your own. Editors are business people and have to keep moving things along the publishing conveyor belt. It doesn't mean they want to stop communication with you, but you may have to make the first move. Let them know of opportunities that arise where your book might get a mention, update your publicity contacts with potential leads, write some blogs and continue your own promotional activity. When you are ready, put all your energies behind producing the proposal, synopsis and draft chapters for the next book you plan to send your editor.

The publisher is not remaining idle either once publication has been and gone. You may have contact with departments you have not previously had dealings with, such as the Finance or Accounts department. They will send you royalty statements a couple of times a year, as outlined in chapter 4. The Rights department will be looking for potential translation deals for your book with foreign publishers and other subsidiary rights that might be exploited. Your publisher may nominate your book for a literary prize – a longlisting or shortlisting can make a big difference to sales.

If your book first appeared in hardback, then eight to twelve months later a paperback is likely to appear. This is an opportunity to discuss any tweaks you think might be useful to the back cover blurb or the cover design that may enhance the way the book is presented. These suggestions might not be incorporated but they do signal to your publisher that you remain engaged with their ongoing management of your book. Assume they know what they are doing, but an author who has useful ideas to contribute to the process is usually welcome to share these. Your book may benefit from some enhanced publicity if additional formats appear after the first print and digital editions, such as the creation of an audio or large-print library version or an adaptation for the schools market. If your title first appeared in hardback then reviews from well-known names or respected publications will be an important promotional tool for a paperback or other edition, and will be included, along with mention of any longlisting or shortlisting for prizes, on the front or back cover.

If you are a self-published author with an ebook whose sales are sluggish, then now is the time to review your cover design, blurb or keyword selection. Could these be improved to help send your title up the Amazon or Google rankings? Take a look again at the box about metadata on page 229 of chapter 6.

Are there other formats or versions that your book might mutate into, or might it be the start of a new series, even if that was not the original intention?

Your next book

Assuming your first book did well enough, your publisher will expect your next book to fall into the same genre as your first one. If the first did win plaudits, they will be hoping for a follow-up quickly that can be marketed using the same, successful, technique. The cover design, style of book title and blurb are likely to mimic that of your debut as your publisher starts to develop you as an identifiable brand. This can all be very exciting and daunting. What if you want to write a picture book next though your first book was a YA dystopian fantasy? My advice is to stick to what you know works. Develop your next teen fantasy novel; keep your picture book ideas safe in a drawer until you are a better-established writer and then consider with your agent how such ideas might best see the light of publishing day. You might need to swap editor or publisher or publish for a different age range under a pseudonym. These are matters that should concern you much further on in your writing life: remember you are still a fledging at this stage.

You, your agent and your publisher can come up with ideas for new books that evolve from the first. Peter Frankopan's *The Silk Roads: A New History of the World* (Bloomsbury, 2015) was a huge success on publication. It was a *Sunday Times* and international bestseller in hardback and subsequently in paperback and was critically acclaimed. This was aimed at adult readers. In 2018 Bloomsbury's Children's Division published a large format, highly illustrated version for children aged 11+. The text was rewritten and adapted to suit this new readership, but the ideas and concept of the original remained. *The Tattooist of Auschwitz* (Zaffre Books, 2018) by Heather Morris was a debut novel that stormed the bestseller charts. It was followed by a sequel in 2019 (*Cilka's Journey*) which developed the story of a character from her first novel into its own narrative. This is something that Rachel Joyce also did successfully when telling the story of Queenie in *The Love Song of Miss Queenie Hennessy: Or the letter that was never sent to Harold Fry* (2014) as a follow-up to her hugely popular *The Unlikely Pilgrimage of Harold Fry* (Doubleday, 2012).

Children's publishers are always on the lookout for series ideas, books and characters that might become wider properties on screen and through merchandising that enhance book sales, and for seasonal and activity book editions of titles. The multiple spin-offs from Julia Donaldson's *The Gruffalo* (illustrated by Axel Scheffler and first published by Macmillan in 1999) is a good example of a single title that developed a publishing strategy of its own. There is a 20th anniversary edition, sticker, board, lift-the-flap, and puppet-book incarnations and it has spawned *The Gruffalo's Child* (2004), a play, a version in Scots and dozens of other languages, and has sold many, many millions of copies (13.5 million at the time of writing this). Your editor will be looking for a hook or theme to build a sequence of titles to satisfy younger readers' appetite for brands, series and familiar concepts. Examples include Holly Webb's *Animal Stories*, Cressida Cowell's *How to Train Your Dragon* and Lucy Courtenay's *Space Penguins*. Do you also have a scalable concept up your literary sleeve?

THE TWO-BOOK DEAL

The two-book deal can be both a pleasure and a curse. Debut crime writers, writers of a fantasy trilogy, children's non-fiction or picture book authors might be signed up by a publisher for more than one title in the contract they agree with an agent. Publishers are seeking authors who they can build as a brand and by committing to more than one book they are signalling a commitment to the author over several years. It is a positive reinforcement of the value of your writing. The reality is that few debut novels make a publisher a fortune; their return on investment may be very small or non-existent. It is expensive to launch an unknown author, but once (the rationale goes) a first novel has been published and has garnered approbation from critics and readers, it is easier to go back to the market with a second book, so bit-by-bit building the author's profile. There is a commonly held assumption that the publishing industry is more impatient than it used to be about the time it takes for an author to 'make it' big. Of course publishers want to sign a new author who will be a soar-away success with their debut novel: the reality is that this is unlikely. Publishers have enough experience under their belts to know how fickle the market can be, and that good writing frequently doesn't receive the acclaim it deserves.

If your debut does win a prize, or gets recommended by the Oprah, Richard and Judy, Zoella or Emma Watson book club, then you could see plentiful sales, putting you in a position to dictate better terms for your next title and possibly look around for a larger, higher-profile publisher to foster your emerging talent for the long term. If you have signed a two-book deal, then you will be wedded to the original publisher for your next title: you might think that only right if they helped secure healthy sales on your debut. It is not uncommon for small, independent presses to have their 'successful' authors poached by the larger houses that can invest greater sums in promotional campaigns and which are likely to have more clout in their negotiations with distributors and booksellers through well-established sales channels.

The write-to-order two-book deal can become a curse when the author has published a first work and then can't seem to get a second to flow. As you write your first novel, the passion to write is what is likely to spur you on, not the desire to be published. You have a fervent need to express yourself through a story that has been whirling around in your imagination and are eager to get your words down: the only thing that is stopping you is time. Writing a second novel might not be such an unassailable creative urge. You may be worrying how to build on your initial success (success being *actually* getting into print – you defied the statistical odds and got an agent and then a publisher!). It can be a tricky act to follow and even trickier if you are aware of the urgency when you have a pre-signed publishing contract hanging over you.

Keep practising

One book does not signal a lengthy and fulfilling writing career ahead. It might, but who can tell at this early stage? You should assume that writing your second book is as hard if not harder than writing the first and requires the same discipline and endeavour, and if you enjoyed writing the first, then that enjoyment should be possible with its follow-up. You need to try and capture some of the passion that helped bring the first to fruition. The trick is not to worry but to continue writing, practising and developing and to remind yourself you are still in the foothills of being a writer. You will not have magically become a fully accomplished author on the strength of one published title. Your writing will still need to be pondered over, redrafted and polished by professional editors. Don't let debut success go to your head. Remain realistic about the challenges of writing and continuing to be published. Take advice where you need it. Practise all types of writing. Do some jobbing writing, jot down the plots for some further novels that your mind is flirting with to keep your brain and pen active. Don't stop writing. Continue to think of yourself as a writer and remind yourself that it is hard work to write and to write well.

The great advantage of already being published is that you know more about the ups and downs of the whole process and the vagaries of the industry. More importantly you now have a set of allies who are there to support and advise you: your agent (if you have one), your editor and her publishing colleagues, and your readers. They are all willing you to do well with your next book.

Networking

In chapter 2, I cautioned against allowing yourself to be distracted from your writing. Post-publication is a perfect time to take stock and enhance your profile and your skills. Writers supplement the money they get from book sales – which, remember, may not come in a steady stream but in chunks a couple of times a year via royalty payments – with a variety of activities and tasks, such as teaching, writing articles, advising on other writers' text through editorial services. You might do work for hire on a fixed-fee basis, such as adapting your own or classic novels for school reading schemes. If you only want to practise your novel-writing or non-fiction style that's fine too: work out what it is you want. You can build a portfolio of paid-for tasks around your creative writing, which over time might become a viable income stream to allow you to devote all your working time to book-related activities. These might include lecturing, appearing at festivals and events linked to writing, publishing or career development.

Now you are published you can share your experiences with other writers just starting out, to encourage and support, mirroring what established writers might have given you once upon a time through their blogs and articles or at events you attended. Look at mentoring schemes, residential and day courses that might help you develop your work and as you improve and get several books under your belt, you might be able to offer advice to others through such schemes. If you write for children, consider offering readings and talks in schools. Try to avoid doing these for free, unless it's for your local school, or is a charity readathon or something similar. Schools have small budgets, but you are doing a disservice to other authors and to yourself if you don't charge for your visit. A fee, which can be negotiated on your behalf by a company, such as Authors Aloud, should reflect the time you spend in the school and preparation and travel time as well as your travel costs.

Nurture your existing contacts in the media and make new ones through online networking and at face-to-face events. This could be your local self-employed networking group (most towns will have one) where you might meet contacts who are looking for someone with writing or editorial skills. Don't be too proud about what you take on. If you are getting paid for writing, even if it is preparing copy for a corporate agency or a manufacturing company's website, then think of it as another opportunity to engage with words and fashion them to fit the audience for which they are intended.

Tell us your story

The team at Writers & Artists spend a fair amount of time talking to authors as well as to agents. I enjoy meeting new writers at the conferences we run and at events we co-host with other organisations and charities. New writers brim with ideas and are passionate about sharing these. We are always keen to hear from you, about your experiences as you try to get published, whether these are positive or grisly ones! Such anecdotes and pieces of advice will help inform the future events we run and the information we provide in our print publications and online at www.writersandartists.co.uk. Do drop us a line if you have useful advice to share with our community of writers, at writersandartists@bloomsbury.com.

In conclusion, here are my three cardinal rules for writers (and publishers too):

1. Read widely and regularly.

2. Use your local library, if you are lucky enough to have one, before it becomes a thing of the past.

3. Buy from your high-street bookshop and independent bookseller when you can, because they too are an essential part of the complicated publishing chain.

Finally, be confident about your writing. Take yourself seriously and others might too. This book is here to arm you with brio and a sense of purpose of 'how-to' and 'will-do'. Good luck on the exciting journey you are about to embark on towards becoming a published writer. If you ask someone what they do and they say they write, admit it, you are rather impressed. And, guess what, they are not a special breed. They are perfectly normal and at the same time exceptional (and probably pretty brave) human beings, just like the rest of us.

Resources

Further reading

Here are some suggestions for books I've found useful and readable and which you might too.

First UK publication date is given. For classic texts, a current edition is listed and original publication details provided too. You might be able to pick up an out-of-print title via the likes of AbeBooks.

The writing life

Being a Writer by Travis Elborough & Helen Gordon (Frances Lincoln, 2018)
> Three centuries of writers offer their thoughts and advice on the highs and lows of a life spent writing.

Why I Write by George Orwell (Penguin, 2004; first published in 1946)
> Orwell outlines the four motives behind every writer's decision to write and explores which of the four most apply to him.

Create Dangerously by Albert Camus translated by Justin O'Brien (Penguin Classics, 2018; first published in French by Éditions Gallimard, 1961)
> In his 1957 lecture Camus insisted that it is the duty of the writer to advocate for those who are denied a voice and who cannot speak out for themselves.

A Room of One's Own by Virginia Woolf (Penguin Classics, 2009; first published by Hogarth Press, 1929)
> Woolf explores the limitations placed upon female writers and upon their creativity, including Jane Austen and Charlotte Brontë, while advocating on behalf of all female creatives.

A Life of My Own by Claire Tomalin (Penguin Press, 2018)
> The acclaimed biographer tells the story of her own life and the impact literature has had upon it.

On Writing: A Memoir of the Craft by Stephen King (Simon & Schuster, 2000)

King tells the story of his path from struggling to successful writer, sharing advice from his experience and the tools which made him the writer he is today.

Stet: An Editor's Life by Diana Athill (Granta Books, 2000)

Athill reflects with honesty and humour on her life as both writer and editor, remembering the authors who shaped her career.

How to be a writer

Writers' & Artists' Yearbook edited by Alysoun Owen (Bloomsbury, every July)

Advice on writing from a range of published authors alongside a wealth of information on every aspect of the publishing process.

Children's Writers' & Artists' Yearbook edited by Alysoun Owen (Bloomsbury, every July)

Writing advice from authors and insight into the publishing industry to guide the aspiring children's writer from amateur to professional.

The Art of Fiction by David Lodge (Penguin Vintage, 2011; first published by Secker & Warburg, 1992)

Lodge explores classic and modern American and British fiction, the authors who wrote it, the ideas they shared and the impact they had upon the practice of writing and literature.

The Paris Review Interviews edited by Philip Gourevitch (Picador US, vol 1: 2007; vol 2: 2007; vol 3: 2008; vol 4: 2009)

The Writer's Chapbook: A Compendium of Fact, Opinion, Wit, and Advice from 'The Paris Review' Interviews edited by George Plimpton (Paris Review Editions, 2018; first published 1989)

Since it was founded in 1953, *The Paris Review* has published essays by and interviews with the literary luminaries of the day. These compilations provide entertaining insights into the minds and craft of some of the 20th and 21st century's greatest writers.

Self-publishing

Not surprisingly many books on this subject are self-published; most poorly
so, though I'm happy to recommend these two.

Successful Self-Publishing second edition, by Joanna Penn (Curl Up Press, 2017;
first published in 2015)

Stress-Free Self-Publishing by Samantha Pearce (SWATT Books, 2019)

Writing for different genres and markets

CHILDREN'S AND YA

Writing Children's Fiction (A Writers' & Artists' Companion) by Linda
Newbery and Yvonne Coppard (Bloomsbury, 2013)

The Magic Words: Writing Great Books for Children and Young Adults
by Cheryl B. Klein (W. W. Norton, 2016)

Writers' & Artists' Guide to Writing for Children and YA by Linda Strachan
(Bloomsbury, 2019)

How to Write a Children's Book and Get it Published third edition, by Barbara
Seuling (John Wiley & Sons, 2004; first published in 1984)

How to Write a Children's Picture Book and Get It Published third edition,
by Andrea Shavick (Little, Brown Group Ltd., 2016; first published in 2011)

NOVELS

How to Write a Novel by John Braine (Methuen Publishing, 2001; first
published by Eyre Methuen in 1974; currently out-of-print)

Plotting and Writing Suspense Fiction by Patricia Highsmith (Sphere 2016;
first published 1966)

How Fiction Works by James Wood (Vintage, 2009)

Novel Writing (A Writers' & Artists' Companion) by Romesh Gunesekera and
A.L. Kennedy (Bloomsbury, 2015)

PLOT

Into the Woods: How Stories Work and Why We Tell Them by John Yorke
(Penguin, 2014)

Story by Robert McKee (Methuen Publishing, 1998)

Seven Basic Plots by Christopher Booker (Continuum, 2005)

NON-FICTION

Literary Non-Fiction (A Writers' & Artists' Companion) by Sally Cline and Midge Gillies (Bloomsbury, 2015)

On Writing Well: The Classic Guide to Writing Non-Fiction by William Zinsser (Harper Perennial, 2006: first published in 1976)

How to Write Non-Fiction: Turn Your Knowledge into Words by Joanna Penn (Curl Up Press, 2018)

POETRY

The Ode Less Travelled: Unlocking the Poet Within by Stephen Fry (Hutchinson, 2005)

How to be a Poet by Jo Bell and Jane Commane (Nine Arches Press, 2017)

What is Poetry: The Essential Guide to Reading and Writing Poems by Michael Rosen (Walker Books, 2016)

A Poetry Handbook by Mary Oliver (Houghton Mifflin Harcourt, 1994)

Poetry in the Making: A Handbook for Writing and Teaching by Ted Hughes (Faber & Faber, 2008; first published in 1967)

PROFESSIONAL (INCLUDING ACADEMIC AND EDUCATIONAL)

Nature Masterclasses: Scientific Writing and Publishing. Available online at: https://masterclasses.nature.com/online-course-in-scientific-writing-and-publishing/16507840

Technical Writing for Business People by Carrie Marshall (BCS, 2018)

Writing Successful Academic Books by Anthony Haynes (Cambridge University Press, 2010)

SHORT STORIES

Writing Short Stories (A Writers' & Artists' Companion) by Courttia Newland and Tania Hershman (Bloomsbury, 2014)

SCREENWRITING

Writing for TV and Radio (A Writer' and Artists' Companion) by Sue Teddern and Nick Warburton (Bloomsbury, 2015)

Screenwriting: Behind the Silver Screen edited by Andrew Horton and Julian Hoxter (I.B. Taurus, 2015)

Screenwriting is Rewriting: The Art and Craft of Professional Revision by Jack Epps (Bloomsbury, 2016)

An editing toolkit

Butcher, Judith; Drake, Caroline and Leach, Maureen, *Butcher's Copy-editing: The Cambridge Handbook for Editors, Copy-editors and Proofreaders* (Cambridge University Press, 4th edn 2006)

Butterfield, J., *Fowler's Dictionary of Modern English Usage* (Oxford University Press, 4th edn 2015)

Ritter, R.M., *New Oxford Dictionary for Writers and Editors: The Essential A-Z Guide to the Written Word* (Oxford University Press, 2nd revised edn 2014)

The Chicago Manual of Style: The Essential Guide for Writers, Editors, and Publishers (University of Chicago Press, 17th edn 2017; www.chicagomanualofstyle.org)

Waddingham, Anne (ed.), *New Hart's Rules: The Oxford Style Guide* (Oxford University Press, 2nd edn 2014)

The Society for Editors and Proofreaders (SfEP), offers training, mentoring, support and advice for editors and proofreaders and a freely searchable directory of editorial professionals, www.sfep.org.uk

Rights, copyright and the law

Cornish, William et al., *Intellectual Property, Patents, Copyrights, Trademarks and Allied Rights* (Sweet & Maxwell, 9th edn 2019)

Bently, Lionel and Sherman, Brad, *Intellectual Property Law* (OUP, 4th edn 2014)

Caddick, Nicholas et al., *Copinger and Skone James on Copyright* (Sweet & Maxwell, 17th edn 2016)

Jones, Hugh and Benson, Christopher, *Publishing Law* (Routledge, 5th edn 2016)

Haggart Davies, Gillian, *Copyright for Artists, Photographers and Designers* (A&C Black, 2010)

Haggart Davies, Gillian, *Copyright for Writers, Editors and Publishers* (A&C Black, 2011)

Owen, Lynette (Gen. Ed.), *Clark's Publishing Agreements: A Book of Precedents* (Bloomsbury Professional, 10th edn 2017)

For a view of copyright from the US perspective:
Netanel, Neil Weinstock, *Copyright: What Everyone Needs to Know* (OUP New York, 2018)

Money matters

GOV.UK
www.gov.uk/national-insurance
For guidance on National Insurance.

DWP benefits
www.gov.uk/browse/benefits

Tax Credits
www.gov.uk/browse/benefits/tax-credits

Child benefit
www.gov.uk/child-benefit

Statutory payments
For SSP, SMP, SPP, SAP and ShPP contact your employer in the first instance.

National Insurance Contributions & Employer Office, International Caseworker
HM Revenue and Customs BX9 1AN
tel 0300 200 3500
For enquiries for individuals resident abroad.

Marketing, publicity and selling yourself

How to Market Books by Alison Baverstock and Susannah Bowen (Taylor & Francis, 2019)
Foundations of Marketing by John Fahy and David Jobber (McGraw-Hill Education, 2015)

Other resources

Organisations, events and services that are useful to writers by providing up-to-date information, advice and spaces in which to share experiences.

The Society of Authors

Members receive unlimited free advice on all aspects of the profession, including confidential clause-by-clause contract vetting, and a wide range of exclusive offers. It campaigns and lobbies on the issues that affect authors. It also administers a range of literary grants and prizes, awarding more than £400,000 to authors annually.

The subscription fee (tax deductible) starts at £25.50 per quarter, or £18 for those aged 35 or under. From the second year of subscription there are concessionary rates for over 65s who are no longer earning a significant amount of income from writing. Annual payment schedules are also available.

email info@societyofauthors.org

website www.societyofauthors.org

WGGB – Writers' Guild of Great Britain

TUC-affiliated trade union for writers. Represents writers working in film, television, radio, theatre, books, poetry, animation, comedy and video games. They offer Full, Candidate and Affiliate membership.

email admin@writersguild.org.uk

website www.writersguild.org.uk

ALLi – Association of Independent Authors

Benefits include self-publishing advice, guidance and community; vetted services, service ratings and watchdog desk; legal and contract appraisal; discounts and deals; professional and business development; and campaigns and advocacy.

They have three membership levels for **authors** – from **Associate** (planning to self-publish) to **Professional** (earning a living as an author-publisher) – and a **Partner** membership for good author services willing to be vetted and approved by their Watchdog Desk.

email info@allianceindependentauthors.org

website http://allianceindependentauthors.org; www.selfpublishing advice.org

Society of Children's Book Writers and Illustrators (SCWBI)

SCBWI is a professional guild with UK and international groups, that represents writers and illustrators for children. It administers a number of awards and grants. You can join for an annual fee.

email membership@britishscbwi.org

website www.scbwi.org; www.britishisles.scbwi.org

Scattered Authors' Society (SAS)

Provides a forum for informal discussion, contact and support for professional writers for children and YA. It consists of a network of around 300 published authors scattered across the UK and welcomes new members that have a publishing deal in place.

email scatteredauthorssociety@gmail.com

website www.scatteredauthors.org

AUTHOR TED TALKS

The Danger of a Single Story, Chimamanda Ngozi Adichie, 2009. Available at: https://www.youtube.com/watch?v=D9Ihs241zeg : As topical and important today as when it was first delivered. Adichie celebrates the power of diverse stories and perspectives and shares her experience of finding her own 'authentic cultural voice'.

Your Elusive Creative Genius, Elizabeth Gilbert, 2009. Available at: https://www.youtube.com/watch?v=86x-u-tzoMA : Gilbert explores inspiration and genius from a cross-cultural perspective and with insights from other writing experts. She recognises the pressures of writing, for a novice and for a bestselling author like herself but reassures her listeners that every writer has a genius within them and the inspiration to unlock it can come from anywhere and at any time.

The Mystery of Storytelling, Julian Friedman, 2012. Available at: https://www.youtube.com/watch?v=al3-Kl4BDUQ&list=PLlH_3Rg-KNr-5J-oWj74Swr_A7JmEJEzs&index=3: As a literary agent with over forty years of experience Friedman is in the perfect position to uncover the mystery of storytelling: it is all about the audience and every writer needs to put their ego aside and realise that in order to succeed.

Adventure is Twitter Fiction, Andrew Fitzgerald, 2013. Available at: https://www.youtube.com/watch?v=J6ZzmqDMhio&list=PLOGi5-fAu8bFJgn8sN

qlTKanV5bcKef9M&index=17 : A new form of experimentation and a new format to experiment with, Fitzgerald encourages writers to embrace unique ways of reaching and engaging with an audience.

What Makes a Bestseller?, Jonny Geller, 2016. Available at: https://www.youtube.com/watch?v=mD-uP2BsVy4: Geller gives aspiring writers an insight into how the book market operates and what it is that literary agents are looking for.

Book sites, blogs and podcasts

Websites and blogs

The Artist's Road
website https://artistsroad.blog
Founder Patrick Ross
Blog created to record the cross-USA road trip that the author Patrick Ross took in the summer of 2010 while interviewing over forty artists with the aim of discussing the motivations, challenges and rewards of their lifestyles, and passing on their creative wisdom. It now details his insights into living an 'art-committed life' through writing and creativity.

Better Novel Project
website www.betternovelproject.com/blog
Founder Christine Frazier
Deconstructs bestselling novels to discover what common elements they all share and shows how writers can use these to create reliable story structures.

Book Patrol
website http://bookpatrol.net
Founder Michael Lieberman
Founded in 2006 in the US as a blog to promote books and literacy, it is now a hub for all things book-related. Posting about book news, book reviews, technology and related content, the site has its own online shop selling a large collection of curated material.

Books & Such
website www.booksandsuch.com/blog
Founder Janel Kobobel Grant
Blog from a literary agent's perspective, advising on writing query letters and improving MSS before submitting them to agents. Also addresses how to find an agent and get published. Highlights the importance of the editing process in adding to writing quality. Discusses the various aspects of traditional publishing and self-promotion for authors.

Nathan Bransford
website http://blog.nathanbransford.com
Founder Nathan Bransford
From the perspective of an author and former literary agent advising about the writing, editing and publishing process, based on his own experience. Added tips on improving plots, dialogue and characters, writing a query letter and synopsis and finding a literary agent. Analyses and debates a range of topics including ebooks and their pricing, social media options, marketing, cover design and plot themes. Includes a publishing glossary and FAQs.

Cornflower Books
website www.cornflowerbooks.co.uk
Founder Karen Howlett
Reviews a wide range of books and has a monthly online book club, debates cover designs and includes a 'writing and publishing' section. Also includes interviews with well-known authors about their books, writing process and routine. Selects 'books of the year' in different genres, and discusses literary festivals and prizes.

Courage 2 Create

website http://thecourage2create.com
Founder Ollin Morales
Ollin Morales shares the experience
of writing his first novel: pitfalls to
avoid, dealing with stress, overcoming
challenges, how his lifestyle benefits
from writing, and inspirational quotes.
Blog chapters describe his creative
journey and what he has learned about
life through the writing process.

The Creative Penn

website www.thecreativepenn.com
Founder Joanna Penn
Focuses on the writing process and how
to market and sell your book. Advises
writers on dealing with criticism, finding
an agent and writing query letters.
Debates traditional publishing, 'hybrid'
and self-publishing options, and also
advises on POD, ebook publishing as well
as online and social media marketing.
Includes audio/video interviews with
mainly self-published authors.

Daily Writing Tips

website www.dailywritingtips.com
Founder Maeve Maddox and others
Publishing new content every day
with articles covering the whole
writing spectrum: from grammar and
punctuation to usage and vocabulary.

Dear Author

website www.dearauthor.com
Founder Jane Litte
Focuses on romantic novels. All reviews
are written in the form of a letter to the
author. Includes interviews with authors
about their writing style.

Fiction Notes

website www.darcypattison.com
Founder Darcy Pattison

Darcy Pattison is a published non-
fiction writer and children's author, as
well as an experienced speaker. Her blog
collates her own articles and thoughts
on children's writing, reviews of her
work and information on her speaking
engagements where she specialises in
novel revision and metamorphosis.

Jane Friedman

website http://janefriedman.com
Founder Jane Friedman
Focuses on digital publishing and
discusses the future of publishing.
Provides tips for writers on how to beat
writers' block, DIY ebook publishing,
marketing your writing and publicising
it online through blogs, social media and
websites to create your 'author platform'
and publish your book. Includes guidance
on copyright and securing permissions.

Goins, Writer

website http://goinswriter.com
Founder Jeff Goins
Focuses on advising authors about their
writing journey and how to enhance
their writing style. Highlights how
authors can build a core fanbase 'tribe'
through a focused approach and adding
value to social media and blogs.

Goodreads

website www.goodreads.com
Founded in 2006 to help people find and
share the books they love. Users can see
what their friends and favourite authors
are reading, rate books they've read on
a scale of one to five stars and write
reviews, and customise bookshelves
full of books 'Read' and books 'To
Read'. Users can receive news on books,
poetry, author interviews and more via
their regular newsletter. Now owned
by Amazon.

Helping Writers Become Authors

website www.helpingwritersbecome authors.com
Founder K.M. Weiland
Tips on story structure, creating memorable characters and plot development. Advice about finding writing inspiration and the writing process, as well as addressing the story revision and MS editing stages. Includes an extensive list of books for aspiring authors.

Live Write Thrive

website www.livewritethrive.com
Founder C.S. Lakin
Set up by a writer specialising in fiction, fantasy and YA, this blog focuses on helping writers discover what kind of copy-editing and critiquing services their work will need once it is finished. As a copy-editor and writing coach, Lakin offers her own editorial services and advice on how to choose the right editor. There are also articles by guest bloggers and tips on grammar.

Lovereading

website www.lovereading.co.uk
Independent book recommendation site designed to inspire and inform readers, all with the aim of helping them choose their next read. Features include: categories broken down by interest; downloadable opening extracts of featured books; like-for-like recommendations for discovering new authors; expert reviews and reader review panels.

A Newbie's Guide to Publishing

website http://jakonrath.blogspot.co.uk
Founder Joe Konrath
Blog by a self-published author which discusses the writing process and focuses

on self-publishing, encourages writers to self-publish ebooks, and looks at developments and trends in this area. Includes interviews with self-published authors about their books and guest posts.

Omnivoracious

website http://www.omnivoracious.com
This blog from Amazon covers an eclectic range of genres. Casting a wide but focused lens over publishing, the posts include: reviews and articles; the best books of the month; current news and discussions; tips for writers; awards in writing and interviews with authors.

Positive Writer

website http://positivewriter.com
Founder Bryan Hutchinson
A motivational and inspirational blog for creatives, particularly writers, focusing on how to overcome doubt and negativity and to unlock your inner creativity. It includes handy tips on marketing and interviews with other authors.

Reading Matters

website http://readingmattersblog.com
Founder Kim Forrester
Created in 2004, Reading Matters offers reviews of modern and contemporary fiction on a clean and navigable website. The site's main focus is Irish and Australian literature and reviews are personable and informative. Every Tuesday the site acts as a platform for guest bloggers to share their favourite books and promote their own blogs.

Romance University

website http://romanceuniversity.org
Co-founders Tracey Devlyn, Kelsey Browning, Adrienne Giordano
An online 'university' for all who are hoping to learn the craft of writing

romance. Three new blog post lectures are added by contributors and industry professionals weekly. Each Monday, posts focus on the theme of 'crafting your career', which include the business of writing, agents, publishing and self-publishing options, and marketing your work on social media and blogs. Wednesdays focus on 'the anatomy of the mind' in relation to different facets of romance writing and Fridays on the elements of the manuscript writing process, e.g. creating characters and plot.

Lauren Sapala

website http://laurensapala.com
Founder Lauren Sapala
This blog gives pep talks to writers in moments of self-doubt. With posts about how to get inspired and stay focused, its aim is to nurture and empower your creative flame.

Savidge Reads

website https://savidgereads.wordpress.com
Founder Simon Savidge
Follows the reading of Simon Savidge whose writing has featured in several literary and lifestyle magazines. Comprised mainly of books in the literary fiction genre from modern classic to contemporary fiction. His chatty reviews are entertaining and open, and give insight into the mind of a self-proclaimed 'book-a-holic'.

Terribleminds

website http://terribleminds.com/ramble/blog
Founder Chuck Wendig
Comical, easy-to-read blog about author Chuck Wendig's trials and tribulations whilst writing.

There Are No Rules

website www.writersdigest.com/editor-blogs/there-are-no-rules
Blog by the editors of *Writer's Digest*. Focuses on the writing process, plot and character development, writing query letters and creating your author platform through social media and public speaking. Tips on how to overcome writing challenges, improve your writing and revise your MS so that it is more likely to be accepted by an agent. Includes a range of regular webinars with industry professionals including agents offering advice. Also discusses and advises on the self-publishing process.

This Itch of Writing

website http://emmadarwin.typepad.com/thisitchofwriting
Founder Emma Darwin
An author's advice on the craft of authoring successful books; both fiction and creative non-fiction.

Well-Storied

website www.well-storied.com
Founder Kristen Kieffer
Articles, resources and podcasts, offering all the necessary tips and tools to turn your writing dreams into reality.

The Write Life

website http://thewritelife.com
Founder Alexis Grant
This blog, by writers for writers, is designed to encourage individuals to connect and share experiences. There is no single expert, but a running dialogue connecting fellow writers during the stages in their writing. Posts tend to focus on how to become a writer rather than the writing process itself, with advice on blogging, freelancing, finding an agent,

promoting and self-publishing amongst other topics.

The Write Practice

website http://thewritepractice.com
Founder Joe Bunting
Focuses on how to get published; includes advice for writers on different stages of the writing process and submitting MSS to agents (e.g. '8 Tips for Naming Characters', 'Your Dream vs. Rejection' and 'Bring Your Setting to Life').

Writer Unboxed

website http://writerunboxed.com
Co-founders Therese Walsh, Kathleen Bolton
Comical tips on the art and craft of writing fiction, the writing process, and marketing your work. Includes interviews with established authors also offering advice.

Writers & Artists

website www.writersandartists.co.uk
You can join over 40,000 subscribers to receive informed and up-to-date news, views and advice on all aspects

of writing and publishing on the site brought to you by the creators of the *Writers' & Artists' Yearbook*. As well as guest blogs, videos and articles from established and debut writers across all genres, there are sections on self-publishing, a community area for sharing work, a calendar of book-related events, and much else besides.

Writers Helping Writers

website http://writershelpingwriters.net
Co-founders Angela Ackerman, Becca Puglisi
Writing tools for authors, to help them visualise and create dynamic characters and improve their plot and writing, including a 'Character Pyramid Tool', 'Character Profile Questionnaire' and 'Reverse Backstory Tool'. Also provides multiple thesauruses such as the 'Character Trait Thesaurus', 'Emotion Thesaurus' and 'Setting Thesaurus' to help authors improve their descriptive writing. Downloadable advice sheets on blogs and social media marketing for authors also available.

Podcasts

This is a small selection of podcast series that are readily available and published on a regular basis. They seek to inform the listener about the publishing industry and provide guidance to aspiring and established writers on how to improve their writing.

Begin Self-Publishing Podcast

website https://beginselfpublishing.com
Host Tim Lewis
Promotes self-publishing by demystifying the whole process and gives advice on how to safely navigate

all services available to self-published writers.

Books and Authors

website www.bbc.co.uk/programmes/po2nrsfl/episodes/downloads

Hosts Mariella Frostrup, Harriett Gilbert
Provider BBC Radio 4
A weekly podcast with highlights from
BBC Radio 4 programmes *Open Book*:
Mariella Frostrup interviews publishers
and bestselling authors about their work;
and *A Good Read*, in which Harriett
Gilbert hosts a lively discussion with her
guests about their favourite books.

The Creative Penn Podcast
website www.thecreativepenn.com/
podcasts
Host Joanna Penn
Published on Mondays, this weekly
podcast informs aspiring authors about
available publishing options and book
marketing through useful information
and interviews.

Creative Writing Career
website http://creativewritingcareer.
com
Hosts Stephan Bugaj, Justin Sloan,
Kevin Tumlinson
Hosted by leading industry professionals
whose credits include writing for Pixar,
FOX and HBO, this US podcast
provides practical advice to writers on
all forms of multimedia writing. Topics
covered include books and comics, video
games, and writing screenplays for
television and film.

Dead Robots' Society
website http://deadrobotssociety.com
Hosts Justin Macumber, Terry Mixon,
Paul E. Cooley
Created *for* aspiring writers *by* aspiring
writers, this fun podcast offers advice
and support by sharing anecdotes and
discussing current topics of interest.

The Drunken Odyssey
website https://thedrunkenodyssey.com

Host John King
Set up as a community hub for writers,
this podcast is a forum to discuss
all aspects of creative writing and
literature.

Grammar Girl Quick and Dirty Tips for Better Writing
website www.quickanddirtytips.com/
grammar-girl
Host Mignon Fogarty
This award winning weekly podcast
provides a bitesize guide to the
English language. Each week
tackles a specific feature from
style and usage, to grammar and
punctuation, all in the hope of
providing friendly tips on how to
become a better writer.

The *Guardian* Books Podcast
website www.theguardian.com/books/
series/books
Hosts Claire Armitstead, Richard Lea,
Sian Cain
The *Guardian*'s book editor, Claire
Armitstead, provides a weekly
podcast that looks at the world of
books, poetry and great writing,
including interviews with prominent
authors; recordings of *Guardian* live
events; panel discussions examining
current themes in contemporary
writing; and readings of selected
literary works.

Helping Writers Become Authors
website www.helpingwritersbecome
authors.com/podcasts
Host K.M. Weiland
As a published author, K.M. Weiland
produces these podcasts on a weekly
basis to help guide aspiring authors on
how to craft and edit a manuscript ready
to be sent to a literary agent.

I Should Be Writing

website http://murverse.com/subscribe-to-podcasts/

Host Mur Lafferty

This award-winning podcast is about the process science fiction writer Mur Lafferty went through to go from a wannabe writer to a professional and published author. It documents the highs and lows of a writing career and provides comprehensive how-to tips and interviews.

The *New Yorker*: Fiction

website www.newyorker.com/podcast/fiction

Host Deborah Treisman

Published monthly. *New Yorker* fiction editor, Deborah Treisman, invites an author whose work is being published by the magazine that month to join her in the podcast. Each author selects a piece of short fiction from the magazine's archive to read and analyse.

The Penguin Podcast

website www.penguin.co.uk/podcasts.html

This series, published fortnightly, gives intimate access to bestselling authors through interviews where they discuss their work and give examples of five things that have inspired and shaped their writing.

Reading and Writing Podcast

website http://readingandwritingpodcast.com

Host Jeff Rutherford

This interview-style podcast encourages readers to call in and leave voicemail messages and questions ready for the host to ask the guest writer, who discusses their work and writing practices.

The Self-Publishing Podcast

website https://sterlingandstone.net/series/self-publishing-podcast

Hosts Johnny B. Truant, Sean Platt, David Wright

As the hosts of this podcast proclaim, self-publishing is a new publishing frontier. The trio explore how a writer can become truely 'authorpreneurial', getting their books published and making money without resorting to agents and traditional publishing models.

Story Grid

website https://storygrid.simplecast.fm

Hosts Shawn Coyne, Tim Grahl

Hosted by a book editor with more than twenty-five years' experience in publishing and a struggling writer, the duo discuss what features bestselling novels have in common and how authors can utilise these to write a great story that works.

Write Now With Sarah Werner

website www.sarahwerner.com/episodes

Host Sarah Werner

A weekly podcast produced specifically with aspiring writers in mind. Sarah Werner provides advice, inspiration, and encouragement to writers to find a suitable work-life balance that will enable them to take their hobby to the next level.

The Writer Files

website https://rainmaker.fm/series/writer

Host Kelton Reid

This long-running podcast explores productivity and creativity, seeing how accomplished writers tackle writer's block and keep the ink flowing and cursor moving.

WRITER 2.0: Writing, Publishing, and the Space Between
website http://acfuller.com/
writer-2-0-podcast/episodes
Host A.C. Fuller
This podcast tackles both traditional and self-publishing. It includes interviews with bestselling authors from every genre, as well as leading industry professionals such as agents, book marketers and journalists to give a broad update on the publishing industry.

The Writership Podcast
website https://writership.com/episodes
Hosts Leslie Watts, Clark Chamberlain
This podcast provides help, support and advice to fiction writers on how they can develop the appropriate skills to self-edit their completed manuscript.

Writing Excuses
website www.writingexcuses.com
Hosts Mary Robinette Kowal, Brandon Sanderson, Howard Tayler, Dan Wells
This weekly educational podcast is written by writers for writers. It offers sensible and strategic advice to all who write, whether for pleasure or for profit, on how they can revise and edit their work to create a better story. Each week there is a homework assignment and suggested reading that complements the theme of each podcast.

Glossary of publishing terms

This is a list of some of the terms you might encounter in your dealings with agents and publishers.

advance
Money paid by a publisher to an author before a book is published which will be covered by future royalties. A publishing contract allows an author an advance payment against future royalties; the author will not receive any further royalties until the amount paid in advance has been earned by sales of the book.

AI (advance information sheet)
A document that is put together by a publishing company to provide sales and marketing information about a book before publication and can be sent several months before publication to sales representatives. It can incorporate details of the format and contents of the book, key selling points and information about intended readership, as well as information about promotions and reviews.

auction
An auction, usually arranged by a literary agent, takes place when multiple publishing houses are interested in acquiring a manuscript and bid against one another to secure the domestic or territorial rights.

backlist
The range of books already published by a publisher that are still in print.

blad (book layout and design)
A pre-publication sales and marketing tool. It is often a printed booklet that contains sample pages, images and front and back covers, which acts as a preview for promotional use or for sales teams to show to potential retailers, customers or reviewers.

blurb
A short piece of writing or a paragraph that praises and promotes a book, which usually appears on the back or inside cover of the book and may be used in sales and marketing material.

book club edition
An edition of a book specially printed and bound for a book club for sale to its members.

book proof
A bound set of uncorrected reading proofs used by the sales team of a publishing house and as early review copies.

C format
A term most often used to describe a paperback edition published simultaneously with, and in the same format as, the hardback original.

co-edition
The publication of a book by two publishing companies in different countries, where the first company has originated the work and then sells sheets to the second publisher (or licenses the second publisher to reprint the book locally).

copyright
The legal right, which the creator of an original work has, to only allow copying of the work with permission and sometimes on payment of royalties or a copyright fee. An amendment to the Copyright, Designs and Patents Act (1988) states that in the UK most works are protected for seventy years from the creator's death. The 'copyright page' at the start of a book asserts copyright ownership and author identification.

edition
A quantity of books printed without changes to the content. A 'new edition' is a reprint of an existing title that incorporates substantial textual alterations. Originally one edition meant a single print run, though today an edition may consist of several separate printings, or impressions.

endmatter
Material at the end of the main body of a book which may be useful to the reader, including references, appendices, indexes and bibliography. Also called back matter.

ePub files
Digital book format compatible with all electronic devices and e-readers (excluding Kindles).

extent
The number of pages in a book.

first edition
The first print run of a book. It can occasionally gain second-hand value if either the book or its author become collectable.

folio
A large sheet of paper folded twice across the middle and trimmed to make four pages of a book. Also a page number.

frontlist
New books just published (generally in their first year of publication) or about to be published by a publisher. Promotion of the frontlist is heavy, and the frontlist carries most of a publisher's investment. On the other hand, a backlist which continues to sell is usually the most profitable part of a publisher's list.

impression
A single print run of a book; all books in an impression are manufactured at the same time and are identical. A 'second impression' would be the second batch of copies to be printed and bound. The impression number is usually marked on the copyright/imprint page. There can be several impressions in an edition, all sharing the same ISBN.

imprint
The publisher's or printer's name which appears on the title page of a book or in the bibliographical details; a brand name under which a book is published within a larger publishing company, usually representing a specialised subject area.

inspection copy
A copy of a publication sent or given with time allowed for a decision to purchase or return it. In academic publishing, lecturers can request inspection copies to decide whether to make a book / textbook recommended reading or adopt it as a core textbook for their course.

ISBN
International Standard Book Number. The ISBN is formed of thirteen digits and is unique to a published title.

ISSN
International Standard Serial Number. An international system used on periodicals, magazines, learned journals, etc. The ISSN is formed of eight digits, which refer to the country in which the magazine is published and the title of the publication.

manuscript
The pre-published version of an author's work; now usually submitted in digital form.

metadata
Data that describes the content of a book to aid online discoverability – typically title, author, ISBN, key terms, description and other bibliographic information.

Mobi files
Digital book format for Kindle devices (owned by Amazon).

moral right
The right of people such as editors or illustrators to have some say in the publication of a work to which they have contributed, even if they do not own the copyright.

MS (*pl* MSS)
The abbreviation commonly used for 'manuscript'.

nom de plume
A pseudonym or 'pen-name' under which a writer may choose to publish their work instead of their real name.

out of print or **op**
Relating to a book of which the publisher has no copies left and which is not going to be reprinted. Print-on-demand technology, however, means that a book can be kept 'in print' indefinitely.

page proofs
A set of proofs of the pages in a book used to check the accuracy of typesetting and page layout, and also as an advance promotional tool. These are commonly provided in digital form, rather than in physical form.

paper engineering
The mechanics of creating novelty books and pop-ups.

PDF
Portable Document Format. A data file generated from PostScript that is platform-independent, application-independent and font-independent. Acrobat is Adobe's suite of software used to generate, edit and view PDF files.

point of sale
Merchandising display material provided by publishers to bookshops in order to promote particular titles.

prelims
The initial pages of a book, including the title page and table of contents, which precede the main text. Also called front matter.

pre-press
Before going to press to be printed.

print on demand or **POD**
The facility to print and bind a small number of books at short notice, without the need for a large print run, using

digital technology. When an order comes through, a digital file of the book can be printed individually and automatically.

print run
The quantity of a book printed at one time in an impression.

public lending right (PLR)
An author's right to receive from the public purse a payment for the loan of works from public libraries in the UK.

publisher's agreement
A contract between a publisher and the copyright holder, author, agent or another publisher, which lays down the terms under which the publisher will publish the book for the copyright holder.

publishing contract
An agreement between a publisher and an author by which the author grants the publisher the right to publish the work against payment of a fee, usually in the form of a royalty.

query or **cover letter**
A letter from an author to an agent pitching their book.

reading fee
Money paid to an editor for reading a manuscript and commenting on it. Reputable literary agents should never charge such a fee.

recto
Relating to the right-hand page of a book, usually given an odd number.

reprint
Copies of a book made from the original, but with a note in the publication details

of the date of reprinting and possibly a new title page and cover design.

review copy
An advance copy of a book sent to magazines, newspapers and/or other media for the purposes of review. A 'book proof' may be sent out before the book is printed.

rights
The legal right to publish something such as a book, picture or extract from a text.

royalty
Money paid to a writer for the right to use his or her property, usually a percentage of sales or an agreed amount per sale.

royalty split
The way in which a royalty is divided between several authors or between author and illustrator.

royalty statement
A printed statement from a publisher showing how much royalty is due to an author.

sans serif
A style of printing letters with all lines of equal thickness and no serifs. Sans faces are less easy to read than seriffed faces and they are rarely used for continuous text, although some magazines use them for text matter.

serialisation
Publication of a book in parts in a magazine or newspaper.

serif
A small decorative line added to letters in some fonts; a font that uses serifs, such as Times. The addition of serifs (1) keeps

the letters apart while at the same time making it possible to link one letter to the next, and (2) makes the letters distinct, in particular the top parts which the reader recognises when reading.

slush pile
Unsolicited manuscripts which are sent to publishers or agents, and which may never be read.

STM
The accepted abbreviation for the scientific, technical and medical publishing sectors.

style sheet
A guide listing all the rules of house style for a publishing company which has to be followed by authors and editors.

submission guidelines
Instructions given by agents or publishers on how they wish to receive submissions from authors.

subscription sale or 'sub'
Sales of a title to booksellers in advance of publication, and orders taken from wholesalers and retailers to be supplied by the publisher shortly before the publication date.

subsidiary rights
Rights other than the right to publish a book in its first form, e.g. paperback rights; rights to adapt the book; rights to serialise it in a magazine; film and TV rights; audio, ebook, foreign and translation rights.

synopsis
A concise plot summary of a manuscript (usually one side of A4) that covers the major plot points, narrative arcs and characters.

territory
Areas of the world where the publisher has the rights to publish or can make foreign rights deals.

trade discount
A reduction in price given to a customer in the same trade, as by a publisher to another publisher or to a bookseller.

trade paperback (B format)
A paperback edition of a book that is superior in production quality to and larger than a mass-market paperback edition, size 198 × 129mm.

trim size or trimmed size
The measurements of a page of a book after it has been cut, or of a sheet of paper after it has been cut to size.

type specification or 'spec'
A brief created by the design department of a publishing house for how a book should be typeset.

typeface
A set of characters that share a distinctive and consistent design. Typefaces come in families of different weights, e.g. Helvetica Roman, Helvetica Italic, Bold, Bold Italic, etc. Hundreds of typefaces exist and new ones are still being designed. Today, 'font' is often used synonymously with 'typeface' though originally font meant the characters were all the same size, e.g. Helvetica Italic 11 point.

typescript or manuscript
The final draft of a book. This unedited text is usually an electronic Word file. The term 'typescript' (abbreviated TS or ts) is synonymous with 'manuscript' (abbreviated MS or ms; pl. MSS or mss).

typographic error or **typo**
A mistake made when keying text or typesetting.

unsolicited manuscript
An unpublished manuscript sent to a publisher without having been commissioned or requested.

verso
The left-hand page of a book, usually given an even number.

voice casting
The process of finding a suitable voice artist to narrate audiobooks.

volume rights
The right to publish the work in hardback, paperback or ebook.

XML tagging
Inserting tags into the text that can allow it to be converted for ebooks or for use in digital formats.

Who does what in publishing?

There are numerous individuals and departments that you will encounter as your book goes through the publishing mill. What do they all do?

agent see **literary agent**

aggregator
Gathers together related content from a range of other sources and provides various different services and resources, such as formatting and distribution, to ebook authors.

art editor
In charge of the layout and design of a magazine, commissions the photographs and illustrations and is responsible for its overall appearance and style.

audio editor
Edits the raw audio from the recording into the final, retail-ready audiobook.

audio producer
Supervises the entire production process of the audiobook.

author
A person who has written a book, article, or other piece of original writing.

book packager see **packager.**

commissioning editor
Asks authors to write books for the part of the publisher's list for which he or she is responsible or who takes on an author who approaches them direct or via an agent with a proposal. Also called **acquisitions editor** or **acquiring editor** (more commonly in the US). A person who signs up writers (commissions them to write) an article for a magazine or newspaper.

contributor
Writes an article that is included in a magazine or paper, or who writes a chapter or section that is included in a book.

copy-editor
Checks material ready for printing for accuracy, clarity of message, writing style and consistency of typeface, punctuation and layout.

desk editor
Manages a list of titles, seeing them through the editorial and production processes, and works closely with authors.

distributor
Acts as a link between the publisher and retailer. The distributor can receive orders from retailers, ship books, invoice, collect revenue and deal with returns. Distributors often handle books from several publishers. Digital distributors handle ebook distribution.

editor
In charge of publishing a newspaper or magazine who makes the final decisions about the content and format. A person in book publishing who has responsibility for the content of a book and can be variously a senior person (Editor-in-Chief) or day-to-day contact for authors (copy-editor, development editor, commissioning editor, etc.).

editorial assistant
Assists senior editorial staff at a publishing company, newspaper, or similar business with various administrative duties, as well as editorial tasks in preparing copy for publication.

illustrator
Designs and draws a visual rendering of the source material, such as characters or settings, in a 2D media. Using traditional or digital methods, an illustrator creates artwork manually rather than photographically.

literary agent
Negotiates publishing contracts, involving royalties, advances and rights sales on behalf of an author and who earns commission on the proceeds of the sales they negotiate.

literary scout
Seeks out unpublished manuscripts to recommend to clients for publication as books, or adaptation into film scripts, etc.

marketing department
Originates sales material – catalogues, order forms, blads, samplers, posters, book proofs and advertisements – to promote titles published.

narrator
Reads a text aloud into a recording device to create an audiobook. This may be the author of the text, or a professional voice artist.

packager
Creates a finished book for a publisher.

picture researcher
Looks for pictures relevant to a particular topic, so that they can be used as illustrations in, for example, a book, newspaper or TV programme.

printer
Produces printed books, magazines, newspapers or similar material. The many stages in this process include establishing the product specifications, preparing the pages for print, operating the printing presses, and binding and finishing of the final product.

production controller
Deals with printers and other suppliers.

production department
Responsible for the technical aspects of planning and producing material for publication to a schedule and as specified by the client. Their work involves liaising with editors, designers, typesetters, printers and binders.

proofreader
Checks typeset pages for presentation and text for errors and marks up corrections.

publicity department
Works with the author and the media on 'free' publicity, e.g. reviews, features, author interviews, bookshop readings and signings, festival appearances, book tours and radio and TV interviews – when a book is published.

rights manager
Negotiates and coordinates rights sales (e.g. for subsidiary, translation or foreign rights). Often travels to book fairs to negotiate rights sales.

sales department
Responsible for selling the publications produced by a publishing

company, to bring about maximum sales and profit. Its tasks include identifying physical and digital outlets, ensuring orders and supplies of stock.

self-publishing services provider
Company that provides (for a fee) the complete range of activities to support a self-publishing author get their book into print or ebook. These include editorial, design, production, marketing and selling: i.e. all tasks carried out by a traditional publisher for their authors (at no cost to the author).

sensitivity reader
Assesses a manuscript with a particular issue of representation in mind, usually one that they have personal experience of.

sub-editor
Corrects and checks articles in a newspaper before they are printed.

translator
Translates copy, such as a manuscript, from one language into another.

typesetter
'Sets' text and prepares the final layout of the page for printing. It can also now involve XML tagging for ebook creation.

vanity publisher
A publisher who charges an author a fee in order to publish his or her work for them, and is not responsible for selling the product.

web content manager
Controls the type and quality of material shown on a website or blog and is responsible for how it is produced, organised, presented and updated.

wholesaler
Buys large quantities of books, magazines, etc. from publishers, transports and stores them, and then sells them in smaller quantities to many different retailers.

Software to support writers

Writing software

Aeon Timeline
www.aeontimeline.com
£42.00
Includes tools and features to help you
understand characters, avoid plot holes
and inconsistencies, and visualise your
story in new ways.

Atomic Scribbler
www.atomicscribbler.com
Free
Organically build your book one scene
or one chapter at a time, then drag and
drop to arrange these on your document
tree. Store your research images, URLs
and notes alongside work for easy access,
plus export your manuscript into a single
Word document when ready.

Bibisco
www.bibisco.com
Community edition – Free; Supporters
edition – pay what you want
Designed to allow a writer to focus
on their characters and develop
rounded and complex narratives, with
particular emphasis on the manuscript's
geographical, temporal and social
context.

Dabble
www.dabblewriter.com
$99 p.a. or $9.99 a month
Gives writers the freedom to plot, write
and edit on a desktop, in a browser or
off-line, and automatically syncs all
versions across your devices. Features

include plot grids, progress tracking and
goal setting.

FocusWriter
https://gottcode.org/focuswriter
Free
Provides a simple and distraction-free
writing environment with a hide-away
interface, so you can focus solely on
your writing.

Novelize
https://getnovelize.com
$45 p.a. or $5 a month
Developed for fiction writers, this
web-based writing app means you can
work on your book anywhere on any
device. Keep your research in one place
in the notebook displayed on the writing
screen and track your progress.

Novel Factory
www.novel-software.com
£24.99
Plan your book with confidence by using
the Roadmap feature which provides
tools and structures to suit your needs.
Includes detailed character overviews
such as biographies and images, as well
as scene tabs and writing statistics about
your work.

Novel Suite
www.novelsuite.com
$99 p.a. or $12 a month
An all-in-one novel writing application
that can be used across all devices.

Manage multiple books using character profiles, scene outlines and writing template tools.

Scrivener
www.literatureandlatte.com
$45
Tailored for long writing projects with everything you need housed in one place; it is a typewriter, ring binder and scrapbook, allowing you to optimise your digital workspace.

Ulysses
https://ulyssesapp
£35.99 p.a. or £4.49 a month

Document management for all writing projects, with flexible export options including pdf, Word, ebook and HTML which are appropriately formatted and styled.

WriteItNow
www.ravensheadservices.com
from $59.95
Includes sophisticated world-building features to create detailed and complex settings and characters. Recommends suitable names for your characters based on the historical period and geographical setting of your story.

Editing software

After the Deadline
www.afterthedeadline.com
Free
A context-driven grammar and spelling checker, it underlines potential issues and gives a suggestion with an explanation of how you can rectify the error.

AutoCrit
www.autocrit.com
From $10 a month
Analyses your entire manuscript and suggests insightful improvements in the form of an individual summary report, showing where your strengths and weaknesses lie.

Grammarly
www.grammarly.com
Premium from $11.66 a month (standard version free via certain browsers)
Provides accurate and context-specific suggestions when the application

detects grammar, spelling, puncuation, word choice and style mistakes in your writing.

Hemingway Editor
www.hemingwayapp.com
$19.99 (desktop), free online
Helps you write with clarity and confidence. This application is like a spellchecker, but for style. It will highlight any areas that need tightening up by identifying: adverbs, passive voice, and uninspiring or over-complicated words.

ProWritingAid
https://prowritingaid.com
from £60
For use via the web, or as an add-on to word processing software, it interrogates your work for a multitude of potential issues such as passive voice, clichés, missing dialogue tags and pace, and

suggests how you can rectify any errors or make style improvements.

SmartEdit
www.smart-edit.com
From $57
Sits inside Microsoft Word and runs twenty-five individual checks whilst you work, flagging areas that need attention, including: highlighting repeated words,

listing adverbs and foreign phrases used and identifying possible misused words.

WordRake
www.wordrake.com
from $129
When you click the 'rake' button in Microsoft Word, the text editor will read your document and suggest edits to tighten and add clarity to your work.

Acknowledgements

I am grateful to the following who have read and commented on the manuscript for this book or have given other advice and in so doing have improved it: Christelle Chamouton, Charlotte Croft, Emma Finnigan, Jonathan Glasspool, Lucy Juckes, Andrew Lownie, Catherine Lutman, Sally O'Reilly and Emma Sky. Thank you to Eden Phillips Harrington, Sophia Blackwell, Jill Laidlaw and Ben Chisnell who shepherded the book through each of its stages from manuscript through to final copies. Especial thanks go to Lisa Carden and Lauren MacGowan who read every word of the manuscript and provided insightful comments, and to Catherine Lutman for designing the book and for creating all the diagrams.

I am most grateful to all the individuals who have, unbeknown to them, helped shape the content of this book. These are the publishing colleagues and authors I have had the good fortune to work with in my career and the agents, established and not-yet-published authors I have met at the dozens of events I have spoken at over the last seven years.

Some material in chapter 1 was informed by the Keynote address I gave to the second Self-Publishing Conference in Leicester in 2014. Part of the text in chapter 3 first appeared online in 2019 as a Reedsy course: 'What Do Agents DO? (and do you need one?)'. Chapter 5 is a much-expanded version of ideas I included in my article for *Inspira* in 2017.

Many of the examples in the text are products of my imagination (such as the Publishing Proposal Form on page 135, cover emails on pages 107 and 109, and sample elevator pitches on page 105). Any similarity to real-life scenarios is purely coincidental.

Index